THE
ROMANTIC
DREAM

William Blake. *Il Penseroso,* plate 5: *Mysterious Dream.* About 1816. The Pierpont Morgan Library. Milton Sleeping on a Bank; Sleep descending, with a strange, Mysterious dream upon his Wings, of Scrolls & Nets & Webs, unfolded by Spirits in the Air & in the Brook. Around Milton are Six Spirits or Fairies, hovering on the air, with Instruments of Music.

Douglas B. Wilson

THE
ROMANTIC
DREAM

*Wordsworth
and the Poetics of the
Unconscious*

UNIVERSITY OF NEBRASKA PRESS

LINCOLN AND LONDON

Acknowledgments for the
use of previously published
material appear on page xx.

The paper in this book
meets the minimum
requirements of American
National Standard
for Information Sciences –
Permanence of
Paper for Printed Library
Materials,
ANSI Z39.48 – 1984.
Library of Congress
Cataloging-
in-Publication Data
Wilson, Douglas B., 1930–
The romantic dream:
Wordsworth
and the poetics of the
unconscious /
Douglas B. Wilson p. cm.
Includes bibliograph-
ical references (p.   )
and index.
ISBN 0-8032-4761-3
(cl : alk. paper)
1. Wordsworth, William,
1770–1850 – Knowledge
– Psychology.
2. Subconsciousness
in literature.
3. Psychoanalysis
and literature.
4. Dreams in literature.
5. Romanticism – England.
6. Poetics. I. Title.
PR5892.S88W54 1993
821'.7 – dc20
92-25123 CIP

For Diana

That abler soul, which thence doth flow,
Defects of loneliness controls.

John Donne

Contents

Our life is two-fold: Sleep hath its own world,
A boundary between the things misnamed
Death and existence: Sleep hath its own world,
And a wide realm of wild reality.
And dreams in their development have breath,
And tears, and tortures, and the touch of joy;
They leave a weight upon our waking thoughts,
They take a weight from off our waking toils.
They do divide our being; they become
A portion of ourselves as of our time,
And look like heralds of eternity;
They pass like spirits of the past,—they speak
Like Sibyls of the future: they have power—
The tyranny of pleasure and of pain;
They make us what we were not—what they will,
And shake us with the vision that's gone by,
The dread of vanish'd shadows—Are they so?
Is not the past all shadow? What are they?
Creations of the mind?—The mind can make
Substance, and people planets of its own
With beings brighter than have been, and give
A breath to forms which can outlive all flesh.

Lord Byron, "The Dream"

Preface

Wordsworth's poetry both narrates and interprets the Romantic dream. Although medieval dream visions and Renaissance figuring of dreams, especially Shakespeare's, have attracted extensive commentary, no study in English, to my knowledge, focuses centrally upon the Romantic dream. The poetics of Wordsworth's unconscious emerges from the historical climate of thinking on the dream—variously defined as reverie, trance, daydream, vision, and nightmare—both during and before his time. Freud depicts the unconscious in *Delusions and Dreams* as the "psychical processes which behave actively but nevertheless do not reach the consciousness of the person concerned."[1] I situate my reading of the Wordsworthian dream between ancient and Freudian dream interpretation in order to gain a perspective on the oneiric moment of Romanticism. Although Blake, Coleridge, Shelley, and Keats might seem the more logical choices for a study of dreaming, Wordsworth, whose use of the dream is more unobtrusive and subtle, embodies virtually all of the dream theory of his time. Wordsworth's Arab dream, *The Prelude* (5), deploys, in the shadow of Cervantes, an apocalyptic nightmare that depicts books endangered by a tidal deluge. In dreaming of books, Wordsworth confronts the hiding places of his power.

By mixing, dissolving, and re-creating rather than discriminating and reordering, the dream in Wordsworth often goes counter to history. Dreams disclose a poetics of the unconscious that provides a depth beneath the surfaces of history. But, like myth, dreams cannot evade

---

1. "Delusions and Dreams in Jensen's *Gradiva*," *The Standard Edition of the Complete Psychological Works of Sigmund Freud,* trans. James Strachey, et al., 24 vols. (London: Hogarth Press, 1953) 9:47. Unless otherwise noted, all quotations from Freud are taken from this edition and will appear parenthetically in the body of the text as *SE*.

xi

history as part of their inner world. Poetry too can in large measure liberate itself from the facticity of history, but imagination is never fully divorced from historical reality. Where poetry's strength was once, in Aristotle's depiction, its freedom from history, recent studies have emphasized the degree to which poetry can be invigorated by uncovering the politics of its history. One thinks of Jerome McGann's tying the action of *Don Juan* to the Siege of Ismael in the closing months of 1790. By marking Byron's swerve into history in the War Cantos (6–8)—with the indictment of Viscount Castlereagh, Britain's foreign minister, as a symbol of a return to the Holy Alliance of regressive monarchy— McGann illuminates the radical politics of the prose preface to Canto 6. In this historical context, *Don Juan* shifts from its earlier cantos of romance into the imbroglio of contemporary politics.[2] Although the suicide of Viscount Castlereagh vindicates McGann's new historical reading of Byron's savage indignation, it is not clear that the earlier cantos can yield such a rich vein of ore to the mining of history.

The poem I have used as my epigraph, Byron's "The Dream" (1816), contains three central Romantic beliefs about dreams—that they represent the waking world, that they have a formative function upon daily life, and that dream activity is analogous to poetic creation. Aligned with Wordsworth's "visionary dreariness" in his "spots of time," Byron's "The Dream" discloses an uncanny dimension: "Sleep hath its own world, / A boundary between the things misnamed / Death and existence." Although Byron is not usually regarded as a poet of dreams, his own "dread of vanished shadows" and his catalog of dream functions epitomize the valences of dreaming in the climate of his time.

That climate, in which "dream" and "vision" so often overlap, fosters nearly all of Blake's poetry. Blake's *Mysterious Dream* (my frontispiece), illustrating Milton's "Il Penseroso," captures, through its visionary swirl, sacred inspiration brooding over the head of the dreamer Milton. The figures surrounding the dreaming poet are playing the instruments of musical harmony. For Blake, the imagination represents God's creativity as manifested in the poet's vision. Blake's prophetic mode differs from

---

2. Jerome J. McGann, "The Book of Byron and the Book of a World," *Poems in their Place: The Intertextuality and Order of Poetic Collections,* ed. Neil Fraistat (Chapel Hill: University of North Carolina Press, 1986) 254–72.

Wordsworth's typical recourse to dreaming. Although Wordsworth rarely deploys myth in a systematic form, he exemplifies the creative function of the Romantic dream. Wordsworth also enacts the creative process of dreams, but he departs from Blake by handling dreams more realistically, tending toward nightmare more than prophetic vision. Although Wordsworth does not reject visionary experiences, his use of dreams, on balance, remains more secular than biblical.

Historical critics such as Marilyn Butler, James Chandler, Marjorie Levinson, Alan Liu, Jerome McGann, and David Simpson resist transcendent moves away from history. These critics have taught us to recognize the pervasive societal and political contexts of Wordsworth. A psychoanalytic context, however, discloses the subjectivity of a poet whose selfhood is bound up with instability and loss. Romantic dreams often depart from history to chart an inner space; they situate authority in the poet's own language, inviting us to listen to a uniquely subjective consciousness.[3] Psychoanalytic readings, however, need not be incompatible with new historicist readings. David Simpson, for example, calls for "a dialectical criticism, one that refuses both the liberal-individualist celebration of the present, with its pseudo-epistemological confirmation of the ubiquity of 'me,' and the more widely discredited and equally implausible fantasy of a past history that is describable with complete disinterest."[4]

Although no inquiry can remain completely disinterested, this awareness does not license us to project an agenda upon the past that patently distorts it. The potency of a work of art to astonish us, to "world us from its world," as Heidegger puts it, deserves an audience. The subjective component of any critical endeavor is undeniable, yet Jon Klancher is right to warn that historical reading should avoid making criticism into

3. Peter L. Rudnytsky, *The Psychoanalytic Vocation: Rank, Winnicott, and the Legacy of Freud* (New Haven and London: Yale University Press, 1991) 134, 158–9, argues cogently for the existence and continuity of self in contrast with the postmodernist denial of self.
4. David Simpson, ed., *Subject to History: Ideology, Class, Gender* (Ithaca: Cornell University Press, 1991) 28–29. I would like to thank David for supplying an early copy of this text and for other courtesies. For a contrary opinion, see Brook Thomas, "The New Historicism and other Old-fashioned Topics," *The New Historicism*, ed. H. Aram Veeser (New York: Routledge, 1989) 201, who states his case as paradox: "The present has an interest in maintaining a belief in disinterested inquiry into our past."

"a transhistorical echo of the politics of the present."[5] A psychoanalytic reading, which acknowledges the transferential investments of both critic and author, can still recognize the value of cultural exemplarity. Like new historicism, psychoanalytic criticism has its own liabilities that require disclosure before it can become a critical instrument. A psychoanalytic study of Wordsworth in his historical context, however, reveals his practice to be at once more rooted in classicism and more modern than we are accustomed to believe.

Chapter 1 of this book, "Dream and the Uncanny," builds on Freud's essay "The 'Uncanny'" to explore Wordsworth's tendency to frame, within the commonplace, moments of self-disruption that paradoxically remain "hiding places of power." Borrowing his definition of *das Unheimliche* from Schelling—"everything is *unheimliche* that ought to have remained secret and hidden but has come to light"—Freud sees the uncanny as "in reality nothing new or alien, but something which is familiar and old-established in the mind and which has become alienated from it only through the process of repression" (*SE* 17:225, 241). For the death-haunted Wordsworth, who typically eschews "gross and violent stimulants" in favor of incidents from common life, their uncanny dimension accounts for the turbulence that characterizes his "spots of time." Like dreams, the uncanny is a royal road to the unconscious, which serves to empower the process of narrativity in Wordsworth's strategy of memory.

Chapter 2, "In Dreams Begin Communities," uses dreams to focus on Wordsworth's loss of sensory power. The question of the authenticity of vision, raised by Wordsworth himself, contests the tendency of new historicists to deny the transcendent possiblities of poetry. Although there is a danger of accepting the discourse of the Romantic poets at face value, we must guard against the opposite danger of projecting our

5. Jon Klancher, "English Romanticism and Cultural Production," in *The New Historicism*, ed. H. Aram Veeser (New York: Routledge, 1989) 77. See also Charles Altieri, *Canons and Consequences: Reflections on the Ethical Force of Romantic Ideals* (Evanston: Northwestern University Press, 1990) 132, who further inveighs against modern critical practice, "the same basic model of historical reasoning prevails: the contemporary scene sets the agenda, then we test the hypotheses in relation to examples drawn from the past." See also Jonathan Bate, *Romantic Ecology: Wordsworth and the Environmental Tradition* (London and New York: Routledge, 1991) 9, who paradoxically tests the ideology of new historicism by his own ecological history.

prejudices onto an earlier historical context. We do a disservice to the Romantics by disparaging their aspirations to the sublime. This chapter confronts the evanescence of vision: the childhood dream in the "Immortality Ode" emerges as a myth of fall from preexistence. In Wordsworth's dialectic of double-consciousness, memories of childhood presence reveal an absence in the adult mind. This dialectic reverses itself in "Elegiac Stanzas," in which grief over the death of his brother, John, causes Wordsworth implicitly to doubt his youthful visionary gleam as brush strokes caught from an imaginary palette. In his elegy, the visionary becomes insubstantial, like a dream, unable to withstand the burden of a brother's death at sea. Freud's "Mourning and Melancholia" enables me to extend the themes of absence and death introduced in the previous chapter. In "Resolution and Independence," the solitary poet's waking dream of the Leech-gatherer serves to check his suicidal tendencies. We come to perceive the precarious merger, mediated by the dream, between the poet and the old man he projects as a surrogate self.

Chapter 3, "Dream Displacement: Projecting the Abandoned Woman," explores the analogy between ventriloquism and dreaming. In *Biographia Literaria,* Coleridge faults Wordsworth for his lack of dramatic skill in creating thinly disguised versions of himself such as the Pedlar in *The Excursion* (1). I defend Wordsworth as ventriloquist, however, particularly in the tale of Margaret, in which he becomes, in turn, the poet, the pedlar, and Margaret. This chapter also contests the claim that Wordsworth simply epitomizes masculinity, as both Coleridge and Virginia Woolf assert. Wordsworth projects himself into the figures of abandoned women. His capacity for ventriloquism also enables the poet to become the suffering other. Freud, similarly, recognizes during his self-analysis that he has projected his own rheumatoid shoulder onto his dream image of Irma. In his early poetry, Wordsworth maintains the balance between male and female elements necessary to the artist. One is no better than the other, yet a deficiency of either becomes a liability.

Two of Wordsworth's reveries in *The Prelude*—of human sacrifice on Sarum Plain and of the Discharged Soldier—inform chapter 4, "The Poetics of Reverie: Carnage and Its Consequences." By summoning darkness and the language of power, the poet brings on his reverie. Here the theme of errant imagination begins as a corruption of Wordsworth's imagination by the fancy. This theme of false imagination leads to a moral collapse in *The Prelude.* Wordsworth experiences nightmares in revolutionary France in which he becomes a sacrificial victim of unjust tribunals (*Prelude* 11). Far from being an indulgence in solipsism, these reveries and nightmares disclose the horrors of the French bloodbath and the corruption of British power, which merge together in the process of dream condensation. Wordsworth seeks to overthrow the yoke of "sensual tyranny," his technical term for a mental fixation upon a single sensory organ that tends to preclude imagination.

Chapter 5, "The Dream Prospect: Imagination Regained," takes as its point of departure Eve's satanically inspired dream in *Paradise Lost*. Adam's interpretation of this dream provides a Renaissance psychology that Wordsworth and Coleridge draw upon for their own modified purposes. In a move that harkens back to Milton's "reason discursive or intuitive," Wordsworth rejects his own seduction by analytic reason. Using Miltonic reason that informs both the human mind and nature, Wordsworth overcomes Cartesian dualism. To restore his impaired imagination, Wordsworth returns to a state of mind analogous to dreaming. This state nurtures imagination and precludes the danger, for example, of the tyranny of the eye. Such sensual tyranny, symptomatic of the disease of false imagination, led Wordsworth to identify himself with the hopes of the French Revolution and thus was responsible for the ultimate betrayal. Dreams subtend the transition from impaired to restored imagination, justifying Wordsworth's paradoxical conclusion that "imagination . . . / Is but another name" for "reason in her most exalted mood."[6] This merger of reason and imagination requires a semantic shift in the meaning of reason.

Dream interpretation informs chapter 6, "Wordsworth's Self-Analysis: The Arab Dream." Wordsworth lodges his own interpretation in the text of the apocalyptic dream of the Arab in Book 5 of *The Prelude*. My examination of the role of the dream interpreter, through a comparison between Freud and Artemidorus, carries further implications for a reading of Wordsworth's texts. After the death of his father, Freud worked through his grief by analyzing his own dreams. This self-scrutiny culminated in a supreme creative achievement, Freud's *The Interpretation of Dreams*.[7] In *The Prelude*, Wordsworth's self-analysis

6. William Wordsworth, *The Prelude 1799, 1805, 1850*, ed. Jonathan Wordsworth, M. H. Abrams, and Stephen Gill (New York and London: W. W. Norton, 1979) 468 (13.167–70).
7. Didier Anzieu, *Freud's Self-Analysis*, trans. Peter Graham (Madison, CT: International Universities Press, 1986) 182, 210–11.

focuses upon his emerging powers as a poet. The Arab dream confronts the threatened extinction of poetry and geometry. Death endangers invention in this nightmare of impending destruction by water. Like Freud, Wordsworth revitalizes his creative stance by working through annihilation, both in this dream and in the episodes of the Drowned Man and the Boy of Winander. The Arab dream epitomizes a process, extending through *The Prelude,* of testing the resilient power of poetry in the face of death. Although Wordsworth's interpretation of the Arab dream progresses toward consolation, its apocalyptic deluge recalls the revolutionary bloodbath and the fracturing of the poet's political hopes.

In discussing the allusions to *Othello* in *The Prelude* (5), I argue that the turbulent depth—which the poet strives to suppress—is more potent than his consolatory surface. Peter Manning recognizes that Wordsworth's revisions "concealed as much as they revealed, and his imagination guarded as much as probed its depths."[8] In Cide Hamete Benegeli, the Arab narrator of *Don Quixote,* Cervantes provides Wordsworth with a prototype for the apparition of the Arab in his dream, which took place after he fell asleep reading Cervantes's novel. Throughout *Don Quixote,* and above all in the Cave of Montesinos episode, Cervantes foreshadows Wordsworth's concern with the perils of reading. But where Cervantes avowedly sets out to destroy "that ill-founded edifice of the books of chivalry" (Prologue to *Don Quixote,* Part 1), Wordsworth quests to preserve the frail vessels of literature. Where Cervantes propels Don Quixote relentlessly toward disenchantment after his reverie in the cave, Wordsworth glimpses apocalypse within an eternal recurrence of nature and imagination.

As this synopsis suggests, I employ a variety of critical approaches, instead of striving for a single all-encompassing perspective, in an effort to do justice to the complexity of dreaming in Wordsworth. Different dreams invite different logics. The language of dreaming, together with its counterpart, imagination, invites a gendered reading for the abandoned woman, a philosophic one for the sublime, a historical one for the reverie of power, and a psychoanalytic one for the uncanny episodes. Reader-response theories also provide useful tools, because the dream, more than any other imaginative form, requires interpretation like that performed on a literary text. Wordsworth's dreamers move us to pose at

8. Peter J. Manning, "Reading Wordsworth's Revisions: Othello and the Drowned Man," *Reading Romantics: Texts and Contexts* (New York: Oxford University Press, 1990) 110.

least three questions: What is the connection between the affinity for dream in Romantic poetry and the paradoxical language of its dream texts? Why do Romantic writers so often explore the creative process through dreams? And, finally, how does the Romantic dream challenge our postmodern sensibility?

Acknowledgments

The following generous friends and scholars have read chapters or contributed timely support for my work: J. Robert Barth, S.J., Jonathan Bate, Harold Beaver, James K. Chandler, Ruth El Saffar, William H. Galperin ("opposition is true friendship"), María Antonia Garcés, Eric Gould, Jan Gorak, Anthony J. Harding, Rachel Jacoff, Kenneth R. Johnston, Anne K. Mellor, Bradford K. Mudge, W.J.B. Owen, Janice Haney-Peritz, Jeffrey C. Robinson, Charles Repka, Stuart Sperry, Raymond P. Tripp, and Leon Waldoff. Peter L. Rudnytsky, apart from expert advice on psychoanalytic readings, helped to fine-tune the logic and style of my preface. Professors Stephen C. Behrendt and J. Douglas Kneale, readers for the University of Nebraska Press, made welcome suggestions that leave me deeply in their debt. Special thanks go to Irene Gorak for her astute work on my index, and to Dr. Sarah Disbrow for her adroit copyediting.

I am grateful to the University of Denver for its financial support of my book's publication, for a sabbatical leave, 1988–89, for an index grant, and for a stipend from its Creative Work Fund to do research at the Stanford and Berkeley libraries, 1989. Gerald Chapman, as departmental chair, helped to facilitate these modes of logistical support. I would like to thank Robert Woof and Jonathan Wordsworth, custodians of the Dove Cottage Library in Grasmere, as well as the librarians at Penrose Library (its Interlibrary Loan staff), the British Library, and especially the Stanford libraries.

I am indebted to Carol Taylor of the Faculty Computer Lab at the University of Denver, as well as to R. Daniel Wilzoch, for invaluable support over the technology of my typescript.

My special gratitude goes to both Peter J. Manning and John Paul

Russo for reading the entire typescript, for ferreting out flaws, and for making timely suggestions and offering indispensable advice. I am grateful to David Buchan, a friend of thirty years since our first meeting at the Child Memorial Library, for his readings, counsel, and animated conversations. Joseph Foote—whose friendship goes back forty years to our college cross-country ski team, and whose concentrated readings have honed my prose—leaves gratitude at a loss for words.

My thanks, also beyond words, go out to our four daughters, now "at the round earth's imagined corners": Antonia, with her conductor's baton, who makes the music that compensates for the hum of the computer; Andrea, who reads with a Greek philosopher's logic and engages in a lifelong dialogue of ideas; Fiona—woodworker, editor, architect—who brooks no empty phrasing and whose early readings were a profound stimulus; and Miranda, for her expert assistance with my index while on leave from her studies composing at the Academy of Music in Prague.

I owe my greatest debt to my wife Diana, beloved colleague and kindred spirit, to whom I dedicate this book.

Versions of a few portions of this book have appeared in print. I am grateful, in each instance, for permission to reprint "The Dreaming Imagination: Coleridge, Keats, and Wordsworth," *Coleridge, Keats and the Imagination: Romanticism and Adam's Dream*, ed. J. Robert Barth, S.J., and John L. Mahoney (Columbia and London: University of Missouri Press, 1989), and "Wordsworth and the Uncanny: 'The Time Is Always Present,'" *The Wordsworth Circle* (Spring, 1985). This last was delivered as a paper at the Wordsworth Conference in Grasmere (1984); I am grateful for feedback from various members of that audience. I am also thankful for permission to quote from an unpublished paper by Carol T. Christ, "Visionary Dreariness and the Female Solitary in Wordsworth's Poetry," MLA Meeting in San Francisco (December 27, 1987).

> I say, then, that the fantasy is the power of the soul
> common to dreams and to poetic verisimilitude.
>
> Jacopo Mazzoni, *Della difesa della comedia di Dante*

Introduction

"Dreams," said Novalis in the same generation as Wordsworth, "are a shield against the humdrum monotony of life."[1] This Romantic vision of dream as a buffer against the ordinary would have startled the ancients, both dream interpreters and poets. It might have seemed strange to Homer, who depicted dreams as prophetic and monitory, as either truthful or delusive. Agamemnon is scarcely shielded from reality during his false dream in the *Iliad* (2.1–84), nor is Penelope when she dreams of her eagle-husband killing twenty fattened geese-suitors in the *Odyssey* (19.509–81). Penelope summed up the ancient monitory theory of dreams in a famous passage, reiterated by Virgil's Anchises, differentiating between the fantastic and illusory dreams that issue from "the ivory gate" and the allegorical but truthful dreams that issue from the "gateway / of honest horn" (*Odyssey* 19.530–31).[2] The most famous dream interpreter in antiquity, Artemidorus of Daldis, author of the *Oneirocritica*, used Agamemnon's dream to illustrate the difference between private and public dreamers, between the prophecies of different classes of men concerning the fortunes of state. Although a king such as Agamemnon would not have been considered a "liar," Artemidorus explains, the dream itself would have been considered a "lie." The council of Achaians was deceived by Agamemnon's false dream because he was not just "any common Achaian soldier."[3] In Wordsworth's historic cli-

1. Friedrich Leopold, Freiherr von Hardenberg, cited by Freud (*SE* 4:83).
2. Homer, *The Odyssey,* trans. Robert Fitzgerald (Garden City, NY: Doubleday, 1963) 370–71.
3. *The Interpretation of Dreams: Oneirocritica by Artemidorus,* trans. Robert J. White (Ridge Park, NJ: Noyes Press, 1975) 17–18 (1.2), hereafter cited in the text by book and section number.

I

mate, on the other hand, a common soldier in *The Prelude* serves as a proper image for a literary reverie. By switching the soldier from the dreamer to the dream, Wordsworth nonetheless uses a private trance to reflect the political discord of his own democratic moment.

In classical literature, oral and written, dreams mediate between gods and humans; they are mysteriously connected with character and fate; they often act as auguries of narrative action. Artemidorus distinguishes between two types of dreaming: "*Oneiros* differs from *enhypnion* in that the first indicates a future state of affairs, while the other indicates a present state of affairs." For this second-century dream interpreter, *oneiros* is a prophetic dream that foretells the future; *enhypnion* merely signifies the state of the soul based upon the experience of the previous day (1.14). The public nature of ancient life, as contrasted with the private cast of modern life, governs the mode of interpretation. But it is reductive to limit the ancient oneirocritic, as Marjorie Garber does in her pointed antithesis: "Artemidorus concentrated his attentions on the associations of the *interpreter*, whereas Freud was concerned with the associations in the mind of the *dreamer*."[4] This distinction blurs because Artemidorus does consider the character of the dreamer: the king will not be interpreted in the same way as a commoner, and the archetypal symbols come from the wider culture, ancient and modern. Like Freud, Artemidorus makes use of puns to suggest interpretation. He also uses association to assign different outcomes for dreamers with various occupations and, hence, in an embryonic way, relies upon individual association. Where Freud typically distrusts dream prophecy and looks back to the past and childhood, Artemidorus rarely interprets the past and sees little value in dreams unless they foretell the future.

Wordsworth's dream interpretation fits the paradigm of neither master interpreter. He neither seeks a forecast of monetary fortune, like Artemidorus, nor does he resort (apart from "Laodamia" and *Descriptive Sketches*) to the sexual dream, the hallmark of Freud. Wordsworth looks back, in the Freudian manner, to his past and to his childhood, but— given the political overtones of his private dreams, reveries, and nightmares—he also shares some common ground with Artemidorus. These

---

4. Marjorie B. Garber, *Dream in Shakespeare from Metaphor to Metamorphosis* (New Haven: Yale University Press, 1974) 6. I am indebted to Garber for providing a Renaissance model of dreaming against which the Romantic dream might be compared.

infantile and political biases in Wordsworth tend to evade the realm of the sexual, a staple of dream life from antiquity to the present. Freud and Artemidorus read sexual dreams in a culturally different way: whereas Artemidorus interprets them as a signifier of economic profit or loss, Freud inclines to read external objects as symbolic codes for the sexual traumas of the individual psyche. Far from striving to fathom the neuroses of his client's personality, Artemidorus aims to foretell pragmatic events in the life of the dreamer. The *Oneirocritica* has abundant detail garnered from a wide experience of Mediterranean culture:

> If a man dreams that he has sexual intercourse with his wife and that she yields willingly, submissively, and without reluctance to the union, it is good for all alike. For the wife represents either the craft or occupation of the dreamer, from which he derives pleasure, or whatever he controls and governs, as he does his wife (1.78).

Far from seeking nuances of sexual repression, Artemidorus considers the status of his dreamer and the role of dreaming about intercourse to predict one's fortune. But status counts too: it is auspicious to "have sexual intercourse with one's servant, whether male or female," because "the dreamer will derive pleasure from his possessions, which will grow greater and more valuable." To be possessed by one's slave, on the other hand "is inauspicious, for it signifies that the dreamer will be despised and injured by that slave" (1.78). Dreams of sleeping with one's mother require much more skill in interpretation, but the shame of the incest taboo does not occur for Artemidorus, who metaphorizes the dreamer's mother along class lines. Thus it is lucky for a craftsman or tradesman to dream incestuously, "for we ordinarily call a person's trade his 'mother'" (1.79). Wordsworth reveals no incestuous dreams of his mother; however, his dream ventriloquy projects into mothers, who are tellingly abandoned and poor. In an oblique way, we may call Wordsworth's trade—his vocation as poet—his "mother."

Far from searching for Oedipal innuendo within the psyche, Artemidorus treats incestuous dreams without shame, as matters of fact. Instead of bridling at incestuous transgression, he uses the position of the dreamer's maternal intercourse as a clue to interpretive outcome. If the mother is standing during intercourse, this position would signify "constraint and oppression . . . (for men use this position only when they have neither bed nor mattress)"; if she is kneeling, her immobility signifies poverty. If a man dreams that his mother is ill, her disease signifies that his "business activities will be weak and disorganized" (1.79). This culturally determined sexual index to financial status runs counter to Freud's therapeutic archeology into sexually conditioned indicators of the individual psyche. Yet these paradigms raise significant questions: What are the sexual indices of Wordsworth's culture? To what extent does Wordsworth share them? Why do Wordsworth's dreams so seldom embody the sexual?

Although Freud strategically tried to distance himself from Artemidorus, similarities between these two dream interpreters nonetheless shed light on the Wordsworthian dream. Both distinguish between the waking consciousness and unconscious awareness and, as John Winkler puts it, both look for a symbolic code "whose elements are drawn from the dreamer's immediate associations":

> The difference is that Artemidoros' [sic] soul is looking to the immediate future, Freud's to the distant past. The mental operations, apart from the future- or past-directedness, are much the same in both systems. What distinguishes them is not so much their theories of the soul's structure or operation, nor their practices of interviewing clients, but the culturally determined value assigned to sex.[5]

The anthropological similarities and differences between Artemidorus and Freud do much to illuminate both their cultures as revealed through the dream lives they choose to interpret. Although Wordsworth's own historical moment conforms with neither of these dream paradigms, in his apocalyptic dream of the Arab [*The Prelude* (5)], he deploys the kind of prophetic dream favored by Artemidorus in predicting a future deluge upon humankind. In his reverie of human sacrifice at Stonehenge in *The Prelude* (12), on the other hand, Wordsworth's retrospect, in the archeological style of Freud, discloses ancient violence infused by contemporary, French revolutionary atrocities. With his dream of the Arab, Wordsworth, like the two dream interpreters who frame him temporally, inserts his own interpretation of the dream and, further, adapts it to epitomize inner authorial experience.

5. John J. Winkler, *The Constraints of Desire: The Anthropology of Sex and Gender in Ancient Greece* (New York and London: Routledge, 1990) 26. I am indebted to Winkler's subtle anthropological reading of Artemidorus's *Oneirocritica* as a cultural indicator of ancient Greece.

Freudian dream interpretation applied to earlier historical texts can, as anthropologists are now making clear, lead to distortions caused by projecting our own values onto an alien culture. The danger endemic to psychoanalytic criticism inheres in its ahistorical claim to universality, its theories of a timeless human nature. This theoretical danger is stated by the classicist S.R.F. Price:

> The acceptance of the universal claims of psychology, and the imposition of its theories on other societies, presents two serious problems. First, given the truth of psychological theory, especially dream theory, the imposition of this theory on ancient Greece is unlikely to be informative historically. It might be illuminating for the biographies of individuals, but it cannot make sense of the cultural configurations specific to that society. In addition, there is the danger of misreading ancient evidence in the light of modern preconceptions.[6]

The misuse of psychoanalytic criticism through the violation of historical context can result in the loss of the vital interchange derived from juxtaposing such matters as the different sexual codes of ancient and modern societies. Freud himself often insists upon proper scientific and historic contextualization.

In this study of the Romantic dream as exemplified by Wordsworth, I draw selectively upon the work of Coleridge, de Quincey, Hazlitt, and especially Keats, whose use of dreams complements Wordsworth's embodiment of dreaming. Where the poetry and biography of Wordsworth warrant the use of psychoanalytic theory, I also draw upon the writings of Freud and other analysts as speculative instruments. Literary dreams, unlike live analytic patients, cannot be probed for the dreamer's patterns of association. But the cryptic language of the dream, animated by

6. S.R.F. Price, "The Future of Dreams: From Freud to Artemidoros," in *Before Sexuality: The Construction of Erotic Experience in the Ancient Greek World*, ed. David M. Halperin, John J. Winkler, and Froma Zeitlin (Princeton: Princeton University Press, 1990) 368–69. For an even stronger warning against unwarranted psychologizing, see Leonard J. Davis, *Resisting Novels: Ideology and Fiction* (New York and London: Methuen, 1987) 14, who cautions against "psychoanalytic readings of texts *per se*": "My feeling is that such readings usually tend to be reductive and, in the case of psychoanalyzing authors, risky at best. The psychoanalytic session is based on a dialectical, face-to-face interaction between patient and analyst—a dialectic that is completely absent in the literary critical method. As such, any psychoanalytic reading of a text is simply risk-taking at best and at worst a violation of psychoanalytic principles."

tropes, is in Wordsworth illuminated by the use of such Freudian papers as "The 'Uncanny,'" "On Narcissism: An Introduction," "Mourning and Melancholia," and "Creative Writers and Day-dreaming" in addition to *The Interpretation of Dreams*.[7]

Two recent books on dreaming, J. Allan Hobson's *The Dreaming Brain* (1988) and Bert O. States's *The Rhetoric of Dreaming* (1988), strongly attack Freudian dream theory. Hobson, a neurophysiologist, attempts to dethrone Freud as the modern arbiter of dreams by demystifying his claims to scientific objectivity and by patronizing his "rich and literary imagination." Hobson conveniently epitomizes his scientific case against Freud:

> By criticizing Freud, this book aims to persuade all theorists who retain the assumption of a disguise-censorship in dream formation to consider the alternative of activation-synthesis. As will be made clear later, this theory does not entail giving up examination of dreams as revelatory of the dreamer's drives, fears, and associations. On the contrary, activation-synthesis acknowledges these processes as highly relevant but finds them, as Jung did, transparently and directly evident in the dream, and thus makes no distinction between manifest and latent content.

Hobson avers that as much can be understood "by direct observation of sleep and dreaming (at the bedside and at night) as by eliciting recollections on the couch the next day."[8] Hobson's attack on Freud centers, with some justice, upon the supersubtlety of Freudian dream interpretation. The manifest and latent content, involving dream condensation and displacement, come under heaviest fire for needlessly complicating what is a much more straightforward process: a neurological triggering of dream thoughts.

---

7. Mark Edmundson, *Towards Reading Freud: Self-Creation in Milton, Wordsworth, Emerson, and Sigmund Freud* (Princeton: Princeton University Press, 1990) 159, reads Freud with "energetic resistance" along with "due admiration." By concentrating upon "On Narcissism: An Introduction" and "Mourning and Melancholia," Edmundson manages to show "Freud the inventor playing off Freud the figure of cultural and scientific authority." This brand of "invention" is akin to Romantic discourse that helps to disclose a subversive boldness in Freud.

8. J. Allan Hobson, *The Dreaming Brain* (New York: Basic Books, 1988) 57 and 68.

In a statement of purpose in the opening paragraph of *The Interpretation of Dreams*—introducing what will become the main point of controversy in the work of Hobson and States—Freud mentions "the processes to which the strangeness and obscurity of dreams are due." From these processes he hopes to deduce "the nature of the psychical forces by whose concurrent or mutually opposing action dreams are generated" (*SE* 4:1). Wordsworth's interpretation of his Arab dream also works by "mutually opposing" actions. Freud's insight that dream logic often discloses opposites that do not cancel each other out—or that emerge disguised as contraries—illuminates this Wordsworthian dream. These opposites in the psyche begin with the rival claims of the ego and the superego: this struggle leads to repression that, according to Freud, produces the displacement and condensation of dream thought. States disagrees, couching his quarrel with Freud in terms that Hobson would endorse:

> We have not done away with drives or neuroses or complexes or repression itself; we have simply demystified the activity of the brain by releasing it from a secret spatial and self-competitive division. And in doing away with the two-mind system, we find that there is no reason to explain the distortions of dreams as products of displacement and censorship.[9]

Freud's bipolar psychic system, with its reliance upon deviance and secrecy, is anathema to Hobson and States. They object to Freud's premise that "the dream is never what it appears to be. It is always . . . a wolf in sheep's clothing." They object, in short, to allegory, to "other" speech. All of this Freudian mumbo jumbo of interpretive decoding, according to States, suggests that some mysterious "intelligence has done the coding for some purpose":

> The dream's symbols and images, then, would be symptoms of the wishes and directives of the unconscious that the dreamer may not

---

9. Bert O. States, *The Rhetoric of Dreams* (Ithaca and London: Cornell University Press, 1988) 37, sums up his approach as a "phenomenological rhetoric of dreaming": "One way to study" dreams is "to see how the principles of rhetoric—the four master tropes, in this case—could be traced *back into* the dream-work, bearing in mind that in applying verbal structures to preverbal structures we are already speaking in an odd sort of metaphor" (6).

understand but that the interpreter may decode and thereby peer into that uncivil realm peopled by drives and presided over by the monstrous id.[10]

States thinks that, given the testimony from sleep clinics, "dreams have much more basic business than preventing the flow of repressed thought to the conscious mind."[11]

In his objection to repression, invented by Freud's opposing psychic forces, States raises the question of dreaming in animals. Are cats, dogs, and horses venting their repressions in dreams? Dreams may not only help to prevent sleep from waking intrusion, but also to reorient the brain by a process of dream thinking that could fit the mind for a better alignment to waking life. Hobson and States both prefer Jung's stance on dreaming as a projection of daytime thinking upon the screen of dream cinema. They also second, with some justice, Jung's objection to Freud's tendency to reduce dreams merely to sexual origins. By reading Freudian dream interpretations as mere projections of womb-and-phallus symbolism, Hobson and States reduce Freud's dream texts to mystifications "of the monstrous id," thereby disparaging the energy of desire generated by new Freudian readings that focus on the gaps, the unstated, the subtexts of literature.

At the opposite extreme from these two theorists, Jacques Lacan, with his linguistic rescripting of psychoanalysis, "returns us to a more unsettling Freud" than the one recognized by Hobson and States. This more disturbing Lacanian reading of Freud, as depicted by Joseph H. Smith, faces "the question of what it is to approach and repeatedly reapproach the assumption of one's subjecthood, only to arrive at a symbolically structured acceptance that the center of one's being is decentered, other, never fully present, never fixed."[12] My position lies between these two extremes: Lacan's disquieting view of Freud helps to account for the uncanny dimension in Wordsworth that is more unsettling than is often recognized. Yet I argue for a Wordsworthian self—no

10. States, *The Rhetoric of Dreams* 21.
11. States, *The Rhetoric of Dreams* 35.
12. Joseph H. Smith, "Epilogue: Lacan and the Subject of American Psychoanalysis," *Psychiatry and the Humanities: Interpreting Lacan,* vol.6, ed. Joseph H. Smith and William Kerrigan (New Haven and London: Yale University Press, 1983) 274; henceforth this volume is cited as *Interpreting Lacan.*

matter how destabilized—that emerges from multiple, shifting dialogues with itself.

Unlike the neurobiology of dreaming, literary interpretation focuses directly upon the matter of language. Even if Freud's dream theory is in some ways outmoded for psychoanalysis today, his work remains more useful than the readings of Hobson and States for meeting the challenge of the linguistic structures of literary texts. States's contention that "dream is not a repressive mechanism and that it is not a form of language" leads him to conclude that "the dream does not speak, it thinks." For him, dream thought is a language of preverbal rhetoric elaborating itself through tropes: "It manifests strategies of thought that if traced upward into language would eventuate in the master tropes. So dreams are a kind of proto-rhetoric, *not yet* a language."[13] Where States elaborates a preverbal rhetoric to account for the genesis of dreams, I deal with constructs that are already linguistic, with dream in literature. Whether or not Freud is correct about the psychic mechanisms of dreaming, his works deal with the circulation of tropes and figures on the verbal surface. Freud teaches us to seek the evidences of desire implicit in the absences or contradictions that unlock the freedom of interpretation. For my purposes, Lacan's claim "that the unconscious is structured like a language"—a claim that represents a "flowering of Freud's linguistic bent"—is closer to the mark for literary dreams than States's proto-rhetoric and exemplifies the idea that "we and our world are constituted by language," that "man is language," and that "our only access to the Real is via language, and the Imaginary and the Symbolic are themselves linguistic orders." These imaginary and symbolic levels of language might seem recalcitrant to ordinary linguistic codes, yet they require interpretation like the images of dreams. Although Lacan resists the referential role of language in favor of the slippage of the signifier, his approach implies an energy of desire beyond the reductive emphases of antiquated Freudian criticism. I hold, as Lacan also did, that language can be referential.[14] My psychoanalytic reading of Wordsworth affirms

---

13. States, *The Rhetoric of Dreams* 6.

14. *Interpreting Lacan* 268. My quotations on Lacan are taken from Smith's lucid article. If Smith understands Lacan's denial of "reference as a move against reification of concepts and as a means of barring inappropriately descriptive reference" (274), he also claims that Lacan believes in a limited referentiality of language: "Attention to both levels [of the language of the unconscious], however, should allow not only for the dominant place

that the dream for him can disclose the impersonal, the visionary and, most important, those uncanny signals from the borders of the mind that are connected with the body. An examination of Wordsworth's historical forerunners on dream thought will now serve to clarify the context from which his own insights emerge.

Medieval and Renaissance Dreams

The links between imagination and dream, culminating in *alta fantasia*—the inspired imagination illuminated by dreams beyond the reach of the waking reason in *The Purgatorio*—have been discussed by Murray Wright Bundy in his magisterial treatment *The Theory of Imagination in Classical and Mediaeval Thought*. Imagination has traditionally been represented as a highly ambiguous faculty: it can distort and remain within the so-called lower part of the soul, or it can become the vehicle of dream prophecy and a path to divine vision. In its negative aspect, imagination reveals a tendency toward errancy—in its root meaning (Latin, *erro, errare*) of "adventuring, wandering, going astray" (*OED*)—of distortion in its precarious relation to reality. Synesius (370–ca. 430 A.D.), aware of imagination's power either to beguile or to inspire, prescribed an arduous discipline: "The best means is to cultivate the speculative life, making life a constant activity of the intellect, and thus preventing the movements of disordered phantasy." By this means, the "soul will no longer be under the influence of external objects, and this intermediary essence, phantasy, is then able to abandon itself to the direction of the Primary Soul, and purifying itself, it mounts to the heavens."[15] This same historical conflict endemic to imagination—for

given to language in Lacan's thought but also for instinct and reference" (269). For a contrary opinion on Lacan's reading of the unconscious, see Didier Anzieu, *Freud's Self-Analysis* 578, who writes of "Lacan's error of interpretation when, basing his argument on passages such as these in Freud, he makes the supposition that the unconscious is structured like a language and that it is a kind of writing: Lacan took for a characteristic of the unconscious what was in fact a feature of Freud's own creative genius." Anzieu contends that the unconscious was not a language until disclosed by Freud, yet dreams as they exist in literature may also reveal the unconscious as a text.

15. Murray Wright Bundy, *The Theory of Imagination in Classical and Mediaeval Thought* (Urbana: University of Illinois Press, 1927) 152, provides superb background to the role of fancy and imagination in classical and medieval thought, leading up to the *alta fantasia*, the

errancy or vitality—informs the poetry of Wordsworth in his struggle with the imagination as it seeks to map newly discovered psychic terrain. Synesius—a philosopher who converted to Catholicism and later became a bishop—also wrote a treatise *Concerning Dreams* (*De Somnis*); he fostered "the acceptable coexistence of pagan and Christian views, especially on divination or prophecy in dreams."[16] It is tempting to linger over dreams in antiquity and the Middle Ages, where dream prophecy and dream vision are the dominant mode, and where allegory, so often initiated by dream vision, qualifies (to borrow a phrase from C. S. Lewis) as "the subjectivism of an objective age."[17] Writing in the subjective age of Romanticism, however, Wordsworth confronts a different objectivity in the rapid advance of modern science. His theme of errant fancy and imagination in *The Prelude,* anticipated here by Synesius, draws upon dreaming as preamble to renovation.

Shakespeare and Milton are for Wordsworth the dominant precursors in the literary dream. Shakespeare rarely writes a play that does not embody dreaming or the supernatural: *Richard III, A Midsummer Night's Dream, Pericles,* and *The Tempest* stand out among the dream plays; all the late romances deal in the dream logic of metamorphosis to construct their intergeneric worlds. Northrop Frye illuminates this blend of poetry and art that comprises Shakespeare's dream sorcery in *The Tempest*:

> The famous speech of Prospero about the dream nature of reality applies equally to Milan and the enchanted island. We spend our lives partly in a waking world we call normal and partly in a dream world which we create out of our own desires. Shakespeare endows both worlds with equal imaginative power, brings them opposite one

---

dream-inspired imagination in Dante's *Purgatorio* (240–41). His work challenges us to discover the role of dreams in Romantic poetry, written in the different climate of individual sensibility.

16. Carol S. Rupprecht, "Our Unacknowledged Ancestors: Dream Theorists of Antiquity, the Middle Ages, and the Renaissance," *Psychiatric Journal University of Ottawa* 15 (1990): 118. Rupprecht also mentions the Renaissance Italian Girolamo Cardano, author of *Somniorum Synesiorum* [Of Synesian Dreams] Basel 1562, who approached dreams from a multidisciplinary point of view; he preferred Artemidorus over Synesius, who "presented many good ideas but neglected to propose specific techniques for interpretation."

17. C. S. Lewis, *The Allegory of Love: A Study in Medieval Tradition* (Oxford and New York: Oxford University Press, 1970) 30.

another, and makes each world seem unreal when seen by the light of the other.[18]

In *The Tempest* and *A Midsummer Night's Dream,* Shakespeare uses the dream as it merges with imagination to shape his worlds of language to suit the demands of the genres of comedy and romance. This language of metamorphosis thrives upon analogy and metaphor as "the stuff that dreams are made on." By building fiction into dreams of art, Shakespeare performs linguistic feats that anticipate the dream modalities of the Romantics.

This dialectic between the heart's wish and the opposing claims of reality will often be pursued by Wordsworth's contemporaries, especially by Keats. In *The Prelude* Wordsworth also traces the distortions and sa-liences of imagination in its dream transformation into psychic growth. The dream for Wordsworth and Keats bears the same relation to reality as the imagination does for Wallace Stevens: "The imagination loses vitality as it ceases to adhere to what is real. . . . It has the strength of reality or none at all." The converse of this proposition also holds true for Stevens as for Wordsworth: "What makes the poet . . . is that he creates the world to which we turn incessantly and without knowing it and that he gives to life the supreme fictions without which we are unable to conceive of it." The assumption underlying this role of the poet is that the imaginary construct and our meditations on the world are as valid as our senses, and what they contribute to our lives.[19] One of the focuses of my study is the reciprocity or contrariety between imagi-nation and reality. If imagination can stray into a barren metaphysical quest, it can also disclose flaws in prevalent cultural patterns. Medieval and Renaissance typologies of dream and imagination anticipate the bearings of these terms in Romantic and Modern poetics.

Eighteenth-Century Dream Theory

In the historical climate of Wordsworth's time, dreams were intimately

18. Alvin B. Kernan, ed., *Modern Shakespearean Criticism: Essays on Style, Dramaturgy, and the Major Plays* (New York: Harcourt Brace and World, 1970) 172.
19. Wallace Stevens, *The Necessary Angel* (New York: Vintage Books, Random House, 1942; rpt. 1951) 6–7, 31.

connected to psychological associationism, particularly in the philosophy of John Locke, Dugald Stewart, and David Hartley. As Hartley
writes:

> Dreams are nothing but the Imaginations, Fancies, or Reveries of a
> sleeping Man; and that they are deducible from the Three following
> Causes; *viz*. First, the Impressions and Ideas lately received, and par-
> ticularly those of the preceding Day. Secondly, The State of the Body,
> particularly of the Stomach and Brain. And, Thirdly, Association.[20]

The trains of ideas occur as a result of all three causes but especially
through the law of association and the stimulating of imagination by
inner images. Rather than forming mental pictures of sensory experience, often a function of the waking imagination, this faculty associates
images from its own mental space. The close connection between imagination as a creative faculty and as a fabricator of dreams stems from this
eighteenth-century psychology of the mind. Wordsworth, Coleridge,
De Quincey, and Keats, in various degrees, share this tendency to include in their poetics an analogy between the creative imagination and
the power of dreaming. The fiction-making power of imagination, amplified from its image-making function of sensory reproduction, shares a
liberating play analogous to that of the world of dream.

Most eighteenth-century theorists of dream shared Dugald Stewart's
idea that the will is absent during sleep and dreaming, that it "loses its
influence over all our powers both of mind and body, in consequence of
some physical alteration in the system, which we shall never, probably,
be able to explain." That the will is absent during sleep, as any insomniac
can attest, is illustrated by our failure at being able "to suspend the acts of
the will" in order to fall asleep. If the will were in fact awake, it would
banish the disquieting ideas from our dreams. The very distinction
between reveries and dreams, for Stewart, depends upon the presence or
absence of the will:

> The *indirect* influence which the mind thus possesses over the train of
> its thoughts is so great, that during the whole time we are awake,
> excepting in those cases in which we fall into what is called a reverie,

---

20. *Observations on Man, His Frame, His Duty, And His Expectations (1749)*, introduction by
Theodore L. Huguelet (Gainsville: Scholar's Facsimiles and Reprints, 1966) 384.

and suffer our thoughts to follow their natural course, the order of their succession is always regulated more or less by the will.[21]

A reverie—a state of mind frequently deployed by Wordsworth in his poetry—differs from a dream by the more or less active presence of the will in guiding its trains of thought. The dream, in contrast, seems to come from elsewhere, as in classical prophetic dreams, as if from some other will. Another eighteenth-century dream specialist, Andrew Baxter, extends this line of thought to embrace the strange notion, already discredited by late antiquity, that dreams come from external spirits acting upon the sleeping mind.[22]

The presence or absence of the will governs the distinction between dreams and reveries. In his *The Poetics of Reverie* Gaston Bachelard, a modern dream theoretician, disparages dreams as "the madnesses of the night." How can such dreamers be sure of being themselves in their irrational lunacies of the darkness? He prefers to maintain the possession of the will in reverie, not to lose control of his own mind in the vagaries of dreaming:

> The night dream is a dream without a dreamer. On the contrary, the dreamer of reverie remains conscious enough to say: it is I who dream the reverie, it is I who am content to dream my reverie, happy with this leisure in which I no longer have the task of thinking.[23]

In Bachelard's poetics of reverie the loss of self in dreaming amounts to putting to sea in a storm. He prefers the quiet waters of reverie, with the helm of his consciousness firmly in hand.

Locke stands at the opposite pole to Bachelard in most respects, yet both tend to disparage dreams. Although we may recall our sleeping thoughts, according to Locke, "how *extravagant* and incoherent for the most part they are; how little conformable to the Perfection and Order of a rational Being, those who are acquainted with Dreams, need not be told." Locke asks an imaginary defender of dreams

---

21. *The Works of Dugald Stewart*, 7 vols. (Cambridge, UK: Hilliard and Brown, 1829) 1:242, 243, 244–45.
22. Cited in *The Works of Dugald Stewart* 1:251.
23. Gaston Bachelard, *The Poetics of Reverie*, trans. Daniel Russell (New York: The Orion Press, 1969) 22.

whether the Soul, when it thinks thus apart, and as it were separate
from the Body, acts less rationally than when conjointly with it, or no:
If its separate Thoughts be less rational, then these Men must say,
That the Soul owes the perfection of rational thinking to the Body: If
it does not, 'tis a wonder that our Dreams should be, for the most
part, so frivolous and irrational; and that the Soul should retain none
of its more Rational Soliloquies and Meditations.[24]

Locke would probably have applied the same logic to reverie as he did to
the eccentric world of dream. As a confirmed rationalist, he shows little
sympathy for openness to the atemporal and irrational unconscious.
Bachelard, like many of his eighteenth-century forebears, cultivates reverie as a means of putting aside the rational, scientific, and fretful world
of daily anxiety that constitutes the bulk of modern waking life.

This study of Wordsworth involves dreams, reveries, trances, and
daydreams. These terms are slippery and require careful definition to
serve the purposes of inquiry. In its originary sense, a trance means a
crossing toward death, a being carried out of oneself, a going across. In
practice, a reverie can slide into a trance, a deeper state of hypnagogic
intensity, in which the will becomes less operative, as in a dream or in a
state induced by hypnosis. The trance is a deeper state lying between
dream and reverie. I shall use the terms *reverie, trance,* and *daydream* (or
waking dream) as cognates of dream. *Reverie* will generally be used in
Bachelard's sense of preserving a governing trace of the will. The daydream, like the reverie, preserves the presence of the will: it is the least
intense of the four terms in hypnagogic power. Any differences from
these working definitions will be explained where the terms appear
in contexts that require further distinctions. Wordsworth's reverie on
Sarum Plain in *The Prelude,* for example, entails an invocation of darkness that involves a loss of will more proper to a trance.

Bachelard draws upon Jung's concept of the anima in defining the

24. *An Essay Concerning Human Understanding,* ed. Peter H. Nidditch (1975; Oxford:
Clarendon Press, 1979) 113. See also John Paul Russo, "Logos and Transience in Franco
Rella," *Differentia* 1 (Autumn 1986): 207. Russo notes how Descartes gave a new lease on
life to "'classical reason' . . . oddly enough, 'by tearing it from the senses,'" and denying
the body, unlike Locke's solid placing of reason within the body. Rella and the modern
Italian crisis-of-reason thinkers would second Locke's reading of reason.

reveries of men as partaking in the repose of the feminine. For Jung, according to Bachelard, "there may be found in any psychism, whether that of a man or a woman, an *animus* and an *anima,* sometimes cooperating, sometimes in dissonance." Although Freud does not share Jung's gender-based definitions of these terms, he stresses bisexual components in all human beings. Unlike the dream, "which is so often marked with the hard accents of the masculine," Bachelard continues, reverie is "of feminine essence. Reverie conducted in the tranquility of the day and in the peace of repose—truly natural reverie—is the very force (puissance) of the being at rest. For any human being, man or woman, it is one of the feminine states of the soul."[25] Although Wordsworth's reveries reveal gender-based insights—especially in his treatment of abandoned women—he does not confine the use of reverie to states of blissful tranquility. Nor does he confine the feminine to gentle trains of association: the reveries of human sacrifice on Sarum Plain and the Discharged Soldier disclose more of flint and iron than of happy repose.

Dreams and Dramatic Illusion: Coleridge and Nietzsche

Coleridge shares with Nietzsche and Freud cognizance of the close affinity between dream and poetry. On the question of audience/reader response during the nineteenth century, Coleridge and Nietzsche provide a dream theory that informs the argument of this book. The texts of literary dreams, more than most imaginative forms, require the activity of reader response to elicit their meaning. Nietzsche's *The Birth of Tragedy,* especially its sections on lyric poetry, builds upon the dream aspect of Apollo to mediate between the audience and the dramatic action. Coleridge models his "willing suspension of disbelief" upon the

25. Bachelard, *The Poetics of Reverie* 18, 19. The quotation from Jung is cited by Bachelard. He writes that *The Poetics of Reverie* is "written in the *anima,*" and should "be read in *anima.*" He can also imagine a book of reverie based on the animus (212). He would probably designate Wordsworth's reverie of Druid sacrifice on Sarum Plain a reverie of animus. Unlike Wordsworth, whose reveries are dark, Bachelard defines reverie in an opposite way: "Thus a whole universe comes to contribute to our happiness when reverie comes to accentuate our repose. You must tell the man who wants to dream well to begin by being happy. Then reverie plays out its veritable destiny; it becomes poetic reverie and by it, in it, everything becomes beautiful. If the dreamer had 'the gift' he would turn his reverie into a work. And this work would be grandiose since the dreamed world is automatically grandiose" (12–13).

reader's experience of dreaming. On the Romantic audience's expectations from the literature of dreaming, David Perkins epitomizes the
contemporary scene. Such visionary poems reveal what is normally
concealed. Because they provide an escape from strict realism, from
ethical accountability, and from mechanical form that is imposed from
without, they deal in the mysteries of folktale and old romance. For
certain Romantic readers, dreams can disclose veiled emotions and
"emerge from a reality deeper than ordinary reality, or express a mind
within us that is more profound and aware than the conscious mind."
Valued for their exoticism, dreams emerge from our unconscious centers
where the individual merges with the collective. The work of Coleridge
reveals the pulse of his own moment by the exemplarity of his dream-
poetry. His introductory note to "Kubla Khan," for instance, apart from
implying a disavowal of responsibility for his poem, would also have led
a large part of his contemporary audience to think of "Kubla Khan" as
"the work of the 'poet hidden' within us" and therefore "a greater work
than if the conscious mind and will had helped to create it."[26] Although
there are dissenting voices, such as Locke's ironic one, those have already
been mentioned in my discussion of eighteenth-century dream theory.

The prevailing tendency among the Romantics to explore psychic
terrain—epitomized by Wordsworth and Coleridge—motivates the latter to deploy dreams in order to unfold a psychology of reader response.
Coleridge explores dramatic illusion by means of dream analogy and,
like Nietzsche after him, invokes dream experience to describe the subliminal engagement of a theater audience. The "willing suspension of
disbelief," for Coleridge, applies as well to the reader of Wordsworth's
lyrics as to the playgoer. Coleridge calls poetry "a rationalized dream"

26. David Perkins, "The Imaginative Vision of *Kubla Khan*: On Coleridge's Introductory
Note," *Coleridge, Keats, and the Imagination: Romanticism and Adam's Dream*, ed. J. Robert
Barth and John L. Mahoney (Columbia and London: University of Missouri Press, 1990)
104–5. See also G. H. von Schubert, *Symbolik des Traumes*, 3rd ed. (Leipzig: F. A. Brock-
haus, 1840) 6. Perkins borrows the phrase "the Poet Hidden within us" from Schubert. See
also Ronald R. Thomas, *Dreams of Authority: Freud and the Fictions of the Unconscious*
(Ithaca: Cornell University Press, 1990) 53, who writes of Wordsworth's Arab nightmare in
order to illuminate contemporary dream theory: the stone and shell in this dream "represent the contending attitudes toward dream experience in the nineteenth century: a
secular, scientific one that seeks to explain the dream and give the dreamer power over it,
and a supernatural, demonic one that seeks to mystify the dream 'with power / To
exhilarate the spirit' of the dreamer."

that unites forms to feelings at a level below conscious awareness: "What is the Lear, the Othello, but a Divine Dream / all Shakespeare, and nothing Shakespeare"?[27] Because dreaming creates the "highest degree" of illusion, Coleridge uses it to describe his own middle position between the French school of dramatic criticism, which insists upon "perfect delusion," and the opposite position of Samuel Johnson—that the audience is always aware of being deceived. Unlike Aristotle, who takes dreams for realities, Coleridge insists upon the incompatibility—except for nightmares and hallucinations—of sleeping and waking perceptions. The sleeper suspends "voluntary and, therefore . . . comparative power": "The fact is that we pass no judgement either way: we simply do not judge . . . [dream images] to be unreal, in consequence of which the images act on our minds, as far as they act at all, by their own force as images."[28] Inquiring further, Coleridge notes that, while awake, a person falls prey to many sensory distractions; often several senses respond simultaneously, and emotions are the after effects of these perceptions. During sleep, however, this process is reversed: "The sensations, and with these the emotions and passions which they counterfeit, are the causes of our dream-images." These nocturnal images benefit from sen-

---

27. *Notebooks* 2086. Quoted in J. A. Appleyard, *Coleridge's Philosophy of Literature: The Development of a Concept of Poetry 1791–1819* (Cambridge, MA: Harvard University Press, 1965) 139.

28. Samuel Taylor Coleridge, *Shakespearean Criticism*, 2 vols., ed. T. M. Raysor (New York: E. P. Dutton, 1960) 1:116. Hereafter cited as *SC*. See also Elisabeth Schneider, *Coleridge, Opium, and Kubla Khan* (New York: Octagon Books, 1966) 98, who notes that Coleridge differs from the *Zoonomia* (1794–96) of Erasmus Darwin, who avers in his chapter on sleep that "in sleep we believe our dreams to be true," whereas Coleridge asserts that "we neither believe nor disbelieve but simply pass no judgement either way." Although Schneider considers Coleridge less sound than Darwin on this point, the change is important to Coleridge's whole concept of "negative faith" as contrasted with positively willed belief. She is certainly convincing in proving Coleridge's debt to Darwin for ideas underlying that of "dramatic illusion": "In sum, Coleridge's celebrated accounts of dramatic illusion might fairly be described as consisting of the ideas of Erasmus Darwin refined at one point by means of [A. W. von] Schlegel—unless it should prove eventually that Coleridge was right in his claim, at present unsubstantiated, to have developed his theory before Schlegel had done so, or at least independently of Schlegel" (102). However, like Shakespeare taking over so much from Plutarch's *Life of Marcus Antonius,* Coleridge, in his final articulation, nonetheless transforms Darwin's analogy between reverie and audience response into a more precise use of dreaming to define the "willing suspension of disbelief." Schlegel had written: "The theatrical as well as every other poetical illusion, is a waking dream, to which we voluntarily surrender ourselves" (96).

sory deprivation: "From the exclusion of all outward impressions on our senses the images in sleep become proportionally more vivid than they can be when the organs of sense are in their active state" (*SC,* I, 116). When we fall asleep, down comes the portcullis upon our judgment and we simply assent to our dream images without questioning if they are real or not. Whether these dream figures emerge from our memories of the previous day or from the repressed part of our psyches, our imagination displaces or condenses them into the tabloids of our dreams. Because our voluntary faculty is in abeyance, we merely assent to such images with "negative faith," not with the positively willed faith proper to religious conviction. Coleridge's playgoer, unlike Johnson's, who is conscious of theatrical deception, gradually responds to a play's illusion with the unconscious intensity of a dream image. The kinship between dream and literary interpretation, elucidated by Coleridge, allows for reading such poems as "Resolution and Independence" and "Ode on a Grecian Urn" as a dialectic of contraries in reader consciousness.[29] In using analogy to dreaming as a basis for generating a theory of dramatic illusion, Coleridge opens the door to the irrational, allowing it to bypass the critical superego, with its censorial tendency to resist the vagaries of imagination.

Coleridge's theory and poetry act as hosts to daemonic currents that release repressed feelings of guilt, remorse, and nightmare conditions of self-enclosure. For Wordsworth, these daemonic energies emerge in his "spots of time" and in other self-annihilating episodes in the "Immortality Ode" and *The Prelude.* The word *daemonic* resists definition, but it definitely signifies amoral creatures or potencies (in Plato's time inferior deities) and acts as a metaphor for unconscious energies that can exert, as it were, another will within the psyche.[30] I use the term as modified by the Freudian definition of daemons, who "might be described as the symbols by which whatever consciousness represses inevitably returns to it, except that unlike the symbols that veil repression, daemons do not need deciphering."[31] In classical cultures, the daemon served to deflect shame from individual responsibility: "The *Daemonic,* then, describes a

29. See Douglas B. Wilson, "Reading the Urn: Death in Keats's Arcadia," *Studies in English Literature* 25 (Fall 1985): 823–44.
30. I am indebted to Charles Patterson, Jr., *The Daemonic in the Poetry of John Keats* (Urbana: University of Illinois Press, 1970) 5–9, for definitions of the daemonic.
31. Lawrence Kramer, "That Other Will: The Daemonic in Coleridge and Wordsworth," *Philological Quarterly* 50 (1979): 299.

state of mind in which one sees his best or worst actions as, in some way, *not part of himself* but thrust upon him from without."[32] The Freudian return of the repressed, unlike the classical displacing of onus upon the daemon, comes from the unconscious tinged with guilt. For Wordsworth, the return of the daemonic is closely shadowed by the uncanny.

Coleridge typically resorts to the dream, as the ancients relied upon the daemon, as stemming from some agency beyond himself. For him the daemon, like the dream, can dominate his poetry beyond his conscious control, and it allows him to disavow responsibility. He tends to counter these daemonic infiltrations, as Lawrence Kramer puts it, with "an answering romantic vision." This uplifting (*Aufhebung*) dialectic allows him "to expose and purge (at least for a while) whatever is questionable, or self-haunting, or debased about the imagination itself."[33] We recognize this conflicting tension in Coleridge's adding the marginal gloss to the "Ancient Mariner"; in his juxtaposing the daemonically possessed poet with the visionary "damsel with a dulcimer" in "Kubla Khan"; in his concluding "Dejection: An Ode," with the calm eddying of Sara's joy after the storm overwhelms the Eolian harp; and in his projecting a happy ending on to *Christabel*. This process of *Aufhebung*—of uplifting the daemonic or of binding the uncanny to the commonplace—also emerges in Wordsworth's "spots of time." In his revery of human sacrifice on Sarum Plain (*The Prelude*, [12]), for example, Wordsworth also modulates this violence back to sacred consolation, with the priests and their ancient music, their white wands pointing to the stars. Yet these priests also preside over the sacrificial rites. This same pattern of uplift appears in Coleridge's criticism: he can envisage Shakespeare's becoming and speaking in the voices of Othello, but he shies away from Dionysiac encroachment by adding that Shakespeare becomes "all beings but the vicious" (*SC*, II, 160). Whereas both Wordsworth and Coleridge tend to counter the daemonic by uplifting, Words-

32. Frank D. McConnell, *The Confessional Imagination: A Reading of Wordsworth's 'Prelude'* (Baltimore and London: Johns Hopkins University Press, 1974) 12, draws upon *The Greeks and the Irrational* to show the change from "shame-culture" to "guilt-culture" as the daemon as "guilt-carrier" gave way in fifth-century Athens to the idea of sin and individual responsibility for good or evil. See E. R. Dodds, *The Greeks and the Irrational* (Berkeley: University of California Press, 1951) 153, who writes that "the function of the daemon is to be the carrier of man's potential divinity and actual guilt."
33. Kramer, "That Other Will" 318.

worth alone continues to value the daemonic as the matrix of his power. No matter how much he may skirt tragedy and move toward consolation, we sense that the daemonic endures, if only as subtext, as the real source of uncanny potency.

The link between dreams and the daemonic also subtends *The Birth of Tragedy*, where Nietzsche portrays the Apollonian dream surface as a means of incorporating the otherwise unbearable Dionysiac depth. Nietzsche unfolds a theory of Apollonian dream surface that discloses a suffering depth and, also, offers a stern test for the Romantic lyric. As applied to the lyric, the mythic valuation of Dionysos provides a standard by which to test Wordsworth's projection of himself into his solitaries and abandoned women. Nietzsche's complex argument requires that these two deities must virtually merge into each other before the fullest tragic experience can occur. Dionysos

> ascends the stage in the likeness of a striving and suffering individual. That he can *appear* at all with this clarity and precision is due to dream interpreter Apollo, who projects before the chorus its Dionysiac condition in this analogical figure. Yet in truth that hero is the suffering Dionysos of the mysteries.[34]

That the tragic hero can appear in the symbolic likeness of this god depends upon the mythic, twice-born aspect of Dionysos: "He of whom the wonderful myth relates that as a child he was dismembered by Titans now experiences in his own person the pains of individuation, and in this condition is worshiped as Zagreus" (*BT* 66). The twice-born Dionysos, then, overcomes the disintegrating process of separation and individuation by second birth, but his mythic paradigm involves going through and beyond the destructive element only to enter it again and again. The Dionysiac epitomizing of suffering should not be romanticized: separated from Apollo, Dionysos stands for the primal wound at the heart of being. The healing catharsis of tragedy is the communal loss of individuation in the separate members of the audience and, hence, the closing of the wound. The nonrepresentational art of music, connected with the dance and chanted poetry of the chorus, allows Greek tragedy

---

34. Friedrich Nietzsche, *The Birth of Tragedy and the Genealogy of Morals*, trans. Francis Golffing (New York: Doubleday, 1956) 66. Hereafter all quotations from Nietzsche are taken from this edition and will be cited parenthetically within the text as *BT*.

to engage Dionysiac, primordial pain. Nietzsche's mythic thinking on dream, as applied to the lyric, raises issues of human anguish that illuminate poems such as "Resolution and Independence" and *The Excursion* (1).

Yet Apollo also takes on the primal curse of individuation, for it is he who "appears to us once again as the apotheosis of the *principium individuationis*, in whom the eternal goal of the original Oneness, namely its redemption through illusion, accomplishes itself" (*BT* 33). This blurring of the boundaries between Apollo and Dionysos, the tragic balance between suffering and the alchemy of imaginative dream, produces tragic drama. Because Dionysos by his dismemberment had undergone a suffering reduction into the four separate elements, his fate discloses "that individuation should be regarded as the source of all suffering," as "the root of all evil." The hope of "the Eleusinian initiates," then, the rebirth of Dionysos from his disintegration, is also part of the mystery of tragedy: "a conception of art as the sanguine hope that the spell of individuation may yet be broken, as an augury of eventual reintegration" (*BT* 66–67). Although Wordsworth tends to displace tragedy, the suffering aspect of Dionysos requires attention because his mythic role in tragedy also subtends the genre of lyric that pertains to Wordsworth's poetry. For the spectator of the drama, the mediation of the dream aspect of Apollo enables the tragic hero to appear on stage in the aura of the suffering Dionysos:

> Instinctively he [the spectator] would project the shape of the god that was magically present to his mind onto that masked figure of a man, dissolving the latter's reality into a ghostly unreality. This is the Apollonian dream state, in which the daylight world is veiled and a new world—clearer, more comprehensible, more affecting than the first, and at the same time more shadowy—falls upon the eye in ever changing shapes (*BT* 58).

The spectator's entering into the Apollonian dream state allows the viewer to engage in the collective state of mind that destroys individual alienation in the members of the theater audience. Although the iconoclasm of Nietzsche places him within the company of Romantic rebels, his disdain of individuation separates him from the dominant bent of Romanticism. He both illustrates and overturns the prevalent ideology of Romanticism. Unlike the condition of individual sensibility inherited by the English Romantics, Nietzsche invokes the communal capacity of the ancient Greeks for suffering. According to him, their unflinching confrontation of human pain renders the suffering of Dionysos accessible through the dream mode of Apollo (*BT* 32–33). Unlike the Freudian dream that reveals an individual psyche, the Greek dream, in Nietzschean discourse, transcends individuation. Because the world of waking life consists of endless suffering and contradiction, the world of Nietzsche's Greek dream, fostered by illusion and under the auspices of Apollo, escapes from the prison of individuation. Dreams for Freud, on the other hand, with their disclosure of repression, can appear more Dionysiac than Apollonian. Although Freud shares with Nietzsche a keen sense of the discontents of civilization, his dreams, unlike the communal ones represented by Nietzsche, tend to reveal the private self. The ancients, with their tragic sense of life, suggested to Nietzsche a dreaming reality more real than waking. For him, the very definition of a lyric poet, who projects himself into his characters, contrasts with that of an epic poet, who stands apart from his characters with a dreamer's delight in appearance. The modern poet, such as Keats saw epitomized in Wordsworth, must confront the egotistical as inherent in the fabric of his or her moment in history. Merely personal egoism was anathema to Nietzsche, but for Wordsworth the lyric "I" can either obtrude or find common humanity in its own voice. Although Nietzsche writes less extensively on the lyric than on the tragic drama, his deployment of Dionysiac turbulence speaks to the historic condition of the Romantic lyric as well as to ancient tragedy. Nietzsche saw the pessimism in Hellenic culture as a mirror of Romanticism: according to Tilottama Rajan, he was "not concerned with historical scholarship, so much as with the use of Greek myth to develop a theogony of creative consciousness."[35] Dream in Wordsworth's poetry and in the poetry of his contemporaries goes a long way toward supplementing Nietzsche's mythic theogony with its own insight into creativity and the unconscious.

35. Tilottama Rajan, *Dark Interpreter: The Discourse of Romanticism* (Ithaca and London: Cornell University Press, 1980) 45. I am indebted to this book for its bold approach to Romantic discourse: "Nietzsche's concern is not to undermine all meanings, but to undermine specifically 'Apollonian' meanings which give 'being' (rather than 'nothingness') a genetic priority" (47, n.46).

> The true poet dreams being awake. He is not
> possessed by his subject but has dominion over it.

Charles Lamb, "Sanity of True Genius"

C H A P T E R   O N E

Dream and the Uncanny

Wordsworth regarded the character of Achilles "as one of the grandest ever conceived" because Achilles was "acting under an abiding foresight of his own death."[1] This expression of affinity for Achilles, far beyond a casual remark made in conversation, reveals a striking correspondence between the English poet and the Greek hero in relation to death. Achilles initiates the tragic mechanism leading to his own early death by allowing Patroclus to don his armor and lead the Myrmidons against the Trojans just as they begin setting fire to the Greek ships. "The death of Patroclus," Cedric Whitman reminds us, "is a shadow play of the death of Achilles, a montage emphasizing with mysterious inevitability the causal relationship between Patroclus' fall and the final stage of Achilles' tragedy."[2] When the ghost of Patroclus appears to Achilles in a dream to rebuke him for leaving his body unburned, Achilles, reminded of his own impending death, urges the mingling of their ashes: "So may the same urn hide our bones, the one / of gold your gracious mother gave"

---

1. *Wordsworth's Literary Criticism*, ed. Nowell C. Smith (London: Henry Froude, 1905) 254. Unless otherwise indicated, the 1805 edition of *The Prelude* is cited throughout. Both the 1805 and the 1850 editions are cited, by book and line numbers, from *William Wordsworth: The Prelude, 1799, 1805, 1850*, ed. Jonathan Wordsworth, M. H. Abrams, and Stephen Gill (New York: Norton, 1979). All other poems are from *The Poetical Works of William Wordsworth*, ed. Ernest de Selincourt and Helen Darbisher, 5. vols. (London: Oxford University Press, 1940). They are cited at first mention by volume and page number, and then in the text by line number.

2. Cedric H. Whitman, *Homer and the Heroic Tradition* (Cambridge, MA: Harvard University Press, 1958) 201.

24

(23.93–94).[3] This Homeric haunting is analogous to many ghostly returns in the poetry of Wordsworth. Whether in recollections of the deaths of others or eruptions of earlier stages of his own self, these disclosures invite a rethinking—on grounds of uncanny experience—of daemonic passages in his poetry. These dark memories function like repetitions in Wordsworth's dialectics of recollection (where present and past feelings are bound together in mutual interaction). Memories for Wordsworth also share with dreams an access to the psychic dimensions in the texts of his poetry. He achieves through the uncanny what Nietzsche discovers in the dream as a vehicle for the Dionysiac. Dream and the uncanny both provide (to borrow from Freud) "the royal road to the unconscious." This chapter maps the Freudian highway into Wordsworth's poetical kingdoms.

The Freudian Uncanny

Wordsworth's insistence upon selecting incidents from common life, and his typical working through the dream landscape of memory, suggest linkages with Freud's theory of the uncanny. Freud borrows his definition from Schelling: "Everything is *unheimliche* that ought to have remained secret and hidden but has come to light" (*SE* 17:225).[4] For Freud, *das Heimliche* becomes its opposite, *das Unheimliche,* when, as in Wordsworth, the commonplace is disrupted by the uncanny. In German

---

3. Homer, *The Iliad,* trans. Robert Fitzgerald (Garden City, NY: Doubleday Anchor Books, 1975) 538.

4. See also J. Hillis Miller, "Critic as Host," in *Deconstruction and Criticism* (New York: Seabury Press, 1979) 217–53, who discusses the "uncanny" relation between critic and text—as host, guest, and ghost merge into each other—and discovers nihilism, defined in Nietzschean terms as the "uncanniest of all guests," lurking beneath any unitary reading (226). Hélène Cixous, "Fictions and its Phantoms: A Reading of Freud's *Das Unheimliche* (The 'Uncanny')," in *New Literary History* 7 (Spring 1976), explores the uncanny doubling in both Hoffmann's "The Sand-Man" and Freud's own doubling in his retelling of Hoffmann. Freud employs his narrative prerogative in selecting "these libidinous regions where the light of law does not yet cast its logic and where description, plural hypotheses, and all the pretheoretical games are given free reign" (538). Neil Hertz, "Freud and the Sandman," in *Textual Strategies: Perspectives in Post-Structuralist Criticism,* ed. Josué V. Harari (Ithaca: Cornell University Press, 1979) 313, usefully draws upon Derrida to define the terrain of the uncanny, "its shifting between the registers of the psychological/daemonic and the literary, thereby dramatizing the differences as well as the complicities between the two."

dictionaries, extremes meet in the definitions of these two words: the "homely" shades into its opposite, "unhomely." "This uncanny," according to Freud, "is in reality nothing new or alien, but something which is familiar and old-established in the mind and which has become alienated from it only through the process of repression" (*SE* 17:241). In the repressed neurotic, the traumas of childhood often betray their guarded, secret presence by revealing themselves in deviant symptoms of compulsion; but the poet taps these unconscious energies and shapes them into fictions. For Wordsworth, who typically seeks "to make the incidents of common life interesting by tracing in them, truly though not ostentatiously, the primary laws of our nature," a predilection for the uncanny might strike the reader as atypical. But Wordsworth's "spots of time," for instance, with their very urgency of repetition, often disclose the turbulent depth of the uncanny rising to the surface of everyday life. Wordsworth deplores the "gross and violent stimulants" needed to overcome "the savage torpor"[5] of modern life in cities; but he also disrupts this bias toward understatement by releasing the psychic energy of the *Unheimliche* from within the commonplace. Past, present, and future do not exist in the timeless world of the unconscious: the uncanny, like the dream, reveals a path to uncharted terrain in the psyche.

"A Slumber Did My Spirit Seal," for example, progresses from Wordsworth's dream absorption in his beloved Lucy toward uncanny awareness of his own death depicted in the loss of a loved object. Charles Rzepka writes of Wordsworth's peculiar solipsistic tendency to displace "his mind's own 'powers' or 'motions' or 'visionary dreariness' into his surroundings, obliterating the embodied boundaries between self and world and appropriating that world as the contents of his own dream."[6] In "A Slumber," however, as in "Strange Fits of Passion," this process works in the opposite direction: Wordsworth moves out of the mental space of dream toward encounter with the reality of loss. In "Strange Fits," as Wordsworth approaches Lucy's cottage, his horse, in its trance-like movement, accelerates the moon's descent as he rides toward the near horizon. The moon's sudden drop into darkness behind "Lucy's cot" provokes a foreboding of Lucy's death:

5. *Literary Criticism of William Wordsworth,* ed. Paul M. Zall (Lincoln: University of Nebraska Press, 1966) 18 and 21. Hereafter cited parenthetically within the text as *LC*.
6. Charles J. Rzepka, *The Self as Mind: Vision and Identity in Wordsworth, Coleridge, and Keats* (Cambridge, MA: Harvard University Press, 1986) 80.

What fond and wayward thoughts will slide
Into a Lover's head!
"Oh mercy!" to myself I cried,
"If Lucy should be dead!"[7]

The poet awakes from his timeless spell and from the ecstasy of a trance induced by love. The word *fond* here includes the sense of the lover as victim of his own amorous condition. The word also picks up its Middle English and dialectic meanings of "infatuated, foolish" and "foolishly credulous and sanguine" (*OED*), closely linked to the vagaries of imagination. The trance usually associated with the inner life of imagination, as with the "wayward" thoughts of Lucy's death, can be shattered by the fondness of the lover's mind, all too prone to deal in extravagance. Going out toward Lucy in love lulls the speaker's mind into a dream, obliterating the boundaries of the self, yet gives way to the limited ego intensified by the shock of Lucy's mortality. This dialectic between dream and reality takes the same form in "A Slumber Did My Spirit Seal," but the sudden fit of passion hinting at Lucy's death now becomes the reality:

A slumber did my spirit seal;
I had no human fears:
She seemed a thing that could not feel
The touch of earthly years.

No motion has she now, no force;
She neither hears nor sees;
Rolled round in earth's diurnal course,
With rocks, and stones, and trees.[8]

When reading this epitaph (as Coleridge termed it) in keeping with Freud's model of the *Unheimliche,* we must try to bring to light what is hidden and secret. In what Rzepka calls Wordsworth's "visionary dislocations," "All outward and unnatural constraints on the poet's identity, all things that reinforce a sense of being among things, are appropriated by a formative, wholly mental power that is taken to be as completely his own as a dream. But the landscape of dream is both intimate and uncanny."[9] This merging of the *Heimliche* and the *Un-*

7. *Poetical Works* 2:29.
8. *Poetical Works* 2:216.
9. Rzepka, *The Self as Mind* 37.

heimliche in the landscape of Wordsworth's memory invites us to disclose the "intimate" connections between dream and the uncanny. This intimacy dovetails with Freud's discovery of the *Unheimliche* in the ordinary individual experience of family romance. Rzepka, who does not make use of Freud's essay on the uncanny, finds that the main result of Wordsworth's egotistical sublimity "is not to make familiar what is strange but to make strange what is familiar, quotidian."[10] For Freud, the familiar becomes *Unheimliche,* or estranged, through the force of repression, which invests it with potency. Although the Lucy poems make the familiar strange, this process is also reversible for Wordsworth: he often makes the strange familiar by lodging the turbulence of the daemonic—unconscious energies that tend to engulf the self—within the homely episodes of everyday life. In these two Lucy poems, the uncanny emerges not from within the beguiling charm of the dream itself, but rather from the harsh awakening from dream to the shock of real or imagined death.

In blurring the boundary between life and death, "A Slumber" represents Lucy as something between the human and the natural. She now literally participates in the Newtonian cosmos ("No motion has she now, no force"), whereas before she hovered in proximity to Wordsworth's fiction of a timeless nature. Wordsworth's mythmaking fiction of Lucy's death does offer some consolation in her becoming one with the "earth's diurnal course," which she had seemed to participate in before she died. Yet in her mortality the poet discovers the grief of his own alienating self-consciousness. Different from the poet in gender and separate as an object of love, Lucy might seem anything but the poet's double; yet her life as myth mirrors Wordsworth's own youth in relation to nature. Lucy dies before she encounters the inevitable human separation from nature incurred by awareness of mortality, but the poet wakes from his dream of Lucy's timelessness into the iron constraint of his unstated grief. The poet's understated poise ensures the quality of this lyric: we must infer Wordsworth's point of view from the poem's second stanza; his loss of love emerges from a diction that avoids the slightest hint of emotion. Wordsworth identifies "himself with another person," as Freud would have it, "so that his self becomes confounded, or the foreign self is substituted for his own—in other words, by doubling, dividing, and interchanging the self." By creating Lucy as a fictional

10. Rzepka, *The Self as Mind* 37.

double who stands in uncanny uncertainty between himself and other, the poet thus confronts his own death in Lucy's demise.

Freud and Otto Rank detect a similar ambivalence in the double "as a preservation against extinction" and as an "uncanny harbinger of death" (*SE* 17:235). By moving from the dream absorption in love, from the mythic exemption from time, Wordsworth awakes to a burden of anx-iety. By mirroring his death in Lucy's, by deploying the detached indi-rection of the double, he also masks his own fear of it. Wordsworth had seemed to participate in natural plenitude until he discovered Lucy's absence: like Blake in his inevitable move from innocence to experience, Wordsworth awakens from timeless dream to confront the fact of tran-sience. In some uncanny and unstated way, the poet *is* Lucy just as Achilles *is* Patroclus: we discover that the fate of the one is predicated as the fate of the other.

Two poems that more overtly deal with the uncanny are "Two April Mornings" and "Surprised by Joy," the first rendered by the poet as an observer *ab extra*, the second as an immediate personal narrative. In "Two April Mornings," Wordsworth and his friend Matthew, the schoolmaster, are hiking in the fells. Suddenly, an involuntary sigh from Matthew betrays a pang of grief: his memory triggered by a purple cloud, he recalls a dreamlike April morning thirty years before. In a typical Wordsworthian moment of double-consciousness, Matthew pauses beside his daughter's grave, overwhelmed by his love for her. Turning from the grave, he encountered 'A blooming Girl, whose hair was wet / With points of morning dew.'[11] We might envision her as a passing country girl, yet Matthew's account implies an uncanny return of his own lost daughter. Apart from her watery spectral appearance, the girl is metaphorically outdoing nature, as had Lucy: "'No fountain from its rocky cave / E're tripped with foot so free'" (lines 49–50). Whatever the ambiguity of this figure, real or imaginary, she doubles as Matthew's image of his love's desire. This vivid image emerges from his uncon-scious, like a dream, as a mythical repetition formed by the intensity of his feeling. By displacing the grief of Matthew, who disavows this girl as his own, the poet infers the schoolmaster's subliminal recognition of a possible ghostly return for the reader, yet withholds the father's con-scious connection of the spectral girl with the dead daughter. As ob-server *ab extra*, Wordsworth preserves his distance from his subject, but

11. *Poetical Works* 4:70–71.

brings this narrative memory to closure by reminding us that Matthew is now in his grave.

In portraying such acts of repetition, Wordsworth foreshadows Freudian insights into the return of the repressed: the creative mind, analogous to dreams, works through the unconscious and its reiterative release of psychic energy. "Surprised by Joy" repeats the father's relation to a dead daughter, but where Matthew's uncanny doubling depends upon a memory chain, Wordsworth's illusory recall of his own dead daughter, Catharine, comes directly, almost by a short circuit, from his unconscious into present experience:

> Surprised by joy—impatient as the Wind
> I turned to share the transport—Oh! with whom
> But Thee, deep buried in the silent tomb.[12]

This sonnet functions like Milton's dream of his dead wife as a living presence, coming to the blind poet as intensified seeing, "Methought I saw my late espoused saint / Come to me like Alcestis from the grave."[13] Just as Milton wakes to the daylight darkness of his blindness, so Wordsworth, tricked by his imaginary conjuring, turns abruptly upon the vacant air. Where Matthew sees a spectral girl drenched in dew, Wordsworth endures a recognition of absence. In "Two April Mornings," Wordsworth's typical stance of "keeping watch on mortality" preserves its distance by casually mentioning Matthew's death. But this repetition, with variation, shows just how closely the uncanny pattern of unconscious release implies for the poet a confrontation with death. Wordsworth bridges sundry stages of clock time by merging various selves, just as the uncanny discloses interior depths beneath the surface of rational assumptions. As often happens in the *Lyrical Ballads,* the uncanny dramatizes inner experience by transfiguring the commonplace.

Memory and the Uncanny

Before further tracing the *Unheimliche* in Wordsworth's poetry, we must first examine the *Heimliche* to show that what appear to be binary

---

12. *Poetical Works* 3:16.
13. John Milton, *Complete Poems and Major Prose,* ed. Merritt Y. Hughes (Indianapolis: The Odyssey Press, 1957) 170. All quotations from Milton's works are from this edition.

oppositions, in keeping with the German words themselves, tend to meld into each other and partake of their opposites. For Freud, the repressed, which ought to have been kept hidden and secret, discloses itself as the familiar in disguise: for this reason, he finds it no surprise that extremes meet, that linguistic usage tends to merge the *Unheimliche* into the *Heimliche* (*SE* 17:241). In the "Immortality Ode," Wordsworth portrays "Earth" as something of a foster mother who plays the "homely Nurse," and with her maternal instincts tries to make the child, "her inmate Man," forget its glorious origin. Her plain and simple virtues are homely in a well-intentioned way: in short, they are *Heimlich*. Despite these kindly offices, the child is acculturated into a "prison-house." Wordsworth's fictional child, who comes out of the "imperial palace" of eternity, must be accommodated to its earthly prison.

Here the *Heimliche,* by opposing human nature to eternal glory, acts within the Platonic myth to disparage the natural in favor of the super-natural. David Ferry regards Wordsworth's "acceptance of temporal nature" as a more accessible and lesser path to the numinous for one who has "lost his mystical capabilities." For Ferry, "nature is at once the source of power for such a poet, since it is the source of his symbols, and a limitation, since his awareness of it is his acknowledgment that he is mortal."[14] Frances Ferguson extends this line of thought to connect the epithet "natural" (the Earth's behavior according to its nature) with the "natural piety" of the epigraph from "My Heart Leaps Up."[15] To dismantle this epigraph into a parody of itself by making it stand for the child's indoctrination into prison does violence to the child's roots in nature, even though they are transplanted from other soil. Lionel Trilling usefully distinguishes "Earth" ("the things of this world") from nature and thus preserves the dichotomy between Earth's societal education and the natural heritage that lies open to the child. "Although Man may be the true child of Nature, he is the 'Foster-child' of Earth."[16]

14. David Ferry, *The Limits of Mortality: An Essay on Wordsworth's Major Poems* (Middle-town: Wesleyan University Press, 1959) 46–47.

15. Frances Ferguson, *Wordsworth: Language as Counter-Spirit* (New Haven and London: Yale University Press, 1977) 119, writes of Wordsworth's epigraph: " 'I could wish my days to be / Bound each to each in natural piety' is, in fact, a malicious epigraph in conjunction with these middle stanzas of the poem, in which 'binding' is so clearly allied with oppression that continuity feels like confinement."

16. "The Immortality Ode," *The Liberal Imagination: Essays on Literature and Society*

Wordsworth's metaphors sometimes involve him in contradictions and he comes to recognize the limits of the naturalized imagination, yet Stanza 6 of the "Immortality Ode" does not constitute a Blakean disdain of nature. The child sees the "glory" both through and beyond nature: he sees it as he had seen Lucy, as it were, in a dream.

Wordsworth transforms the homely into an ironic catalog in his negative portrayal of the ages of man (Stanza 7). Even the notorious opening lines "Behold the Child among his new-born blisses / A six year's Darling of a pigmy size," sometimes misread as sentimentality, actually mimic the language of parental baby talk. Wordsworth's irony pervades the stanza and invites an ironic reading of these lines. Further, the child is "Fretted by sallies of his mother's kisses," as if mother love had become a military invasion of the child's proper space. Lines such as these confirm David Ferry's insight that Wordsworth's "genius was his enmity to man, which he mistook for love," that he disdained aspects of ordinary society without knowing it.[17] Although sometimes singled out as a blemish upon the poem, Stanza 7, with its withering depiction of the stages of life, is crucial to the dialectical pattern of the ode. Wordsworth's fictional child, who has access to a perceptual "glory" that diminishes with growth, is all too prone, in its restless desire to imitate adult roles, to abet the process of its own imprisonment. The child will all too soon carry its burden of "earthly freight, / And custom lie upon thee with a weight, / Heavy as frost, and deep almost as life."[18] If the mimetic pattern of childhood play thus loses its savor, Wordsworth also reveals how memories of the early years, like dreams, can tap the uncanny as a means of resisting this bondage of societal acculturation. The civilizing mimesis of the child's playing adult roles, under the homely offices of "Earth,"

(Garden City, NY: Doubleday Anchor Books, 1957) 146. Barbara A. Schapiro, *The Romantic Mother: Narcissistic Patterns in Romantic Poetry* (Baltimore and London: Johns Hopkins University Press, 1983) 116–18, objects to Trilling's differentiating *earth* and *nature* by showing uses of *earth* in the first four stanzas of the ode that are synonymous with *nature*. Even if one takes this point, the ode contains inconsistencies such as those found in its metaphors of light, and Trilling's point may still be valid for Stanzas 6 and 7. Yet her point that Wordsworth's childhood glory must be relinquished in favor of a mature compassion for human society never addresses the force of the ironic catalogue of negative theatrical imitation that acculturation into society produces in Stanza 7. Trilling makes a point similar to Schapiro's about the inevitable progress toward the burden of human suffering, yet he also recognizes how some aspects of society also detract from the heritage of the child.

17. Ferry, *The Limits of Mortality* 173.   18. *Poetical Works* 4:281–82.

goes counter to the unearthly origin of the child, inferred from the Platonic myth of preexistence.

How does the *Unheimliche* work through memory in the "Immortality Ode" to act as therapy for impoverished adult life? Exactly what events from his past does Wordsworth single out for highest praise? The difficulty of his subject makes it easier to say what they are *not* than what they are. For it is not "delight and liberty, the simple creed / Of Childhood," nor is it youth's fountain of ever-replenishing hope. As an adult looking back, he gives "thanks and praise," not for these rhetorically enforced, highly prized blessings,

> But for those obstinate questionings
> Of sense and outward things,
> Fallings from us, vanishings;
> Blank misgivings of a Creature
> Moving about in worlds not realised . . .
> (lines 142–46)

The style of these self-destroying experiences works best through negation in the classic pattern of mysticism; such recurrent negations describe what defies language by rejecting valuable possible alternatives that imply an unmediated encounter. Here the valorized event remains enigmatic and must be inferred from examples of what it is not. To the child, these experiences were terrifying, but to the grown man they are the more valued because they undo the bondage to socialized life. The child had the experience but missed the meaning. The poet, by moving beyond the child's impercipience and fear, has it both ways. Coleridge remarks in *Biographia Literaria* that only they can understand the "Immortality Ode" who have learned the discipline of reflection upon inner states of consciousness, "to which they know that the attributes of time and space are inapplicable and alien, but which yet cannot be conveyed save in symbols of time and space." Trilling discerns in these moments the liminality between the oceanic feeling that Freud identifies as common to most human experience, and our maturing discovery of the limits of our own bodies.[19] As I shall explore in chapter 5, Helen Vendler in opposition to Trilling reads Wordsworth's "fallings from us, vanish-

19. On Wordsworth's mysticism see Ferry, *The Limits of Mortality* 47; Samuel Taylor Coleridge, *Biographia Literaria,* 2 vols., ed. John Shawcross (London: Oxford University Press, 1907) 2:120; Trilling, "The Immortality Ode" 139–40.

ings" as a move beyond the senses: "Wordsworth was able to complete the Ode only by at last recalling the first motions of *non*-sensuous instincts as the most valuable of his childhood experiences."[20] Although each of these readings bears upon Wordsworth's economy of mental states, all neglect the uncanny turbulence peculiar to the poet. Because these living embers of memory are in danger of being smothered by ashes, Wordsworth would bring to light what is, in the relentless process of growth, becoming ever more hidden and secret.

In *Civilization and Its Discontents,* Freud describes this blurring of the boundaries of identity—of the oceanic experience—as follows: "There are cases in which parts of a person's own body, even portions of his own mental life—his perceptions, thoughts and feelings—appear alien to him and as not belonging to his ego; there are other cases in which he ascribes to the external world things that clearly originate in his own ego and that ought to be acknowledged by it. Thus even the feeling of our own ego is subject to disturbances and the boundaries of the ego are not constant" (*SE* 21:66). Wordsworth recalls these obliterating encounters as tentative evidence of immortality, of oceanic moments unlike but akin to the dream-invested visions of childhood as sources of energy. Yet the influx of power in these ordeals puts the child's identity at risk, and thus disorients and frightens him. As Wordsworth remembers them, these episodes return as uncanny repetitions in his adult life. What makes these moments vital is their ambivalence: Wordsworth undergoes a numinous expansion, but his awareness of mortality intensifies as a byproduct of the invasion of self. If such sublime moments imply intimations of

20. Helen Vendler, "Lionel Trilling and the *Immortality Ode,*" *Salmagundi* 41 (1978): 83, also buttresses her point by citing a canceled passage from the ode: "This hints at the difficulty of our attempt to liberate ourselves from 'the spell / Of that strong frame of sense in which we dwell'" (82). See also Jeffrey C. Robinson, *Radical Literary Education: A Classroom Experiment with Wordsworth's "Ode"* (Madison: University of Wisconsin Press, 1987) 114–17, who sees a problem in Wordsworth's downgrading of bodily sense in favor of Platonic myth: "Perhaps the most revealing revision is the elimination of the phrase, 'strong frame of sense in which we dwell.' Like the definition of the child's power as a 'might / Of untam'd pleasures,' this line states emphatically that the body defines us and organizes our relationship to the world." Wordsworth had revised the "untam'd pleasures" of 1807 to "heaven-born freedom" in 1815. Robinson's insight is welcome in that these revisions do indeed downgrade the claims of the body by reinforcing the Platonic fiction (117). Even in the revised version, however, the uncanny continues to assert the claims of the body.

immortality, they also bring a sense of mortal shame for returning from such overmastering exposure. The uncanny can restructure the impoverished life of the adult who remains keenly aware of his own loss of perceptual power. The adult transforms and releases the threatening energy of childhood fear into a power capable of freeing him from the constraints of civilization. These "fallings from us, vanishings" represent for Wordsworth an *Unheimliche* journey into the abyss of himself.[21]

A psychoanalytic reading typically arouses critical suspicions about taking a writer such as Wordsworth at face value, by questioning how a text might provide a depth that would subvert or complicate the surface level: "In particular, they [the analyst and the psychoanalytic critic] share a sensitivity to all the ways in which a conventional, naturalistic, literal-minded expectation about meaning is defeated; both have become wary of the 'referential fallacy,' and they look to other dimensions of a text besides the seemingly obvious literal meaning to which it refers."[22] Modern critics sometimes express just such suspicion of Wordsworth's "Fallings from us, vanishings; / Blank misgivings of a Creature / Moving about in worlds not realised." These are not merely screen memories—which are formed later but mask as original occurrences—but a rescripting of childhood trauma from an adult perspective. Michael Friedman, for example, aptly stresses the terror in the earlier experience of the child, but he resists reading these moments of self-obliteration as numinous idealism. If the poet's surroundings appeared to fall into an abyss of unreality, "it was because he was contracting into solipsism, into a self devoid of relation to anything outside the self. Wordsworth felt himself to be in a world in which all objects were unreal and dead."

Friedman stresses the border between self and other; he refuses to take literally the poet's remarks to Isabella Fenwick about the "obstinate

---

21. For a different opinion, see William H. Galperin, *Revision and Authority in Wordsworth: The Interpretation of a Career* (Philadelphia: University of Pennsylvania Press, 1989) 157, who demystifies the myth of memory and childhood. Instead of using Freud's "oceanic feeling" or the uncanny to disclose the energy of childhood, Galperin accentuates Freud's portrayal of the adult world of the superego. Instead of seeing, along with Trilling, the poet's adult gain in tragic experience, Galperin sees Wordsworth retreating into a world of fictional memory: "Contrary to those readings in which the poet's power and immortality are a 'response' to Freud, the speaker of the Ode ultimately resists this very trajectory."
22. Meredith A. Skura, *The Literary Use of the Psychoanalytic Process* (New Haven and London: Yale University Press, 1981) 231.

questionings"; he rejects the depiction of such experiences in the discourse of "philosophical idealism." In the end, he dismantles Wordsworth's enigma: "An abyss of idealism suggests a realm filled either with the subject's spirit or with some transcendent spirit. But the world the terrified youngster contemplated, far from being filled with spirit, was drained of it, was void."[23] Although Friedman captures the childhood shock now refashioned by the adult poet, his hermeneutics of suspicion (to borrow a phrase from Paul Ricoeur) here violates the text. To call this "abyss of idealism" *solipsism* has its own logic, yet the blurring of the boundary between self and other in Freud's "oceanic feeling," far from producing a void, discloses the power of otherness invading the borders of his identity. This mental abyss suggested by Wordsworth's "obstinate questionings" now invites our revaluation by means of the uncanny.[24]

As Freud expands on it, "an uncanny experience occurs either when infantile complexes which have been repressed are once more revived by some impression, or when primitive beliefs which have been surmounted seem once more to be confirmed" (*SE* 17:249). Wordsworth's self-destroying moments qualify as "primitive" experience from his childhood that he has outgrown but can now reencounter as uncanny vestiges of implanted energy. Whereas Freud seeks to dislodge the *Unheimliche* from the bondage of repression, Wordsworth strives in the "Immortality Ode" to recuperate the uncanny moment for a different purpose—to rekindle his spirit through the agency of memory. What we

23. Michael Friedman, *The Making of a Tory Humanist* (New York: Columbia University Press, 1979) 22.

24. Rzepka, *The Self as Mind* 37–38. Rzepka's account of the Penrith Beacon incident, even though not written about the "Immortality Ode," provides a corrective to Friedman's reading of the "void": "It is his [Wordsworth's] sense of the uncanny that strikes the poet as the surest sign of other-worldly intervention. The dreamscape and the figures in it etch upon his passive mind a cryptic, often undecipherable message that he must struggle to understand because *he* means nothing thereby: the imaginative 'Powers' of mind working *in* him do" (38). My application of the uncanny to Wordsworth's spots predates Rzepka's book (1986). See Douglas B. Wilson, "Wordsworth and the Uncanny: 'The Time is Always Present,'" *The Wordsworth Circle* (1985): 74–84. Although he does not make use of Freud's "The 'Uncanny,'" I welcome his support for recognizing the uncanny in Wordsworth's spots. I am indebted to Rzepka's seminal work on the dream. See also Barbara A. Schapiro, *The Romantic Mother* 100, for an astute psychoanalytic reading of the uncanny in Wordsworth as "the emergence of repressed libidinal and destructive feelings toward the mother imago." These hostile energies derive from "the original narcissistic wound" incurred by separation from the mother.

find here in Wordsworth—the lyric poet's depersonalization—is described by Nietzsche as a "dream scene": "The artist had abrogated his subjectivity earlier, during the Dionysiac phase: the image which now reveals to him his oneness with the heart of the world is a dream scene showing forth vividly, together with the original pain, the original delight of illusion." Wordsworth derives from the uncanny what Nietzsche mediates through dream as the Dionysiac. The kinship between the *Unheimliche* and the dream here reveals itself: either route to the unconscious has the power to vitiate solipsism. In his words, "The 'I' thus sounds out of the depth of being; what recent writers on esthetics speak of as 'subjectivity' is a mere figment" (*BT* 38). What Friedman calls a solipsistic emptiness is actually its sublime opposite, Dionysiac otherness filling the initial vacuum with redundant power.

Wordsworth further complicates these already baffling lines on his "obstinate questionings" by alluding to the ghost of Hamlet's father: "High instincts before which our mortal nature / Did tremble like a guilty Thing surprised" (lines 146–47). What does a young boy's fearful encounter have in common with Old Hamlet's ghost, forced back to the nether regions by a rooster's crowing, starting, as Horatio says, "like a guilty thing / Upon a fearful summons" (1.1.148–49)? Because this ghost has crossed the boundary between the living and the dead, it trembles at a summons back to the underworld. By uncanny analogy, the boy's mortality trembles at an encounter with a world beyond death. The boy's guilt provokes an intricate reaction: Wordsworth has lost his father and takes unseemly guilt upon himself, whereas Old Hamlet incurs his own guilt—cut off with "foul crimes" upon his head, without benefit of communion, confession, or extreme unction. As Jonathan Wordsworth puts it, "the poet associated the 'blank misgivings' and 'high instincts' of childhood with his father's death, and with the guilt that has been taken over from the ghost."[25] Yet it is actually his own uncanny guilt that incites him to make common cause with the Danish king's ghost. One would expect the young Wordsworth, who lost both parents by the age of thirteen, to become preternaturally aware of mortality and to internalize guilt as the understandable response of a son assuming irrational blame for his father's death.

Hard questions stem from this astonishing connection. Why is the

25. Jonathan Wordsworth, *William Wordsworth: The Borders of Vision* (Oxford: Clarendon Press, 1982) 64.

boy, in the role of a son, not compared to Hamlet himself, rather than to the paternal ghost? Why can the adult poet draw sustenance from this childhood trauma that had disrupted the normal course of his life like a usurping ghost? The hidden and secret sources of power for Wordsworth, like the enigmatic guilt of the old king's ghost, emerge from a no-man's-land on the border between this world and beyond. Adult consciousness assumes an alien presence in the face of an unconscious and indifferent cycle of nature, and all too easily seeks refuge in the numbing armor of habit. But in retrospect, the self-destroying encounter changes the poet's adult consciousness by an *Unheimliche* intimation that had shaken the frame of his identity to its foundations.

Memory and Psychoanalytic Narration

Freud and Wordsworth, both preoccupied with the role of memory, mutually illuminate its implications for narrative patterns. A psychoanalytic reading of Wordsworth's uses of memory, while recognizing the problematic changeability of the self, requires the assumption of an endangered but nonetheless legitimate self. In the historic climate of the Romantic poets, as the self becomes increasingly perplexing, the word *self* occurs as part of a struggle to maintain identity in a world that tends to put it at risk.[26] Just as the telling in analysis (like Wordsworth's central mode of constructing poems) provides a structure for disclosing the patient's protean identity, so disclosure of the repressed uncanny affords useful insight into the poet's practice of composition. In articulating the function of memory in his poetry, Wordsworth provides the clue to his imaginative changes by wedding his internal emotion to external event: "Poetry is the spontaneous overflow of powerful feelings: it takes its origin from emotion recollected in tranquillity: the emotion is contemplated till by a species of reaction the tranquillity gradually disappears, and an emotion, similar to that which was before the subject of contemplation, is gradually produced, and does itself actually exist in the mind" (*LC* 27). The function of memory is never an exact recollection of the past, but in recalling a potential subject for poetry, thought and imagination both actively participate in recreating the event. Unlike a

---

26. Rzepka, *The Self as Mind* 1–30, provides a philosophical discussion of the endangered self in the Romantic period.

neurotic patient, whose emotion may be blocked or displaced, Wordsworth achieves distance and control over his partly subconscious powers. As Charles Lamb sums up the difference between madness and
genius: "The true poet dreams being awake. He is not possessed by his
subject but has dominion over it."[27] The poet does not—like the neurotic dreamer—tend to disclose the deviant repressed. The artist taps
unconscious desires, including repression, by the dream process of imagination.

Wordsworth himself was acutely aware of the slippages and distortions of memory, as witnessed by his figure of himself in a rowboat
looking down into a transparent lake:

> solacing himself
> With such discoveries as his eye can make
> Beneath him in the bottom of the deeps,
> Sees many beauteous sights—weeds, fishes, flowers,
> Grots, pebbles, roots of trees—and fancies more,
> Yet often is perplexed, and cannot part
> The shadow from the substance, rocks and sky,
> Mountains and clouds, from that which is indeed
> The region, and the things which there abide
> In their true dwelling; now is crossed by gleam
> Of his own image, by a sunbeam now,
> And motions that are sent he knows not whence,
> Impediments that make his task more sweet . . . .
> (*The Prelude* 4.249–61)

Such are the incumbencies of Wordsworth "o'er the surface of past
time," as he relishes the retelling in Books 1 and 2 of *The Prelude* of his
childhood memories among the lakes and fells. In thus lingering over the
episodes of his youth, he implies the aging process of diminishing
powers within his guarded recognition of possible distortion. Although
particular details may fade or change, the residue of sublimity remains
unscathed.

Memory, apart from informing the dialectic between man and boy in
the "Immortality Ode," provides a counterpoise to the civilized world
of "endless emulation." Yet Frances Ferguson's deconstructive reading

---

27. Quoted in Lionel Trilling, "Freud and Literature," in *The Liberal Imagination* 169.

raises the objection that the poet is merely projecting a naive fictional childhood out of his adult need. Such a reading would discredit Wordsworth's use of memory by questioning his creation of a false polarity between a fiction of childhood "glory" and the "dead forms" of adulthood: "But memory forms no part of these projections [these polarities] unless they are both seen as negative moments which intimate by their oversimplification the difficulties of accepting memory as a truly temporal consciousness of the self's identity and difference from itself."[28] This reading would coincide with a Nietzschean dismantling of the self: far from a unitary self, or even any self-knowledge, we have only a multiplicity of unknowable selves. A psychoanalytic reading, however, recognizes the liabilities of memory, yet cleaves to an identity that emerges from all the protean retelling of past and present recollection because one *lives* it, inhabits it.

In recognizing, for instance, that most memories are in fact screen memories rather than accurate reproductions of the past, Freud is aware of the potential distortions of memory: "It may indeed be questioned whether we have any memories at all *from* our childhood: memories *relating* to our childhood may be all that we possess. Our childhood memories show us our earliest years not as they were but as they appeared at the later periods when the memories were revived. In these periods of revival, the childhood memories did not, as people are accustomed to say, *emerge*; they were formed at that time" (*SE* 3:322). Wordsworth provides his own analogy to screen memories by marking the overlay of shadows upon the water and his imaginary additions to the lake bottom. Yet his representation of himself in poetry is not strictly analogous to a patient's telling his or her story to an analyst, with all the attendant complications of transference and counter-transference. The

28. Ferguson, *Language as Counter-Spirit* 122. See also Joseph H. Smith in *Interpreting Lacan* 274, who discovers a decentered self in Lacan's linguistic reading of "a more unsettling Freud—A Freud who would face American ego psychology with the question of what it is to approach and repeatedly reapproach the assumption of one's subjecthood, only to arrive at a symbolically structured acceptance that the center of one's being is decentered, other, never fully present, never fixed. For a different opinion, see Charles Taylor, *The Sources of the Self: The Making of the Modern Identity* (Cambridge: Harvard University Press, 1989) 429, who writes, "There are forms of subject-centeredness which don't consist in talking directly about the self. . . . The very nature of epiphanic art can make it difficult to say just what is being celebrated: the deep recesses beyond or below the subject, or the subject's uncanny powers."

poet, unlike the analytic patient, often fictionalizes autobiographical fact in shaping recollected events. Irrespective of a strict rendering of his own personality, Wordsworth produces representative fictions of the stages of human growth—childhood, youth, and adulthood. Even if these fictions are screen memories, they validate, in the retelling, their own dialectical interaction of two different stages of feeling.

Screen memories, then, may influence both the tellings of Freud's patients and Wordsworth's modes of recollection. Roy Schafer, a modern analyst, seeks to revise the mode of psychoanalytic narrative in a way that avoids a tendency toward determinism in a case history told in the "simplified form of traditional biography." Instead of pseudoscientific fact-finding in a positivistic manner, the dialogue between analyst and patient should take the form of "hermeneutically filled-in narrative structures. The narrative structures that have been adopted control the telling of the events of the analysis, including the many tellings and retellings of the analysand's life history. The time is always present. The event is always an ongoing dialogue." This exchange between patient and analyst differs, of course, from Wordsworth's dialogues with himself or from his rendering of implications for a reader, yet Schafer's theory of narrative memory vindicates the practice of Wordsworth's poetry in dealing with recollection. Just as Schafer rethinks the narrativity of Freudian analysis, so Wordsworth employs the polemics of recall to generate a dialectic between his various temporal selves. Like revisionary analysis, Wordsworth's poetry tends to begin with the present as the point from which to generate his fictions. Schafer's analytic narrative begins with a constant retelling of the present—within the transference—in order to bring about change in the analysand: "Under the provisional and dubious assumption that past, present, and future are separable, each segment of time is used to set up a series of questions about the others and to answer the questions addressed to it by the others. And all of these accounts keep changing as the analytic dialogue continues."[29]

Such an account of analytic narration suggests salient ways in which Wordsworth typically uses recollection. "To the Cuckoo," "Tintern Abbey," "Resolution and Independence," the "Immortality Ode," and "Elegiac Stanzas" all operate from changing conditions in the present that dictate different relations to past and future. Like analytic dialogues,

29. Roy Schafer, "Narration in the Psychoanalytic Dialogue," in *On Narrative,* ed. W.J.T. Mitchell (Chicago: University of Chicago Press, 1980) 49.

retold from multiple perspectives, the story of the self is often revised. The telling of the self requires these dialogues with itself—with its past, present, and future—for the reader to achieve a sense of the poet's identity. No single account of the self in recollection can be reified into absolute status: comparisons among these poems become one of the most useful tools for interpreting fictional identity. This model of the analytic dialogue serves to validate the return of the uncanny for Wordsworth within the dialectics of his double-consciousness.

The Uncanny and the "Spots of Time"

The Prelude, with its "spots of time" and its repetitive resort to memory, is fraught with Wordsworthian disclosures of the uncanny. They contain therapeutic and restorative energy for the modern mind, weighed down by "trivial occupations, and the round / Of ordinary intercourse" (11.262–63). In describing these spots, these temporal and spatial islands "in the unnavigable depth / Of our departed time" (the Norton *Prelude* 493), Wordsworth implies a daemonic underpresence:

> This efficacious spirit chiefly *lurks*
> Among those passages of life in which
> We have had deepest feeling that the mind
> Is lord and master, and that outward sense
> Is but the obedient servant of her will.
> (*The Prelude* 11.268–72, my italics)

The verb "lurks," with its hint at disclosing what is hidden and secret, baffles the senses, with their bondage to appearance, and implies an unsettling component in Wordsworth's idea of education by fear. A "master-mistress" incongruity (to borrow a turn from Shakespeare) emerges here with what Wordsworth surprisingly represents as a *lordly* mind, of feminine gender, portrayed as mastering the potentially unruly senses. As E. Douka Kabitoglou nicely puts this matter, there is an "inner tension present in the poet's mind—and text—by the parallel adoption of a patriarchal authoritarian model, and the recognition of the feminine values of affect and emotion—a simultaneous repression and exaltation of the 'female.' "[30] This exalting and repressing of the feminine

---

30. E. Douka Kabitoglou, "Problematics of Gender in the Nuptials of *The Prelude,*" *The Wordsworth Circle* 19 (1988): 134.

in the implicit "master-mistress" coincides with the verb "lurks," as if the spots contain unconscious salience not entirely under the poet's control, as betrayed by his incongruous crossings of gender. In the patriarchal structure that might occlude the feminine, we identify the rational assumptions of the normal power structure. But in the subversive, partly repressed feminine—in the mind fertilized by the spots—Wordsworth's female matrices of creativity break through the barriers of repression with doubly charged power. Given the poet's adult tendency to become further enmeshed in excessive masculinity, we can understand why the androgynous energies in his uncanny recollections must not be allowed to escape into oblivion. On the one hand, the imagination comes from beyond nature and craves a lodging in the external world.[31] But on the other, uncanny vestiges of the mind, emerging from unconscious depths, unhinge the complacency of the adult conceptual mind all too liable to the burden of custom. Like the neurotic patient, Wordsworth requires his own repetitive therapy, but while the sick mind is crippled by the deviant return of the repressed, the poet shapes his mythic repetitions into the sinuous wanderings of his own mental journey.

Wordsworth's periodic returns to the psychic past, his spots of time, trace the growth and bonding of his imagination to *Unheimliche* sources of power. In an essay on Freud and narrative, Peter Brooks remarks upon the "daemonic and the uncanny nature of repetition" in a way that distinguishes the creative artist from the compulsive neurotic: "Repetition in all its literary manifestations may in fact work as a 'binding,' a binding of textual energies that allows them to be mastered by putting them into serviceable form within the energetic economy of the narrative." Wordsworth's spots are not, of course, literal repetitions, yet their common investment with psychic energies rooted in childhood fear lets them work like mythic repetition with variation. The poet's struggles with time are the acts of "memory—or more precisely, we could say with Freud, of 'remembering, repeating, working through.'"[32] Although Wordsworth is writing an autobiographical poem in *The Prelude,* these Freudian dynamics are primarily functions of textuality rather than biography. Unlike the neurotic individual, who lives at the mercy of

31. Geoffrey H. Hartman, *Wordsworth's Poetry 1787–1814* (New Haven: Yale University Press, 1964) 229.
32. Peter Brooks, "Freud's Masterplot: Questions of Narrative," in *Literature and Psychoanalysis,* ed. Shoshana Felman (Baltimore: Johns Hopkins University Press, 1977) 289, 299.

repressions that return compulsively, Wordsworth writes a narrative of his life that creates its own textual desire to invite the reader to participate in the acts of "working through" now embedded in the poem. Readers must then make their own connections among the episodes that circle backwards and forwards among themselves. And there is also a reader figured in the poem, the admonishing but sympathetic Samuel Taylor Coleridge. In this "poem to Coleridge" he is the imagined other (like the analyst in the transference) through whom the narrator/patient develops his self.

In recalling his spots of time from early childhood, Wordsworth typically returns to human desire as an alien presence within the calm of nature. The "presences of Nature" strangely haunted his boyhood actions, and

> Impressed upon all forms the characters
> Of *danger* or *desire,* and thus did make
> The surface of the universal earth
> With triumph, and delight, and hope, and fear,
> Work like a sea . . .
> (*The Prelude* 1.490–501, my italics)

By "haunting him," these presences of nature operate below the level of ordinary sensory experience and infuse a turbulent power within the commonplace. These hauntings return, like the apparition of Old Hamlet's ghost, as a metaphoric analogy supplied by the adult poet for the unnerving impact of those disruptive moments in his childhood. Before giving way to a strong desire to steal a bird from another's snare, he had felt alienated from the "moon and stars" and found his presence "a trouble to the peace / That was among them." Hanging perilously above the raven's nest on the "naked crag," the "strange utterance" of the wind incidentally penetrates his mind as he pursues his craving for the bird's eggs. As he takes part by night in an ice-skating party, "every icy crag" tinkles "like iron" from the tumult of the skaters, but "the distant hills" send "an alien sound / Of melancholy" back into the noisy throng (*The Prelude,* 1.321–24; 1.346–49; 1.468–71). These separate incidents function like a repetition with variation, as the alien note of human desire echoes against the austerity of nature.[33] Desire is associated with the voiceless

33. Frederick Garber, *Wordsworth and the Poetry of Encounter* (Urbana: University of Illinois Press, 1971) 19, writes of Wordsworth's role as an alien observer in encounters with man and

44

DREAM AND THE UNCANNY

uncanny in the repeated pattern of the spots of time. In the narrative action of *The Prelude*'s text, "desire must be considered the very motor of narrative, its dynamic principle."[34] Desire, in effect, motivates narrative and *re*-motivates earlier events. The reader responds to encoded desires as a by-product of the act of reading. As an adult looking back upon his past in world-weariness, Wordsworth craves the very energy of desire as a source of creativity. In his maturity, he indulges himself in the wish that we might give "to duty and to truth / The eagerness of infantine desire" (*The Prelude* 2.25–26). Because *infant* in its derivation means "without speech" (Latin *in-fans*), Wordsworth here aims to transform the energy of silence into the language of poetry. Desire itself tends to hide from disclosure in language and to invite its connection with dream and the uncanny: "Since desires hide themselves in dreams, interpretation must substitute the light of meaning for the darkness of desire." In this sense, *desire* refers to its primitive habitation in the unconscious, or as Paul Ricoeur would have it: "If dream interpretation can stand as the paradigm for all interpretation it is because dreams are in fact the paradigm of all the strategems of desire."[35] Thus the language of desire emerges in symbols amenable to dream interpretation, but remains hidden from ordinary language and must be inferred.

Wordsworth's spots of time, infused with the uncanny, retain traces of desire; these spatial and temporal landing places in the landscape of memory contain evidence of imaginative potency. As a child not yet six years old, Wordsworth becomes separated from his guide, honest James. This incident fits the recurrent topos of the mental traveler in *The Prelude*. His encounter with the moldering gibbet, with the victim's name still visible in the plucked turf, adds the haunting presence of death to his mounting fears. All this preparatory detail invests his next encounter, with the woman, with a dreamlike, mythic quality, as if it takes place in another world: "A girl who bore a pitcher on her head / And seemed with difficult steps to force her way / Against the blowing wind" (*The*

---

nature: "The observer is consistently a stranger, an outsider alone and with difficulty becoming aware that he is separate and has to learn to live with that too. In some cases the stranger takes the role of an intruder, breaking in where he has no business, into a life that shares no part of his life but may be forced to notice him."

34. Brooks, "Freud's Masterplot" 281.

35. Paul Ricoeur, *Freud and Philosophy: An Essay on Interpretation*, trans. Denis Savage (New Haven and London: Yale University Press, 1970) 159–60.

Prelude 11.305–7). The episode has all the inevitability of dream logic, for we never think to ask why he does not call out to her. The action takes place in the visionary scene of his own mind, with all the absorption one would expect from the unfolding sequence of a dream where there is no chance to revise the pattern of events.[36] As in "Tintern Abbey" ("I cannot paint / What then I was," [lines 75–76]) and "Elegiac Stanzas," he resorts to the analogy of painting (which I shall explore in the next chapter) to describe what here is really beyond description, because the ordinary has become uncanny:

> It was, in truth,
> An Ordinary sight, but I should need
> Colours and words that are unknown to man
> To paint the visionary dreariness
> Which, while I looked all round for my lost guide,
> Did at that time invest the naked pool,
> The beacon on the lonely eminence,
> The woman, and her garments vexed and tossed
> By the strong wind.
> (*The Prelude* 11.307–15)

Wordsworth's rhetoric of the unpaintable resembles that of the negations leading up to the "fallings from us, vanishings" of Stanza 9 of the "Immortality Ode." Both passages, similar in effect to the aftermath of the boat-stealing episode, render ordinary sensory experience invalid or inapplicable. Yet, unlike the other two incidents that are equally freighted with the uncanny, this encounter with the woman transfigures the "ordinary sight," which, paradoxically, the poet paints with more than usual care.

Some years ago, Janet Spens described this incident in *The Prelude* as providing a corroborating impetus for her understanding of Spenser's *The Faerie Queene* as an action in mental space: "Faery Land then is the mind, the inner experience of each of us, and the subject of *The Faerie Queene* was the same as that of Wordsworth's projected *magnum opus* more than two centuries later—the apprehension, description, and or-

36. Jean-Paul Sartre, *The Psychology of Imagination* (New York: Philosophical Library, 1948) 246, distinguishes waking from dreaming consciousness: "In an imaginary world there is no dream of *possibilities* since possibilities call for a real world on the basis of which they are thought of as possibilities."

ganization of the inner world." Like Spenser, Wordsworth devises a language for inner space: whereas Spenser peoples his allegorical dream-scape, Wordsworth makes landscape the vehicle of spots invested with a redundance of imagination. Whereas Spenser tends to deploy the natural world as an extension of the human, the girl with a pitcher on her head is assimilated into the dreary scene.[37]

In this respect, the episode illustrates Wordsworth's premise about these spots' deriving their "efficacious spirit" from those moments in life that confirm our conviction that "the mind / Is lord and master, and that outward sense / Is but the obedient servant of her will" (*The Prelude* 11.270–72). From the perspective of the young boy, the dreamlike enactment of the scene operates beyond the rational control of the mind. Clearly, here the adult is looking back upon his past and rescripting the episode from the mature poet's vantage point. Yet this transformation of biography by no means vitiates Wordsworth's use of his boyhood experience: only an adult understanding of this eerie vision resolves the enigma of deploying sense in order to go beyond it.[38] The senses here have been transfigured by uncanny imagination, although the young boy in the grip of his fear would have been far from recognizing this insight.

Psychoanalytic readings of the first spot of time have focused upon the Oedipal symbolism implicit in its spatial figuration. Onorato's is an exemplary reading of this kind: "It is surprising, first of all, how very simply the images are very common dream symbols: the naked pool in a landscape enclosed by hills as woman or the mother; the mountain with the beacon on the top as phallic man or the father. The girl who bore a pitcher on her head is also woman or the mother; the pitcher, as something which holds and pours fluid to drink, is the symbol of the breast, here, as often in dreams, displaced but emphasized by that displacement."[39] This episode of the girl with the pitcher on her head brings

37. Janet Spens, *Spenser's Faerie Queene: An Interpretation* (New York: Russell and Russell, 1934) 52–60, discovers a source for the atypical detail of Wordsworth's woman carrying a pitcher on her head in Una, separated from the Redcross Knight. The Knight, "wandering among the grey chill shadows that cling to the by-ways of the mind," encountered a "damsel" "that on her shoulders sad pot of water bore" (*Faerie Queene*, 1.3.10).

38. William Empson, "*Sense in The Prelude*," the Norton *Prelude* 636, notes how "sense" gives way to an "inner sense" to the "supreme sense of imagination." I take Empson's point, yet find it disappointing that he never addresses the opposing question of "sensual tyranny."

39. Richard Onorato, *The Character of the Poet: Wordsworth in 'The Prelude'* (Princeton: Princeton University Press, 1971) 214.

47

together in a single focus the dynamics of family romance in this Oedipal reading. Even without resorting to dream symbolism, Onorato writes, the "gentle aspects of the landscape" would suffice to suggest "'the Presence' that is the mother in Nature"; also, the distant mountain "dominating the landscape stand[s] for the father." These readings stress the young boy's traumatic separation from his guide above the awareness of death infused by the gibbet. Onorato elides, however, the uncanny potency of the death-marked spot with which memory has imbued the adult consciousness.[40] The connotations of the Freudian *Unheimliche*, although implanted in childhood, derive their resonance from the poet's adult rescripting of his narrative, as Schafer's model implies, in keeping with the artistic design of his older self.

The moldering gibbet in Wordsworth's first spot of time acts as a screen memory: the poet looking back upon the roots of his imagination, as when he confronts the shock of Lucy's death, infuses a ghostly image of mortality and activates the "visionary dreariness" in the timespot of the mental traveler. As a bridge passage between these two spots of time, Wordsworth discloses the fragility of memory as though it shares in the evanescence of dreams:

> The days gone by
> Come back upon me from the dawn almost
> Of life; the hiding-places of my power
> Seem open, I approach, and then they close;
> I see by glimpses now, when age comes on
> May scarcely see at all . . .
> (*The Prelude* II.333–38)

This insight reflects the peculiar stance of keeping watch over mortality that informs Wordsworth's poetry of recollection: this mortal consciousness is the subtext on the verge of breaking through the surface of "Tintern Abbey"; perhaps nature will indeed "betray / The heart that loved her." These elusive and uncanny memories carry the full impact

---

40. Richard Onorato, *The Character of the Poet* 213, writes persuasively about the boy's possible impercipience in such matters as the murderer, the reading of the letters in the turf, and even all the visual details. He thinks the boy's separation and estrangement primarily account for his fear, and of the gibbet that "a large piece of moldering farm equipment that was strange to the child might have frightened him as much."

of hidden things disclosed and infuse the dialectic of the double-consciousness.

The second spot of time, centering on the death of Wordsworth's father, emerges again with strong fidelity to sensory detail:

> 'Twas a day
> Stormy, and rough, and wild, and on the grass
> I sate half sheltered by a naked wall.
> Upon my right hand was a single sheep,
> A whistling hawthorn on my left, and there,
> With those companions at my side, I watched,
> Straining my eyes intensely as the mist
> Gave intermitting prospect of the wood
> And plain beneath.
>
> (*The Prelude* II.355–63)

Because I will discuss "sensual tyranny" in more detail in chapter 5, a few words about it here in relation to the spots of time will suffice. Wordsworth uses "sensual tyranny" in a special sense, to denote a fixation upon a particular sense, such as sight, that obstructs the mental activity of imagination. The uncanny dreamscape of the first spot offers a counterpoise to the different mood of courtship with Mary and Dorothy that is later overlaid upon the same spot. This later event superimposes a different temporal level upon the same spot and provides another example of *Aufhebung,* previously discussed in relation to Coleridge: the poet attempts to merge the *Heimliche* into the *Unheimliche,* as if to lodge the uncanny within the quieter stream of human events, to juxtapose the offices of beauty and fear. In the second spot, "outward sense," the senses of sight, hearing, and touch mutually counteract each other, with the paradoxical *drinking* in of the retrospect adding a metaphorical function of taste. Wordsworth never claims to obliterate "outward sense" as he is "laid asleep in body" in "Tintern Abbey"; on the contrary, the senses act as a path to imaginative power.[41]

---

41. David Ellis, *Wordsworth, Freud and the Spots of Time: Interpretation in 'The Prelude'* (Cambridge: Cambridge University Press, 1985) 127, after discussing both spots in sensitive detail, remains reluctant to take Wordsworth at his word on the mind's mastery over the senses: "The second spot provides a dubious illustration of the mind's mastery, and in the first [spot] all the advantages seem to lie with 'outward sense.'"

Uncanny Ghosts

How do these types of "visionary dreariness," by virtue of their *Unheimliche* aspect of fear, free the mind from potential tyranny by the senses? In the second spot, the ordinary scene of anxious waiting in the storm and mist would have remained just another everyday event, had not the death of Wordsworth's father invested the episode with retrospective force. Just prior to Christmas 1783, John Wordsworth was riding back from a remote part of Cumberland when "he lost his way in the darkness on Cold Fell and was obliged to spend a winter night shelterless on a fell side, with the result that he arrived home in the grip of mortal illness."[42] As if in unconscious disclosure of the uncanny's tendency to function as psychic repetition, Wordsworth repeats the "bleak" and "blasted" details of the scene, but now under the shadow of the fact of death. The spot now, paradoxically, becomes a fountain of recuperative drink:

> the wind and sleety rain,
> And all the business of the elements,
> The single sheep, and the one blasted tree,
> And the bleak music of that old stone wall,
> The noise of wood and water, and the mist
> Which on the line of each of those two roads
> Advanced in such indisputable shapes . . .
>
> (*The Prelude* II.375–81)

Here uncanny repetition informs the dreariness of the spot, yet the spots themselves function as mythic recurrence, as if their compulsion to repeat derives from psychic urgency. If the concealed sources of power are endangered by occlusion, there is more compelling need to recollect and to make them into poetry before the gates of memory are forever closed. Although Freudian theory clarifies Wordsworth's uses of memory and the uncanny, an important difference emerges between the poet and the neurotic in relation to the death instinct. Alice Miller, a modern analyst, brings this difference into focus: "Much has been written about the negative aspect of the compulsion to repeat: the uncanny tendency to reenact a trauma, which itself is not remembered, at times has some-

---

42. Mary Moorman, *William Wordsworth: A Biography: The Early Years 1770–1803* (Oxford: Oxford University Press, 1957; rpt. 1968) 68.

thing cruel and self-destructive about it and understandably suggests associations with the death instinct."[43] The neurotic's repression emerges within the disintegrating shadow of the death instinct. Although he conjures up the ghost of his father, Wordsworth reverses the slide toward death that is revealed in the uncanny symptoms of compulsive neurosis. Wordsworth's strength derives from his ability to transform a potential death instinct into a "hiding place of power." Heidegger describes this stance (in words written for another purpose) as "freedom-toward-death" or "resoluteness": "Touched by this interior angel of death, I cease to be the impersonal and social One among many, as Ivan Ilyich was, and I am free to become myself. Though terrifying, the taking of death into ourselves is also liberating: It frees us from servitude to the petty cares that threaten to engulf our daily life and thereby opens us to the essential *projects* by which we can make our lives personally and significantly our own."[44] This passage might have been written to account for the antisocial strain in Wordsworth, implying his affinity with Heidegger's thought about being. But Heidegger's passage also defines Wordsworth's own project as a poet, for his ability to tap the numinous and daemonic uncanny acts as a hedge against the encumbrances of the social envelope. Wordsworth employs the recollection of his spots to alleviate the depression of his burden of self-consciousness: he accepts the struggle with the discontents of civilization as the condition of existence. Unlike Freud's negatively driven patient, Wordsworth imaginatively recollects and tranquilizes his traumas. This resort to the *Unheimliche* is not merely an arrogant retreat into subjectivity, because it allows him to write the poetry that has a social impact upon his reader.

In the previous quotation from *The Prelude*, Ernest de Selincourt identifies the line, "Advanced in such indisputable shapes," as an allusion to "Thou camst in such a questionable shape" from *Hamlet*.[45] Some readers might question whether this line qualifies as a valid echo of Shakespeare, yet—even if it is unconscious on Wordsworth's part—its

43. Alice Miller, *The Drama of the Gifted Child*, trans. Ruth Ward (New York: Basic Books, 1981) 78.
44. Cited by William Barrett, *Irrational Man: A Study in Existential Philosophy* (Garden City, NY: Doubleday Anchor Books, 1962) 225–26, who restates these ideas from *Being and Time*.
45. *Wordsworth: The Prelude or The Growth of a Poet's Mind*, ed. Ernest de Selincourt and Stephen Gill (Oxford: Oxford University Press, 1970) 314.

psychological aptness reinforces the justice of the reading. Because the second spot of time naturally invites association with the "obstinate questionings" passage of the "Inmortality Ode," I find de Selincourt's proposal of an allusion to *Hamlet* convincing for the light it throws upon the strange invocation of the ghost in the ninth stanza of the ode. Upon the "questionable" presence of Old Hamlet's ghost hinges the authority of the past: it may invite questioning, on the first level, yet on the second it provokes uncanny misgivings about its authenticity.[46] It strikes the keynote for the radical disparity between surface and depth that marks the entire play. Is the ghost a true ghost or a devil inhabiting a pleasing shape? Is Gertrude an accomplice in the crime or merely a sensual timeserver helping Claudius to consolidate power for his kingship? Is Hamlet mad or merely putting on an "antic disposition"? The uncanny return of Old Hamlet not only puts in question the legitimacy of Claudius's reign, but it also creates a dilemma as to the authority of the ghost. In some strange way, in the context of the ode, Old Hamlet's ghost may be a displacement for Wordsworth's own lost father, for his own ambivalent relation to the authority of the past as symbolized by the father. By identifying with the ghost of Hamlet's father, instead of with Hamlet the son, Wordsworth shares an ambivalent purgatorial guilt. But by uncanny analogy, in the second spot of time, the ghost of the dead king crosses on the bridge of allusion to merge with the haunting presence of the lost father.

In his preface to *The Interpretation of Dreams*, Freud avers that one of the more important elements of his self-analysis required him to work through his reaction to the loss of his father, "that is to say, to the most

46. Marjorie B. Garber, *Shakespeare's Ghost Writers: Literature as Uncanny Causality* (New York: Metheun, 1987) 163–65, writes about Hamlet's doublebind produced by the questioning of authority itself in the uncanny ambiguity of Old Hamlet's ghost; the questioning is turned back upon the ghost, contributing to questioning also of the law as symbolized by the father and contributing to Hamlet's own paralysis. See also J. Douglas Kneale, *Aspects of Rhetoric in Wordsworth's Poetry: Monumental Writing* (Lincoln and London: University of Nebraska Press, 1988) 183, who links the second spot of time with a verbal echo of lines in *Hamlet:* "If there is a reminiscence here of the play that Wordsworth knew so well, it suggests that he may be appropriating the unfathered aspect of Hamlet's character, giving intertextual status to his narrative experience." Of the rhetorical repetition of "visionary dreariness" in the second spot involving his father's death, Kneale writes, "The successive appearances of all these images demonstrate the power of language to re-present experience, to hallow it with rhetorical decoration of ideal grace. What gives man 'profoundest knowledge' (12.221) of the mind is language itself" (179).

important event, the most poignant loss of a man's life." Whether the loss of a father would exceed all other losses for every man is beside the point: the loss certainly presented Wordsworth with peculiar circumstances. His father died when the poet was thirteen, untimely even in those days; he seems to have been distant from his father, who was often absent on business; Wordsworth also lived away from home for extended periods while attending school in Hawkshead. The trembling "like a guilty thing surprised" in the ninth stanza of the "Immortality Ode," shared by the ghost and the young boy, immediately brings to mind the guilt that Wordsworth feels for his own father's death.

In the second spot of time, Wordsworth requires the chastisement of God to humble his pride, to correct the extravagance of his "desires" (*The Prelude* 11.374). These enigmatic "desires" invite Freudian Oedipal speculation as to their tantalizing obscurity. In writing of the primitive "omnipotence of thoughts," Freud observes "that an uncanny effect is often and easily produced when the distinction between imagination and reality is effaced, as when something that we have hitherto regarded as imaginary appears before us in reality, or when a symbol takes over the full functions of the thing it symbolizes, and so on." Uncanny feelings may also occur in reaction to the death of a person toward whom one has had aggressive thoughts: conscious or unconscious guilt stems from the thought, "So, after all, it is *true* that one can kill a person by the mere wish [by desiring a person's death]!" (*SE* 17:244, 248) The *Unheimliche* also includes the hostility that a son might feel toward his father, as if his own imaginary attitudes might lead to self-blame for his father's death.[47] In an early poem, *The Vale of Esthwaite* (1787), Wordsworth portrays his reaction to his father's death as one of belated tears: this relief comes because he could not mourn at the time of his father's death.[48] Both the likelihood of Wordsworth's having felt hostility toward his father, and the belatedness of his repressed grief, point toward distance from and

47. David Ellis, *Wordsworth, Freud and the Spots of Time* 23, cites Freud's "omnipotence of thoughts" (*Allmacht der Gedanken*) to explain filial hostility toward a father as a source of the son's irrational self-incrimination when the father dies.
48. Mary Moorman, *William Wordsworth—A Biography: EY* (Oxford: Oxford University Press, 1957; rpt. 1968) 67–73, provides an account of Wordsworth's father's death and also discusses *The Vale of Esthwaite*. The following lines from this poem include Wordsworth's belated mourning: "Flow on, in vain thou hast not flow'd, / But eased me of a heavy load; / For much it gives my heart relief / To pay the mighty debt of grief, / With sighs repeated o'er and o'er, / I mourn because I mourned no more." (*Poetical Works* 1:280, 428–33).

aggression toward his father as sources of guilt, as part of those unexplained "desires." On the first level, of course, the poet might merely have held excessive hopes for holiday festivity.[49] The ultimate separation from both parents, however, leaving him an orphan along with his brothers and sister Dorothy, makes his father's death the source of even stronger anxiety. The force of such a separation, projected upon the "indisputable shapes" of mist inexorably advancing like fate along the road, reinforces the strangeness disclosed from the reiterated detail of the scene. Wind, rain, mist, and noise of water no longer function as sensory markers: instead, cast as an *unheimliche* dream, they acquire the skewed spatial disorientation that often informs the sublime. Wordsworth's common cause with Old Hamlet's ghost merges with his guilt over the loss of his own father: this immersion in the destructive element allows him to vanquish the paternal threat in order to free the authority of his own voice.

Wordsworth's affinity for *Hamlet* corresponds to Freud's own affinity for Hamlet as an Oedipal model. Freud musters the courage for his self-analysis—leading to his most intense creative moment in writing *The Interpretation of Dreams*—out of despondency over his father's death.[50] Wordsworth similarly releases vast creative energy in confronting his own melancholia, brought on by *his* father's death. The close connection between dream and the uncanny resolves a disturbing paradox: how does Wordsworth obtain nurturance from sublime memories that disrupt identity? In resorting to interactions of the self through his characteristic patterns of memory, Wordsworth enacts for his reader a process analogous to a patient's reshaping memories for an analyst. He molds his screen memories like the alchemy of dreams, according to the fictional demands of his mental self-portrait. His enchantment by the tale of Achilles—of his living under an abiding awareness of his own early death—as is now clear, is one of the most self-revealing affinities ever disclosed by the poet. His sharing with Achilles in the uncanny conjuring of ghosts allows him, unlike the ill-fated Greek, to choose poetry over silence, life over extinction. As I will argue, Wordsworth exorcises, rather than succumbs to, voices from the grave.

49. See also Alan Liu, *Wordsworth: The Sense of History* (Stanford: Stanford University Press, 1989) 448, who sees God's correction of Wordsworth's desires as an "atonement for the Imagination's complicity in imperialism."

50. Didier Anzieu, *Freud's Self-Analysis* 182, 210, traces Freud's creative burst derived from self-analysis to the process of working through the death of his father.

The Dionysiac or lyric-dramatic poet,
who *is* in what he contemplates, . . . projects his
Dionysiac life into Apollonian images in order to
find himself in them, whose images are in fact
nothing but *his very* self.

Nietzsche, *The Birth of Tragedy*

CHAPTER TWO

In Dreams Begin
Communities

Wordsworth extends his changing valuation of "the visionary gleam" across four poems: "Tintern Abbey" (1798), "Resolution and Independence" (1802), the "Immortality Ode" (1804), and "Elegiac Stanzas" (1806).[1] These poems show the poet questing either in solitude or in contact with a figure such as Dorothy or the Leech-gatherer. The visionary gleam, absent in the "Immortality Ode," appears disparagingly in "Elegiac Stanzas" as a poet's dream. This change, which departs from the dream-invested spaces of the "spots of time," suggests a movement from the melancholy awareness of loss to a skeptical questioning of the dream. In all poems under discussion, Wordsworth implies, or explicitly introduces, the poet's calling in relation to his subject. "Resolution and Independence" focuses upon the vocation of poetry, adds a new perspective on the visionary gleam, and speculates upon the early death of improvident poets. This chapter illustrates how Wordsworth criticizes the liabilities of dream consciousness while verifying the authenticity of vision. This dynamic reappears in Keats, whose "La Belle Dame" encrypts dream within dream only to have the dreamer awaken to the impoverished reality of a hopeless lover. Conversely, "Resolution and

---

1. *Poetical Works* 2:259; 2:235; 4:279; 4:258.

Independence" deploys a dream of the Leech-gatherer to dispel suicidal thoughts brought on by the hazards facing poets.

The dream can be the vehicle of the uncanny, nearer to nightmare than to illusory happiness. As Wordsworth well knew, absence can be a subtler form of presence. "Tintern Abbey," the "Immortality Ode," "Resolution and Independence," and "Elegiac Stanzas" all relate to "the visionary gleam," yet they express it by its absence rather than its presence. Jay Clayton recognizes the pain of absence alive in Wordsworth's present memory, the pain of different selves as a function of identity: "If this claim is sublime in its willingness to embrace great sorrow as the burden of identity, it is egotistical in its insatiable desire to absorb all differences into the self."[2] In the politics of vision, the economy of gain and loss builds Wordsworth's identity, but at the price of suffering and solipsism. We have already seen, in chapter I, the dialectics of memory creating identity; it remains to unfold how the poet employs dream both to critique and to advance his visionary project. If Wordsworth himself exemplifies Clayton's rendering of the perils of vision, the visionary power emerges the more strongly from such an ordeal of self-scrutiny. Wordsworth absorbs such visionary power not merely as salient memory of absence but also as presence:

> For I would walk alone
> In storm and tempest, or in starlit nights
> Beneath the quiet heavens, and at that time
> Have felt whate'er there is of power in sound
> To breathe an elevated mood, by form
> Or image unprofaned; and I would stand
> Beneath some rock, listening to sounds that are
> The ghostly language of the ancient earth,
> Or make their dim abode in distant winds.
>
> (*The Prelude* 2.321–29)

This "ghostly language" permeates Wordsworth's mind as a sublime vestige and inhabits the terrain of his song, *The Prelude*. But these ghosts do not always come when Wordsworth calls them: memory fades like the

2. Jay Clayton, *Romantic Vision and the Novel* (London and New York: Cambridge University Press, 1987) 71. The phrase, "absence can be a subtler form of presence," is from Sergio Perosa.

remembrance of dreams; Wordsworth attempts to capture these moments before they fade, which is like attempting to grasp the "distant winds."

Passages such as the one above, on "the ghostly language of the ancient earth," are all the more moving and poignant because Wordsworth, like Keats, does not leave his own visionary project unexamined. Because the visionary dream and the epiphany occur to the narrator or poet in private, they are often dismissed as liabilities of solipsism. These limitations of solitude may deserve exposure, but the factor of the reader's active role in the writer's dream may alter the dynamics of such evaluative judgments. As Peter Manning puts it, the reading act includes its own community: "To excise all registers of language but that of represented 'social fact' leads to overlooking the community the poem creates among its readers, a community that has no specific historical location but exists as the forever renewable potential of poetic response itself."[3] Yet the problem of history always remains, leaving us to choose among the variety of these historical locations.

The new historicist critics, by excavating the archeological and historical contexts of literature, expand the scope of texts. If a critic begins with a modern disdain for transcendence, however, such a materialist history may present a blinkered reading of the past. As Jerome McGann reminds us, our task is to detach ourselves from the chosen discourse of the Romantic poets in order to achieve a balanced critical stance. What he writes of the "Immortality Ode" exemplifies his view of Wordsworth's ideology: "The paradox of the work is that it embodies an immediate and concrete experience of that most secret and impalpable of all human acts: the transformation of fact into idea, and of experience into ideology." By transforming historical fact into an ideology made out of what cannot be spoken, Wordsworth believed he had solved his problems: "What he actually discovered was no more than his own desperate need for a solution." McGann epitomizes his argument: "That Wordsworth's is as well a false consciousness needs scarcely to be said, nor is it an indictment of the poem's greatness that this should be the case."[4]

3. Peter J. Manning, *Reading Romantics: Text and Context* (Oxford and New York: Oxford University Press, 1990) 309.
4. Jerome J. McGann, *The Romantic Ideology: A Critical Investigation* (Chicago and London: University of Chicago Press, 1983) 90–91. See also Marjorie Levinson, who, "far from

By using the evasion of history as the standard by which to undermine the illusion of Wordsworth's ideology of transcendence, McGann
risks imposing a distorting generality upon the poetry. Poems are enhanced by being placed within their historical context, but such prescrip-
tive ideology tends to blur the nuances of such works as the "Immortality Ode." New historical readings often succeed in disclosing fresh
insight into poems that are illuminated by their reception, history, and
facts of publication. But one can defend Wordsworth's poetry against
reductive ideological judgments on psychological grounds. In my concluding remarks on "Resolution and Independence," I shall return to the
reader's encounter with dream ventriloquy as a move by Wordsworth
beyond McGann's ideology, beyond solipsism toward community.

Dream and Delusion: The Betrayal of Nature

Wordsworth's "Elegiac Stanzas Suggested by a Picture of Peele Castle, in
a Storm, Painted by Sir George Beaumont" (1807) was inspired by the
drowning of his brother, John, in a storm at sea. In this work, the poet
rejects his earlier dream prospect of Peele Castle to intensify his own
irreparable loss: "Farewell, farewell the heart that lives alone, / Housed
in a dream, at distance from the Kind!" "Elegiac Stanzas" illustrates this
tendency to disparage the dream in its most extreme form. The stoical
image of the ruined castle and the menace of a sailboat skirting the rocky
surf—painted in the somber colors of sublimity—suggests a predatory
nature and a symbol of endurance analogous to the poet's weathering an
intensity of grief. "Tintern Abbey," which also employs the trope of
painting, by comparison provides critical perspective on "Elegiac Stanzas." In the latter poem, the poet as painter punishes himself, as Keats

---

seeking to depreciate Wordsworth's transcendence or to trivialize profoundly moving
works," hopes instead "to renew our sense of their power by exposing the conditions of
their success: that recalcitrant facticity with which they had to contend, explicitly *and*
unconsciously" (*Wordsworth's Great Period Poems: Four Essays* [Cambridge, UK: Cambridge University Press, 1986] 3). In practice, the new historicists sometimes tend to
neglect this wise balance between the visionary and the reality from which it emerges. See
also Jerome J. McGann, *Social Values and Poetic Acts: The Historical Judgment of Literary
Work* (Cambridge, MA: Harvard University Press, 1988) 82–92, for a superb new historicist reading of Arnold's *Sorab and Rustum* as taking part in "an important contemporary,
and continuing, argument about poetry and its relation to culture, and it took a definite
position on a series of relevant issues in that debate" (90). This reading reclaims *Sorab and
Rustum*, by its history, from our misreading it as a narrow piece of antiquarianism.

will do in *The Fall of Hyperion,* by reacting against an earlier poetry of dream. In his solitary stance in relation to a sacramental universe (as Whitehead puts it, grasping "the whole of nature as involved in the tonality of the particular instance"), Wordsworth had ignored the violent aspect of "nature, red in tooth and claw." In the particular circumstances of his grief, Wordsworth paints the poetry of dream as "the fond illusion of . . . [his] heart." The drama of "Elegiac Stanzas" lies in its subtle depiction, in the idiom of an idyllic beauty, of nature masking its betrayal.

"Elegiac Stanzas" is particularly germane for its disclosure of imagination's sensory relation to dream. In a poem of 1806, which moves in a direction diametrically opposite to that of "Tintern Abbey," Wordsworth returns by way of the painting of Peele Castle in a storm to an earlier memory (August 1794) of having lived across the narrow straits from the castle on Piel Island. Whereas in "Tintern Abbey" he spoke in 1798 of recollection as a mode of reviving alienated periods of self-consciousness, in "Elegiac Stanzas," as he anguishes over John's death, he indicts his dreamscape as a benign delusion that intensifies his grief. But the link between these two poems is even more direct. As an adult looking back upon his earlier visits to the Wye Valley, he stresses the gulf in time by resorting to a trope from painting, "I cannot paint / What then I was." At the time of his visit to Peele Castle, the unusual tranquillity of the weather, prolonged for four weeks, beguiled him into solipsistic unreality. He wryly recounts how he would have painted the castle's image on "a glassy sea":

> So pure the sky, so quiet was the air!
> So like, so very like, was day to day!
> Whene'er I looked, thy Image still was there;
> It trembled, but it never passed away.
>
> (lines 5–8)

These exclamation points, atypical in the lover of litotes, counter Wordsworth's usual puritanical qualms about excess. The subtle overdoing that builds throughout the poem's progression foreshadows a doomed illusion. He lingers over the fantasy of the idyll he would have painted, letting his irony unfold dramatically in a prolonged trajectory. The progression of overstatement, repetition, and conditional verb tenses serves to suggest the fragility of the "glassy sea," limned in the brush strokes of an imaginary palette. Not until halfway through the poem does he reveal that this imaginary canvas comes from the "fond illusion" of the youthful poet's dream. This dramatic disclosure leaves the reader free, however, to anticipate the half-loving disparagement implicit in the portrait. Wordsworth's ambivalence toward his dream emerges. When he submits "to a new control," the dream becomes a lost potency: "A power is gone, which nothing can restore; / A deep distress hath humanized my Soul" (lines 34–36). Coupled with this lost power in himself, the irrevocable loss of John completes the definition of humanization that had functioned earlier as a speaking silence in "Tintern Abbey."

Both poems include the topos of revisiting an earlier scene, but with differences. "Tintern Abbey" is begotten not by a mental journey but by an actual return to the Wye Valley to revisit a beloved landscape. "Elegiac Stanzas"—encompassing eleven years of change in the poet from his visit to Rampside in August 1794 until the writing of the poem in 1805— derives its subject from Sir George Beaumont's sublime painting: the castle in a storm begets a *memory* rather than a physical visit to an earlier time of serenity. Yet Wordsworth views the prospect of the Wye landscape in a fashion comparable to the antithetical canvases of Peele Castle: by juxtaposing his memory of the Wye against his present sight in "Tintern Abbey," he feels "somewhat of a sad perplexity." He both endures "gleams of half-extinguished thought" and finds "many recognitions dim and faint" (lines 58–60). His sadness derives from a double vision. He has changed in the interim: his present seeing lacks the intensity that it had during his visit to the Wye Valley five years earlier and the intensity of his sister Dorothy's perceptions at the time of his second visit. Dialectically, his sister acts as a stand-in for his own stage in life five years before; she dramatizes his double-consciousness by physically enacting his previous stage of sensibility. Even in the act of revisiting, Wordsworth reveals the impact of his loss, as if the subtext of the poem might imply a potentially incompatible marriage between mind and universe.[5] From a Freudian perspective, this subtext provides the energy of "Tintern Abbey": the depth beneath the surface of the poet's words discloses the menace of decay in human nature.

5. Stuart M. Sperry, Jr., "From 'Tintern Abbey' to the 'Intimations Ode': Wordsworth and the Function of Memory," *The Wordsworth Circle* 1 (Spring 1970): 47, makes an apt distinction: "It is the strong awareness of loss itself, rather than anything recollected, that proves so moving."

Wordsworth, like Keats after him, employs a condition of alienation to form one pole of a dialectic against which various strategies of myth and imagination can act as counterpoise. Two examples from Keats serve to define this alienation: in "Ode to a Nightingale" he contrasts the clinical reality of youth growing "pale, and spectre-thin" and dying with the ecstatic release symbolized by the nightingale's song; in the "Ode to Psyche" he injects a dialectic between Psyche's mythic world of visionary dream and his own iron time, "these days so far retired / From happy pieties." In "Tintern Abbey" an alienated Wordsworth—confined to "lonely rooms" amid "the din / Of towns and cities," "amid the many shapes / Of joyless daylight," and amid "The fretful stir / Unprofitable, and the fever of the world" (lines 25, 52–53)—recalls the Wye Valley to rekindle his spirit. The poet echoes here the mood of political gloom at the beginning of Book 7 of *Paradise Lost*, where Milton, in the alien climate of the Stuart Restoration and amid "the barbarous dissonance / Of *Bacchus* and his Revellers," carries on his song with unaltered voice. Milton continues to write his epic, trusting his divine muse to overcome his estrangement in the political world of the drunken court of Charles II, now prevailing over the Puritan revolutionary cause. Milton's alienation speaks directly to Wordsworth's solitary condition:

> though fall'n on evil days,
> On evil days though fall'n, and evil tongues;
> In darkness, and with dangers compast round,
> And solitude . . .
> (7.24–33)

Like Milton, Wordsworth was a revolutionary "fall'n on evil days" as well as "evil tongues," his own former allegiances tainted by the miscarriage of the French Revolution, now lapsed into an internecine bloodbath, as France swerved toward empire. On his first visit to the Wye Valley, Wordsworth was more like a man fleeing "from something that he dreads than one / Who sought the thing he loved" (lines 71–72). Although this flight could imply a retreat from fearful aspects of nature, it also suggests the political climate of 1793.[6] To mention only two

---

6. W.J.B. Owen, "The Most Despotic of Our Senses," *The Wordsworth Circle* 19 (Summer 1988): 137–39. I am indebted to this impeccably researched article for its suggestion of a political dimension to Wordsworth's flying from "something that he dreads" and for its

examples, the bloodletting of Robespierre had already taken place and the English had declared war on France in December 1793. Alienated and dejected, Wordsworth required the memory of the landscape above Tintern Abbey to stave off his depression, so

> that neither evil tongues,
> Rash judgments, nor the sneers of selfish men,
> Nor greeting where no kindness is, nor all
> The dreary intercourse of daily life,
> Shall e'er prevail against us, or disturb
> Our cheerful faith, that all which we behold
> Is full of blessings.
>
> (lines 128–34)

Milton's covenant with Urania, the heavenly muse, is far less endangered than Wordsworth's projected wedding between his mind and the external world. Even phrasings such as "Our cheerful faith" fail to carry conviction, "conveying a will to believe, rather than belief."[7] Wordsworth's impassioned addresses to Dorothy also reveal disquiet, as if he were trying to conjure up his former self in her: "thou my dearest Friend, / My dear, dear Friend; and in thy voice I catch / The language of my former heart" (lines 115–17). This ardent repetition adumbrates Keats's repeated *happy*s in the "Grecian Urn." The very rhetorical urgency of this *epizeuxis* (doubling with a view toward amplification or to excite pity) discloses the kind of alienation that provokes Keats to conjure up the dream discourse of a timeless world of Grecian art. For both Wordsworth and Keats, the depth emerges, within the surface level of language, to reveal what is unstated. Words on the brink of veering out of control yield a hermeneutic by-product in voicing the unvoiced. Wordsworth's dialectic relies upon the "quietness and beauty" of the Wye Valley to resist the snarls of political intrigue and the discontents of civilization.

The visionary gleam does not overtly appear in "Tintern Abbey," but

---

designation of 1793 as the definitive date for the poet's visit to the vicinity of Tintern Abbey as described in the poem, rather than his "visit to North Wales in 1791." See also Harold Bloom, *The Visionary Company* (Garden City, NY: Doubleday, 1961) 146. He writes that Wordsworth "sped as if to out-distance time, and sought an immediacy he was doomed to lose."

7. Peter Malekin, "Wordsworth and the Mind of Man," *An Infinite Complexity: Essays in Romanticism*, ed. J. R. Watson (Edinburgh: Edinburgh University Press, 1983) 11.

the loss of perceptual power represents the same issue as the lost gleam in the "Immortality Ode," which becomes "the Poet's dream" in "Elegiac Stanzas." As Wordsworth reaches the climax of his rhetorical invocation of Dorothy, his urgency leads us to the cause of his expostulation "Oh! Yet a little while / May I behold in thee what I was once" (lines 119–20). This absence in himself prompts an enigmatic prayer: "this prayer I make, / Knowing that Nature never did betray / The heart that loved her" (lines 121–23). We expect a strong affirmation in the future tense, yet the emphatic past tense renders the future vulnerable to chance and calamity. Even the heart's love for nature is oddly couched in the past rather than the present tense, implying a possible breach in continuous action. But this trope of nature as a lover, capable of bad faith, reveals the very anxiety that the poet seeks to forestall. Unless the wishes for Dorothy, fourteen lines later, constitute the prayer "Therefore let the moon / Shine on thee in thy solitary walk; / And let the misty mountain-winds be free / To blow against thee" (lines 134–37), as Jack Stillinger suggests, Wordsworth never clearly states what he intends to pray for.[8] If these lines are the prayer, they come as a curious displacement, as if the real subject were being elided. Given his preoccupation with continuity, Wordsworth probably intends to pray for nature's unimpaired fidelity, but instead he attempts to convince himself "that all which we behold / Is full of blessings" (lines 133–34). By omitting the expected prayer, Wordsworth reveals himself as a distracted lover, one reluctant to subject the beloved to an ordeal of faith to which she might prove unworthy.

"Elegiac Stanzas" (1806) forms a kind of diptych with "Tintern Abbey" (1798), together serving as a contrasting pair, like Milton's "L'Allegro" and "Il Penseroso." Where Milton uses the binary day and night, Wordsworth uses waking and dreaming. He would have painted the castle as "the soul of truth in every part"; he would have depicted "a stedfast peace that might not be betrayed," but he would have done so "in the fond illusion of his heart." Nature is no longer overtly the beloved, as in "Tintern Abbey." The "stedfast peace that might not be betrayed," however, operates as a metonymy for nature, because the

---

8. William Wordsworth, *Selected Poems and Prefaces* (Boston: Houghton Mifflin, 1965) 517. See also Bloom, *The Visionary Company* 148, who writes on the matter of Wordsworth's prayer, "We begin to understand the prayer he intends but does not make explicit. It is 'Do not forget, or the life in me, the creative joy, will die.'"

rejected canvas of the "smiling sea" actually reflects "silent Nature's breathing life." Over this motif of fidelity to the poet's mind, "Elegiac Stanzas" completes the trajectory of the subtext of "Tintern Abbey": the unthinkable betrayal has come to pass in the violent death at sea of Wordsworth's brother John. As for this test of fidelity, we might question the role of Wordsworth as lover as much as the constancy of his beloved nature. "It is quite true that nature led him on, to a conception that proved false; but it is clearly his own soul which betrayed him through the 'fond delusion' that nature is more than it can be." Under the auspices of the "heart's desire," the poet's demands upon nature exceed the reality principle.[9] Wordsworth tends to ascribe changes to nature that are, in fact, changes in himself. Freud's concept of narcissism throws light on Wordsworth's trope of erotic love as applied to his relation to nature. According to Freud, the typical male pattern of "object-love"—i.e., love for the female—"displays the marked sexual overvaluation which is doubtless derived from the child's original narcissism and thus corresponds to a transference of that narcissism to the sexual object. This sexual overvaluation is the origin of the peculiar state of being in love, a state suggestive of a neurotic compulsion, which is thus traceable to an impoverishment of the ego as regards libido in favor of the love-object" (*SE* 14:88–89).

Although love of nature may not be the same as love for a woman, Wordsworth tended to overinvest libido upon the natural world as compensation for losing his mother at the age of eight. Rather than impoverishing his ego, in contrast to Freud's narcissistic paradigm, his love of nature (in 1798) tends to produce an opposite effect: his alienation is overcome and his self-esteem is enhanced. After John's death in 1806, this pattern is shattered. At least in "Elegiac Stanzas," his fondness for nature abets its betrayal and his mourning for John diminishes his self-esteem. "A person who loves has, so to speak, forfeited a part of his narcissism," Freud writes, "and it can only be replaced by his being loved. In all these respects self-regard seems to remain related to the narcissistic element in love" (*SE* 14:98). Self-esteem requires an economy of healthy narcissism. As long as the balance between mind and object is maintained, nature returns the ardor of reciprocal love. By turning upon his own youthful poetry of dream, Wordsworth deplores John's death as

9. Geoffrey Hartman, *Wordsworth's Poetry* 284.

it discloses his own violation of community by living in solitary estrangement. The energy previously cathected upon nature now seems like a wishful illusion, a dream not as a creative matrix but as a lovely misguided indulgence. He seems to violate recognition of nature's otherness in favor of projecting his own extravagant desires upon it. But when his brother dies, violent nature causes this untimely fate, redefines the poet's youthful vision as narcissistic solipsism, and polarizes his earlier solitary life against the feeling of suffering endemic to society. The endurance of suffering becomes an antidote to narcissism, and Wordsworth reveals the overvaluation typical of male narcissistic love in his disparaging of the visionary dream.

Recanting the Visionary Gleam

In Beaumont's painting of the sublime castle in a storm, Wordsworth discovers a stoical image that counters his earlier poetry of visionary dream. In its progression toward illusion—in its use of brush strokes as dream images—"Elegiac Stanzas" reacts against the visionary gleam of the "Immortality Ode." "Elegiac Stanzas" represents the gleam as a mere additive of the painter's brush rather than an absent quality that had previously seemed intrinsic to the landscape. The poet now adds

> the gleam,
> The light that never was, on sea or land,
> The consecration, and the Poet's dream . . .

The ode begins with four stanzas marked by a nagging melancholy that emerges in the midst of the poet's encounter with a pastoral scene on a May morning. In a setting that could have been a prelude to a medieval dream vision, the poet alone feels "a thought of grief"; "On every side" he discovers evidence "That there hath past away a glory from the earth." As in "Tintern Abbey," he looks upon a landscape with double-consciousness: although he sees and hears with joy, the single tree and field and pansy tell the same story of loss. The absent glory, far from a painter's choice of color, is here represented as a vacancy in landscape. "Whither is fled the visionary gleam? / Where is it now the glory and the dream?" In mythic terms, the glory represents residual light from the world of preexistence still visible to the child. What had been a glory— an aura in natural objects analogous to a halo in the iconography of sacral painting, a residue from the soul's eternal home—has in "Elegiac Stanzas" become an insubstantial dream, a mere brush stroke applied as an afterthought from the palette of the painter-poet.

In a puzzling violation of context, Coleridge in *Biographia Literaria* uses Wordsworth's lines on the disparaged dream of "Elegiac Stanzas" ("The light that never was, on sea or land, / The consecration and the poet's dream") as evidence and illustration of Wordsworth's preeminent power of imagination, a power that places him closest of all contemporaries to Shakespeare and Milton. Like other romantics such as Charles Lamb, de Quincey, and Keats, Coleridge employs *dream* as a code word for the transforming power of imagination, the power that distinguishes fiction from fact. Shawcross finds it singularly unfortunate that Coleridge should cite a passage to illustrate the "essence of imaginative power" that Wordsworth had deployed to denote the "errors, or at least the limitations, of imagination in youth." On the strength of this instancing of imagination by Coleridge, critics have, according to Shawcross, misread Wordsworth, conceiving that the poet believed the "charm of art as something adventitious, which the artist or poet puts into nature and does not find there." Wordsworth revised his poem in 1827, watering down its strong spirit to show the painter as highlighting aspects of nature that already contained their own intrinsic value. Now the poet tepidly adds

> a gleam
> Of lustre, never known to sea or land,
> But borrowed from the youthful poet's dream.[10]

Evidently, Wordsworth found this revision wanting, because in later editions he reverted to his original lines; his very ambivalence toward the dream betrays his misgivings over the optics of the gleam. Coleridge cared so much for John Wordsworth that neither sly malice nor ignorance of context are likely reasons for his using "the consecration and the poet's dream" to illustrate a triumph rather than an impairment of imagination. Coleridge welcomes dream as deliverance from strict realism: he "follows the tradition of the European Romantic poets who saw in the dream a means of transcending the limitations of the senses."[11] He

10. *Biographia Literaria* ed. Shawcross 2:293–94.
11. Max F. Schulz, *The Poetic Voices of Coleridge* (Detroit: Wayne State University Press, 1963) 128.

perhaps felt that the dream was an apt equivalent for the transfiguring power of secondary imagination.

Part of the powerful impact of "Elegiac Stanzas" stems from Wordsworth's casting aspersions upon his own earlier self—upon his own imagination—as a conflict mirroring his grief over the loss of John. That earlier time of serenity, displaced by Beaumont's dark painting, epitomizes Wordsworth's own solitary condition before John's death. It represents, even in its defensive posture as a "fond illusion," his youthful visionary power, disparaged even as it wanes. Coleridge's admiring remark on "The consecration and the Poet's dream" fits Wordsworth's position on the visionary gleam in 1802, but ironically misses his disparagement of imagination as dream in the "Elegiac Stanzas" of 1807. Richard Gravil takes the language of this elegy at face value: "It is immediately apparent that what Coleridge terms imaginative is in Wordsworth's mature judgement illusory."[12] But rather than accepting this illusory dream as temporal evidence of Wordsworth's maturity, we might read the poet's transforming the visionary into a dream as an overreaction upon his youthful imagination in the act of expressing the extremity of his grief. That both Coleridge and Shawcross cannot accept Wordsworth's disillusion with imagination in "Elegiac Stanzas" underscores the shock value of mourning in these lines.

His brother's death distressed him far more deeply than the earlier death of his father. In a letter to Sir George Beaumont about John's death, Wordsworth questions God's justice as compared to human morality: "Would it not be blasphemy to say that upon the supposition of the thinking principle being destroyed in death, however inferior we may be to the great Cause and ruler of all things, we have *more of love* in our nature than He has? The thought is monstrous; and yet how to get rid of it except upon the supposition of *another* and *better world,* I do not see."[13] In seeking to pass through the stages of mourning, Wordsworth impugns his solitary quest for nature, as if his loss jeopardizes the natural sublime except insofar as it acts as a vehicle for the human sublime. The bold daring of his Job-like questioning of God, in the depths of his grief, is matched by his recantation of the visionary gleam.

12. Richard Gravil, "Imagining Wordsworth: 1798–1807–1817," in *Coleridge's Imagination* 138.

13. *Early Letters of William and Dorothy Wordsworth: The Early Years 1787–1805,* ed. Ernest de Selincourt, 2nd ed., rev. Chester L. Shaver (Oxford: Clarendon Press, 1935) 556.

Freud's "Mourning and Melancholia" suggests a possible source for the particular intensity that Wordsworth brings to his dream here as it withers under the effects of mortality. In grieving for the loss of a loved person, one may become reluctant to relinquish the libidinal energy one has invested in the human object of loss. Such reluctance can be so strong "that a turning away from reality takes place and a clinging to the object through the medium of a hallucinatory wishful psychosis [occurs]. Normally, respect for reality gains the day. Nevertheless its orders cannot be obeyed at once. They are carried out bit by bit, at great expense of time and cathectic energy, and in the meantime the existence of the lost object is psychically prolonged" (*SE* 14:244–45).

Although Wordsworth speaks "with mind serene" in "Elegiac Stanzas," he projects his grief upon Beaumont's painting. He commends its dark sublimity, "This sea in anger, and that dismal shore." He "psychically prolongs" the libidinal energy formerly cathected upon his brother ("The feeling of . . . [his] loss will ne'er be old") by fixing it upon the storm-tossed boat on the canvas, barely visible among the deep blacks of its pigment. His elegy represents the act of working through his mourning rather than lapsing into Freud's idea of melancholia: "The distinguishing mental features of melancholia are a profoundly painful dejection, cessation of interest in the outside world, loss of the capacity to love, inhibition of all activity, and a lowering of the self-regarding feelings to a degree that finds utterance in self-reproaches and self-revilings, and culminates in delusional expectation of punishment" (*SE* 14:244). All of these traits occur in mourning as well as in melancholia, except the final "expectation of punishment." Writing a year after the death of John, Wordsworth forces himself away from the crippling isolation brought on by his grief and melancholia, and moves toward the social act of embracing the ills to which mortal flesh is heir. For Wordsworth, the act of writing this elegy is therapy. What he says about epitaphs shows how his refusal to be "housed in a dream," in "Elegiac Stanzas," leads to his taking comfort from Beaumont's castle, which is ensconced in "the unfeeling armour of old time": "For the occasion of writing an epitaph is matter-of-fact in its intensity, and forbids more authoritatively than any other species of composition all modes of fiction, except those which the very strength of passion has created; which have been acknowledged by the human heart, and have become so familiar that they are converted into substantial realities" (*LC* 115). In

"Elegiac Stanzas," the dream, as a fragile fiction, gives way before the fact of death. Wordsworth resorts to the fiction of painting, yet the language of feeling—of "the human heart"—emerges from the dialectic between the idyll of his retrospective dream and the present poetry of bald statement. If Wordsworth did not have the gift of elegiac discipline, his mourning might well have crossed the border into melancholia. An orphan before adolescence, he perhaps never totally completed the mourning process that would free his libidinal energy. Whereas mourning is grief for a consciously known lost object, melancholia often includes object losses that remain hidden in the unconscious. As his "Essays on Epitaphs" attest, Wordsworth's uncanny imagination cohabits with death, leaving poems such as his elegy for John in that no-man's-land between mourning and melancholia. In "Elegiac Stanzas," as in "A Slumber Did My Spirit Seal," the iron restraint in the poetry of loss, contrasting with the inflated dream, verifies the act of mourning.

In "Tintern Abbey," the "Immortality Ode," and "Elegiac Stanzas," the dream encounter emerges from within Wordsworth's typical stance of reflecting upon the stages of his own life. Not one of these poems includes an encounter with another human being. The presence of Dorothy in "Tintern Abbey" might appear to be an exception, yet she primarily represents a confrontation with the poet's own earlier self. Like Coleridge in "The Eolian Harp," the poet speaks for another character who is also present: Dorothy is never given a chance to reply in her own voice. The visionary gleam of the ode, in accordance with its platonic fiction, invests the landscape of childhood with a residual glory, an aura of "celestial light," that has become lost to the adult. In "Tintern Abbey," early childhood has none of the trappings of eternity; in fact, it is even dismissed for its robust, physical character: "(The coarser pleasures of my boyish days, / And their glad animal movements all gone by)" (lines 73–74). In the ode, the later stage of youth, exemplified by Dorothy, shares the visionary perceptual power of the child. In both "Tintern Abbey" and the "Immortality Ode," the use of memory, itself endangered, enables the adult to access the earlier dream from the enhanced vantage point of imagination acquainted with grief. In "Elegiac Stanzas," by contrast, Wordsworth downgrades the visionary, in a drama of a dream going sour, to a private indulgence in solitude. His own earlier heart's wish has been deceived by an environment under a chance spell of tranquility. Employing the sublimity of proximity to

69

death, this poem verifies the "still, sad music of humanity" of "Tintern Abbey" but, in contrast to that poem, its concord turns "harsh" and "grating." Implicit in this quoted phrase are Wordsworth's economic straits, political setbacks, guilt over his desertion of Annette, and the crisis stemming from failure of his revolutionary hopes. The dialectic of "Elegiac Stanzas"—this conflict between solitary imagination and social grief—is what "stamps the quality mark" (to borrow a phrase from Keats) upon the poem. The visionary gleam, the source of poignant absence in the "Immortality Ode," becomes in "Elegiac Stanzas" a dream disparaged. The gleam itself comes in for a skeptical testing that implies a poetics of suspicion toward the visionary. Whereas the dialectic works within single poems for Keats, for Wordsworth it extends to engage other poems. In the changing spectrum of his poetry, the absent gleam of the "Immortality Ode," the more valorized for its loss, is transformed in "Elegiac Stanzas" into a dream chimera. Wordsworth's own attempt to put down the dream in "Elegiac Stanzas," as revealed in the very style of his half-loving dismissal, discloses repressed energy reluctant to be curbed.

Critique of the Visionary

In "Elegiac Stanzas," Wordsworth presents a critique of the visionary imagination in the form of a dream painting, yet his critique is secondary to the act of deploring John's death. Because Keats draws upon Wordsworth's *Lyrical Ballads* as inspiration for poems that he adapts to the dream mode, a comparison between these two poets on the critique of the visionary imagination is revealing.

Keats deploys the ballad genre not only to create a paradox of impersonal personality, but also to disclose the liabilities of hungering for the infinite. His well-known letter on Adam's dream in *Paradise Lost* provides a model for the discourse of desire: Adam's dream imparts the "conviction that Imagination and its empyreal reflection is the same as human Life and its spiritual repetition."[14] A tendency to metaphorize imagination as dreaming—unlike Wordsworth's practice, where this merging occurs more sparingly—pervasively informs Keats's specula-

14. *The Letters of John Keats 1814–1821*, ed. Hyder E. Rollins (Cambridge: Harvard University Press, 1958) 1:185.

tions on poetry. Yet only four months after writing this letter, Keats deplores, in his "Epistle to John Hamilton Reynolds," the tendency of his "dreamings," whether "of sleep or wake," to assume nightmare proportions instead of remaining content with the "material sublime." Although Keats's disclosures on dreams also include their permeability to imagination, such dreamings can transform reality for either good or ill. The overtaxed visionary imagination, by striving relentlessly "to see beyond our bourne," may leave the poet "Lost in a sort of purgatory blind," his imagination subject to bouts of disease in departing from "its proper bound," the sublimity of this world. One thinks of Shakespeare's playful commentary through the irony of Theseus on the imagination as it "bodies forth / The forms of things unknown, . . . and gives to aery nothing / A local habitation and a name." As this rational king ruefully chides the common denominator of frenzied subjectivity in "lunatics, lovers, and poets," he speaks for a late classical and a medieval tradition—invested in the vagaries of imagination—in a play whose essence is dream logic. For Keats, the imagination partakes of Theseus's unruly moments: "in the night, imagining some fear, / How easy is a bush suppos'd a bear!"[15]

In "Elegiac Stanzas," Wordsworth reluctantly questions his earlier visionary imagination as an illusion, as a charming dream unable to withstand the pain of his brother's death at sea. Unlike Keats's dream merging with imagination, Wordsworth's dream here becomes the mirage of a painter's artifice. In "La Belle Dame," Keats carries even further this skeptical tendency of the Romantics to subject the dream to fierce criticism. In contrast to "The Eve of St. Agnes," which rises toward dream consummation, "La Belle Dame" plunges downward from super-natural, erotic encounter through dream to impoverished reality. If the former poem follows the paradigm of Adam's dream by enabling the lovers' escape into legend, the latter implies a reverse movement from dream back to a barren reality. The closure, however, of "The Eve of St. Agnes"—with the setting of St. Agnes's moon, the elfin storm, and the deaths of Angela and the Beadsman and, by implication, the later deaths of Madeline and Porphyro—foreshadows the movement of "La Belle Dame." But the lovers nonetheless escape into fulfillment: the magical

15. *A Midsummer Night's Dream, The Riverside Shakespeare,* ed. G. Blakemore Evans, et. al. (Boston: Houghton Mifflin, 1974) 242 (V.i.14–22).

storm presumably works in their favor, for there is no evidence that they perish in the storm. Only their mortality, introduced in the poem's closure, subverts the dream of romance by a swerve back into history. Although the retrospective story in "La Belle Dame" begins in the mode of Adam's dream, Keats's idyllic romance evaporates within a dream that triggers the Dionysiac subtext of this unearthly vision. The knight begins his tale of a liaison with an unearthly lady, his absorption in romantic love carrying him beyond the boundaries of everyday life into supernatural terrain. Only after the knight relates his dream does the reader discover that this narrative is also an imaginary quest, that the lover's image of desire was itself a dream, one that the knight himself depicts as "The latest dream I ever dream'd / On the cold hill's side." The feverish brow of the knight links him now with the "death pale" kings, princes, and warriors as ghostly trophies of an inaccessible love. This deflation of the visionary quest, with its spectral figures and feverish consciousness, undermines the chivalric code. Instead of discovering reality on an ideal level in "a finer tone," the dream dismantles the paradigm of Adam's dream. If Keats's attraction for the visionary imagination is analogous to the knight's love for an unearthly beauty, then the common menace lies in the imagination's own burden of illusion, not in a seductive trap set by a Circean archetype.[16] The knight as dreamer conjures up the image of his own desire, but his dream of spectral thralldom, within a decadent chivalric order, releases the voice of bitter incompatibility. Where Wordsworth deploys the dream as a surrogate for the visionary, Keats uses the dream to reveal the Dionysiac jeopardy of imagination. Where Keats typically employs a sexual dream, Wordsworth, except in his erotic relation to nature, tends to eschew (with the exception of "Laodamia") the overtly sexual dream, revealing a bias

16. See Bloom, *The Visionary Company* 405–6, for a contrary view of the elfin lady as sinister seductress, and David Perkins, *The Quest for Permanence* (Cambridge: Harvard University Press, 1959) 263, who tentatively finds a suggestion of Circe's victims in the "starv'd lips" of the "pale warriors" who appear in the knight's dream. See also Karen Swann, "Harassing the Muse," in *Romanticism and Feminism,* ed. Anne K. Mellor (Bloomington and Indianapolis: University of Indiana Press, 1988) 89, who avers that a feminist critic might find romance "at least as fatal to the lady as the knight. Not only does its logic work toward her disappearance from the scene, romance blinds most readers to the woman's point of view—a point of view from which the exchange between lady and knight looks less like a domestic idyll or a fatal encounter and more like a scene of harassment."

toward displacement.[17] In Keats's "La Belle Dame," the overtaxed visionary imagination, subjected to a stern self-critique by the poet, becomes a place where "no birds sing."

Unlike "Elegiac Stanzas," in which the private delusion of dream gives way to the consciousness of pain to which humanity is prone, the dream within the dream of "La Belle Dame" displaces the narrative to a mental landscape that is finally a vehicle of barren love. According to Freud, a dream within a dream allows the dreamer a protective mechanism to disclose repressed material that could not otherwise emerge from the unconscious by dream condensation or displacement. Whether or not it is fair to apply such insights to a fictional character, the concrete details of the ballad's text support the validity of this insight in relation to the knight. Freud's ideas, in this instance, are not incompatible with Wordsworth's culture: "The intention is . . . to detract from the importance of what is 'dreamt' in the dream [within a dream], to rob it of its reality" (*SE* 4:338).[18] The menace of this elfin lady comes, then, not from the exterior plot of a Circe-like figure, as in Spenser's Bower of Bliss or Milton's *Comus,* but rather from her lodging at the core of the knight's unconscious. The peril of the feminine and/or the visionary leaves him starved and feverish, obsessively striving to repeat what his own subliminal nature vilifies. The imagination discloses its own Dionysiac underside: Keats gives voice to its daemonic claims through the medium of dreaming. If the hopeless courtly love of the knight-at-arms is analogous to the poet's overstrained wooing of the metaphysical muse, Keats implies the strain upon a psychic economy in the politics of vision. Both Keats and Wordsworth subject the visionary to an arduous ordeal:

17. Jean H. Hagstrum, *The Romantic Body: Love and Sexuality in Keats, Wordsworth, and Blake* (Knoxville: University of Tennessee Press, 1985) 73, 75, makes a case for strong implicit sexuality in Wordsworth's poetry and prose: "It is the central view of this book, particularly of this chapter, that natural and bodily energy inspires and shapes the poetry of both tender familial affection and transcendental vision and that when it does not, the reason is not that nature is *exhaustible* but that the poet is *exhausted*" (74).

18. David Simpson, "Keats's Lady, Metaphor, and the Rhetoric of Neurosis," *Studies in Romanticism* 15 (1976) 276, cites Freud's "dream within a dream" that "is presented in this recessive or distanced form because it is unpleasant or disruptive." See also Leon Waldoff, *Keats and the Silent Work of Imagination* (Urbana: University of Illinois Press, 1985) 94–95, n.9. Although Waldoff questions the treatment of a literary dream as analogous to one by a living person, he concludes that this "analogy . . . reinforces the notion that the knight's dream, rather than an illusion, has considerable psychological authority in the poem."

Keats's knight is driven from dreaming to melancholic isolation; Wordsworth, on the contrary, rejects the dream of solitude for the gnawing pain of community. Keats's knight wakes from a dream of supernatural love doomed to endure his waking death-in-life, his dream turned waking nightmare; Wordsworth's dream of the heart's desire, of "a smiling sea," gives way to a nature suddenly turned predatory that vitiates a solipsistic escape from mortality. The dream of an isolated subject had masked the ultimate betrayal lurking in a shipwrecking storm.

Dream Prelude to Ventriloquy

Unlike the poems discussed thus far in this chapter, "Resolution and Independence" adds an external other, the Leech-gatherer, impinging upon the suicidal qualms and the mental terrain of the poet's dream. Unlike "Elegiac Stanzas" and "La Belle Dame" in their critique of the visionary, "Resolution and Independence" tests the dream against a destitute figure of endurance. Far from acting as an onlooker of the Leech-gatherer at safe remove from a suffering human object, the narrator is now himself the melancholic sufferer in search of solace. The subject of writing poetry is never far from the surface of the poems under discussion. "Resolution and Independence" proceeds to question a poet's melancholy in the midst of a storm-rinsed landscape of rare splendor. The encounter with the Leech-gatherer, a subtle blend of realism and dream consciousness, includes its own special drama of mutually exclusive discourses. The old man functions as a typically understated image of stoical distress, acting as a foil to the self-conscious narrator. A peculiar instance of a Wordsworthian dream epiphany serves as a mediator in the subliminal merging (as will later become clear) of the alien worlds of the poet and of the Leech-gatherer.

Unlike "Elegiac Stanzas," which begins with a dream, "Resolution and Independence" opens with a memory of a traveller wandering over the moors. The first two stanzas, recounting the overnight mountain storm, emerge vividly in the present tense, evoking the hare's antics in response to the sunshine, raising from "the plashy earth" a mist that forms a "glittering" cloud in its wake. Not until the third stanza does it become clear that this clarification of the storm into fine weather occurred in the past, "I was a Traveller *then* upon the moor" (italics added). The capitalization of the generic *traveler* corresponds with Wordsworth's extension of his own role to represent the condition of the solitary poet, beyond "the ways of men, so vain and melancholy."

Wordsworth passes from intense delight in this watery landscape, mirrored in the frolicking hare, into a fit of despondency. As these extremes meet, his melancholy exceeds the pangs of visionary absence disclosed in the opening stanzas of the "Immortality Ode." Wordsworth's pursuit of the dream of the youthful poet, cavorting with the gleeful hare, gives way to thoughts of Chatterton's suicide and Burns's premature death in poverty, examples of poets spurned or unrecognized. The covenant between mind and nature, even at the peak of ecstatic joy, begins to unravel. Where the gleam had figured as an absence from the outer pastoral scene in the "Immortality Ode," the visionary dream here becomes a frank projection of the poet's mind:

> By our own spirits are we deified:
> We Poets in our youth begin in gladness;
> But thereof come in the end despondency and madness.
> (lines 47–49)

Wordsworth the observer begins this poem by questioning the resilience of his own spirit, by recognizing the diminishing returns of his solitary quest for natural renovation, and by brooding upon the treachery of a breach in "natural piety" that might endanger his survival as a poet.

This speculation on the vocation of poets takes on added point if we accept the conjecture of James Dykes Campbell (Coleridge's biographer) "that Wordsworth may possibly have had Coleridge rather than himself in view" when he added to "The Leech-Gatherer" (an earlier version of the poem) the following lines:

> My whole life I have lived in pleasant thought,
> As if life's business were a summer mood;
> As if all needful things would come unsought
> To genial faith, still rich in genial good;
> But how can He expect that others should
> Build for him, sow for him, and at his call
> Love him, who for himself will take no heed at all?[19]
> (lines 36–42)

19. James Dykes Campbell, *Samuel Taylor Coleridge: A Narrative of the Events of His Life* (London and New York: Macmillan, 1894) 132–33, n.2.

75

This passage portrays the Romantic quest as an extremity of heedless solipsism. In the summer of 1802, when Wordsworth wrote these lines, and in the previous spring, when Coleridge was writing his "Verse Letter to Sara," Coleridge was at a low point from his opium addiction, his crumbling marriage, and his precarious financial affairs, not to mention his envy of Wordsworth's impending marriage to Mary Hutchinson. Coleridge's hopeless love for Sara Hutchinson, Mary's sister, intensified his dejection. Even if he had been free to marry Sara and she had accepted him, the chances were good that his opium addiction would have doomed that relationship as well.[20]

But the specifics of Coleridge's plight are not the point. Unlike Campbell, I think Wordsworth is also writing about the generic category of poets, including himself, facing financial problems and other worries on the eve of marriage. Wordsworth advisedly includes himself, along with Burns and Chatterton, in the generic pronoun "He," capitalized to enforce the point. The narrator both is and is not Wordsworth (I use their names interchangeably in discussing this poem), but the main subtext is the unnamed Coleridge, who fits the improvident predicament like a glove. Gene Ruoff's exploration of the intertextual relations between two of Coleridge's poems, the "Verse Letter to Sara Hutchinson" and "Dejection: An Ode," and two of Wordsworth's, "Resolution and Independence" and the "Immortality Ode," reinforces my point about the inclusion of the unnamed Coleridge as the primary target among the generic class of endangered poets. Ruoff epitomizes the intertextuality in Wordsworth's poetic dialogue with Coleridge: "If 'The Leech-Gatherer' and 'Resolution and Independence' had attempted to counter Coleridge's despair by trivializing it, the ode attempts the more remarkable task of countering it by intensifying it."[21] Although a sheet is

20. Molly Lefebure, *The Bondage of Love* (London: Victor Gollancz, 1986; rpt. 1988) 195. In 1809–10 "Sara Hutchinson had struggled to prevent . . . [Coleridge] from drowning himself in laudanum; had coaxed, cajoled, scolded, upbraided; in short she had played the part which had earlier been Sara Coleridge's, and with the same results: as Dorothy described it to Catharine Clarkson, 'His love for . . . [Sara Hutchinson] is no more than a fanciful dream. . . . He likes to have her about him as his own, as one devoted to him, but when she stood in the way of other gratifications, it was all over.'"

21. Gene W. Ruoff, *Wordsworth and Coleridge: The Making of the Major Lyrics, 1802–1804* (New Brunswick: Rutgers University Press, 1989) 252. The draft version of "The Leech-Gatherer" (ca. April–May 1802), mentioned by Ruoff, comes from Dove Cottage manuscript DC Ms.41; see also *Poems in Two Volumes, and Other Poems, 1800–1807*, ed. Jared R. Curtis (Ithaca: Cornell University Press, 1983) 316–23 for a facsimile and transcription.

torn from an earlier draft of "Resolution and Independence," called "The Leech-Gatherer," there is no mention in the existing pages of the Leech-gatherer's pervading Wordsworth's daydream. Ruoff captures the gravity of Wordsworth's depiction of loss in the first eight stanzas of the "Immortality Ode." What concerns us now, however, is whether Coleridge is the subtext in "Resolution and Independence" as a figure of a melancholy Romantic in need of reclamation. I differ here from Ruoff (at the risk of violating the subtlety of his larger context), who implies that Wordsworth had contrived his despair for Coleridge's edification. Wordsworth makes his message the more palatable for Coleridge by including himself as the main subject of a poet's nightmare.[22]

The peculiar drama of Wordsworth's encounter with the Leech-gatherer unfolds as if by providential design. The old man, "feet and head / Coming together in life's pilgrimage," heightened by his imaginative merging with rock, sea beast, and cloud, appears alongside "a pool bare to the eye of heaven." This strange encounter includes the facts of the old man's condition, as if a "more than human weight," wrought by "pain" and "rage" and "sickness" in his history, had left him as one who had outlived his suffering. In the odd emergence of the Leech-gatherer, Wordsworth encounters an image of the human sublime, enforced by metaphors fused by imaginative alchemy.[23] The self-conscious poet meets a figure of endurance who exists in a world beyond subjectivity. Wordsworth here occupies a mental space, wholly alien to the Leech-gatherer, which leads to an epiphany manifested in a trance:

> The old Man still stood talking by my side;
> But now his voice was like a stream
> Scarce heard; nor word from word could I divide;

22. See Charles Rzepka, "A Gift that Complicates Employ: Poetry and Poverty in *Resolution and Independence*," *Studies in Romanticism* 28 (1989): 225–47, who makes a strong case for Wordsworth's severe economic needs in the months preceding his marriage to Mary Hutchinson in October of 1802. This article reinforces my point that Wordsworth includes himself, along with the implicit Coleridge, as vulnerable to poverty.

23. Susan E. Meisenhelder, *Wordsworth's Informed Reader: Structures of Experience in His Poetry* (Nashville: Vanderbilt University Press, 1988) 67–69, uses Wordsworth's essay on the sublime, its inclusion of resistance overcome, to show how the reader learns to identify the Leech-gatherer as an image of the human sublime: "Wordsworth's evocation of the force animating the Leech-Gatherer transforms him into an image of visionary dreariness. The equilibrium achieved as his internal force opposes external pressures makes it possible to see the sublimity of his suffering."

And the whole body of the Man did seem
Like one whom I had met with in a dream.
(lines 106–10)

Like James Joyce we may define epiphany as a "showing forth," or
like Robert Langbaum as something that "reveals spirit, and breaks—
whether, as in the plan for *Lyrical Ballads,* we start with a fact or a phase
of mind—*suddenly,* in a *moment* of insight, upon a sensitive observer and
through him upon the reader."[24] In strict accuracy, the line "Like one
whom I had met with in a dream" is really a simile likening Wordsworth's mental prospect to a dream image. The imaginative transformation, however, takes the will for the deed: Wordsworth's style converts
metaphor into a trance. In recasting the old man as a specter of inner
consciousness, the dreamer now loses contact with external reality. With
the encounter seemingly staged by divine grace, this trance or waking
dream provides the reader with insight into the narrator's consciousness.
The reader, in the mode of reception theory, watches the narrator
reading the Leech-gatherer. Although the action takes place in Wordsworth's mind, the sensory presence of the Leech-gatherer continues to
invest the image in the dreamscape. The dual levels of realism and
imagination, managed so skillfully by Wordsworth, produce the comedy
of the Leech-gatherer's smile as the poet's distraction leads him to repeat
his question to the old man, 'How is it that you live, and what is it you
do?' (Line 119). The question is not, however, redundant for the reader,
who recognizes the hazardous mental expanse (one thinks also of Coleridge) that the traveler must cross.

Don Bialostosky surmises that the Leech-gatherer recognizes the
poet's distress: "It is almost as if the old man had heard the young man
confess his own loneliness in his sympathetic acknowledgment of the old
man's loneliness, or at least as if the narrator thinks he noticed a response
which indicated recognition of his plight."[25] The courtesy of the old man
in responding to the poet's repeated question may support the notion
that he notices the narrator's need. But the unself-consciousness of the
Leech-gatherer, coupled with the typical lack of subjectivity in Words-

24. Robert Langbaum, *The Word from Below* 36. See also Lionel Trilling, *Sincerity and Authenticity* (Cambridge, MA: Harvard University Press, 1971) 89–91.
25. Don H. Bialostosky, *Making Tales: The Poetics of Wordsworth's Narrative Experiments* (Chicago: University of Chicago Press, 1984) 156.

worth's solitaries, makes it unlikely that the old man notices the poet's trauma. The *sentimental* character of the narrator contrasts with the *naive*—in Schiller's parlance—Leech-gatherer: the latter is, in a sense, beyond psychology. The surprise caused by two incompatible discourses functions ironically, with the reader perceiving what the Leech-gatherer does not, and the poet's dream existing side by side with the old man's literal presence.

Anthony Conran thinks that in "Resolution and Independence" Wordsworth himself expresses "his disillusionment with the romantic imagination considered as an end in itself." This "condition" is "a recurring sickness among all the Romantics, who tended to value daydreaming above activity."[26] In order to disparage romantic excess, Conran also indicts dreaming as willful escape. In the context of the poems discussed in this chapter, Wordsworth's "melancholia, " connected with the untimely fate of poets, scarcely deserves Conran's pejorative relegation to "trance." The melancholy mood actually occurs before the trance provoked by the encounter with the Leech-gatherer. Conran defines both the encounter and the poet's melancholy as "part of a dream."[27] Far from beginning in a dream, however, the encounter begins with the narrator greeting the old man with the everyday salutation appropriate to a stranger in real life. The narrator's despondency, on the other hand, rhetorically dismissed by Conran as a daydream, might more justly be termed a nightmare.[28] If Wordsworth is trying to overcome Romanticism, he is not doing so at the price of disparaging the dream. A sublime epiphany transforms the lofty utterance of the Leech-gatherer into the waking dream of the narrator. This image of deliverance rescues his

26. Anthony E. M. Conran, "The Dialectic of Experience: A Study of Wordsworth's *Resolution and Independence*," *PMLA* 75 (1960): 66, 68, epitomizes the poem as "the comedy of a solipsist faced with something outside himself" (74). For a different view, see Albert O. Wlecke, *Wordsworth and the Sublime* (Berkeley: University of California Press, 1973) 148–49, n.3, "One way of looking at 'Resolution and Independence' might be to see it as a poem that tells of the movement of the poet's mind from an anguished preoccupation with thoughts of death to a state in which, because of the strangely visionary resonances of the Leech-gatherer, the fear of death is transformed into a triumphant sense of man's ability to live in spite of the encroachments of mortality."
27. Conran, "The Dialectic of Experience" 66.
28. Ruoff, *Wordsworth and Coleridge* 159, hits the mark: "It may be possible to correct daydreams with good sense, but good sense will not, as Anthony E. M. Conran argues in an otherwise excellent study of the poem, chase nightmares."

mind from its nightmare and modulates back to the Leech-gatherer's alterity, to the otherness of the old man's language.[29] If Wordsworth comes to laugh at his melancholy humor, his dream serves to unmask his former Romantic excesses. The poet's melancholy may border on the histrionic, yet the dream requires its dialectical contrary in the Leech-gatherer, who provides an alien social incursion into the poet's solitary quest. Conran disparages the narrator's Romantic daydreaming (i.e., suicidal theatrics that Wordsworth frowns on), yet the dialectic of the poem that he describes as "one argument, one emotion or belief, pitted against another" invites a different evaluation of the dream.[30]

In his discussion of the lyric poet—mediated through the dream aspect of Apollo—Nietzsche provides a fresh means of looking at the dialectic between the narrator's melancholy and the Leech-gatherer's stoical endurance. Nietzsche's theory shows us how, in the context of "Resolution and Independence," Wordsworth's dream functions in a more auspicious form than romantic escape. For Nietzsche, the subjective passions of the lyric poets, paradoxically, play no part in their proper vocation: "Being the active center of that world he may boldly speak in the first person, only his 'I' is not that of the actual waking man, but the 'I' dwelling, truly and eternally, in the ground of being. It is through the reflections of that 'I' that the lyric poet beholds the ground of being" (*BT* 39). The lyric artist manages to see, through dream appearance, the Dionysiac pain that inheres also in music. "The 'I' thus sounds out of the depth of being; what recent writers on esthetics speak of as 'subjectivity' is a mere figment" (*BT* 38). The dream, for Nietzsche, uses its surface illusion to modulate the Dionysiac depth. The dream comes from some other *will* outside the lyric poet, who moves beyond his private subjectivity through the medium of dream. Because Wordsworth's narrator begins with suicidal qualms that stem from solitary withdrawal, the merger in a trance between speaker and Leech-gatherer vitiates solipsism

29. For a reading that stresses the narrator's recognition of otherness in the closure, see Rzepka, *The Self as Mind* 96, who distinguishes Wordsworth's visionary usage of the Leech-gatherer from his nonvisionary reality in the poem's closure: "Whatever Wordsworth's conscious or unconscious intent, the Leech-gatherer demonstrates another kind of perseverance than that which the poet so obscurely apprehends at the visionary level: the persistence of a mind outside his own, inviting him to return to a shared world, pressing him to acknowledge his own embodied presence there."
30. Conran, "The Dialectic of Experience" 70.

and acts as a vehicle leading to the narrator's restoration. He can ultimately laugh at himself and at the luxury of any suicidal escape. This vitiation occurs because the physical body of the Leech-gatherer—of whom Wordsworth is a part, just as the Leech-gatherer is a part of the poet—creates a dialectic with the trance.[31]

The analogy between Wordsworth and the Leech-gatherer, reading the latter as a projection of the former, suggests other plausible displacements: the scarcity of leeches parallels the poet's waning inspiration, and the old man's reduction to the lowest common denominator of human survival represents an embodiment of what Wordsworth or Coleridge could become. The economic straits of the Leech-gatherer, his struggle for mere subsistence, suggest a frightening gap that poets must bridge for themselves. Similarities, of course, must not blur differences: the self-conscious poet is unlike the primitive, enduring old man; the active vocation of finding leeches contrasts with the contemplative life of the poet. This perspective of lyrical characterization casts a different light upon Wordsworth's meeting with the Leech-gatherer. As he will in "Elegiac Stanzas," the poet deploys in "Resolution and Independence" an awakening from a dream that impugns his reclusive rendezvous with nature aloof from community.

The poet's encounter with the Leech-gatherer is, by the standards of oneiric logic, a self-projection. This fusion between Wordsworth and the Leech-gatherer requires, however, the collaboration of the reader. Before we arrive at this point of merger, we have already responded to the full progression of the poem as a language of matter-of-factness, signified by the Leech-gatherer's talk, interacting with a language of myth, shown by the narrator's trance. Jared Curtis shows how Wordsworth balances these two discourses: "What Wordsworth discovered in writing this poem, as he worked his way from the ballad-like beginnings to the fable-like effect of the last version, was the special power of figurative language not only to delight the mind but also to transform it, to give it a range and depth it did not have before the man became metaphor."[32]

31. Robert Langbaum, *The Word from Below* 63. This two-in-one function of lyrical characterization in Wordsworth has been pointed out by Robert Langbaum: "The observed figure becomes a projection of himself; so that the two solitaries become in effect one figure."
32. Jared R. Curtis, *Wordsworth's Experiments with Tradition: The Lyric Poems of 1802* (Ithaca: Cornell University Press, 1971) 111.

The old man's metamorphosis from stone to sea beast to cloud, the refiguring of imagination, lifts the style into mythic action within the mental space of the narrator. The progression of the poem, with its unfolding interchange between Wordsworth's imaginative response and the Leech-gatherer's "ballad-like" objectivity, must play its part in the reader's experience before the final merging of the poet with his creation can be disclosed. Just as the epiphany demands its repetition in the act of reader-response, the reader now moves beyond Curtis's reconciliation of opposing styles to entertain the paradox of the poet's becoming the object of his own narration.

Far from luxuriating in the Romantic daydream, the poet, working through a mythic transformation of the Leech-gatherer, emerges from a crisis of solitude to connect with a figure of sublime endurance. The biographical link with Chatterton and Burns historicizes the narrator's suicidal fits. But Wordsworth does not displace history in favor of an ideology of sublimation, as McGann's theory would lead us to expect. Even in his dream, Wordsworth both embraces the Leech-gatherer as an embodiment of human poverty and constitutes him as a cautionary figure. Waking from dream epiphany in "Resolution and Independence," Wordsworth turns a stoical irony upon himself, an act of therapy for the melancholia endemic to poets. By aligning himself with the Leech-gatherer, that "poor, bare, forked animal," Wordsworth discovers himself—the limits of his endurance, the excesses of his Romantic posturing—in dream.

> But Misery still delights to trace
> Its semblance in another's case.

Cooper, *The Castaway*

CHAPTER THREE

Dream Displacement: Projecting the Abandoned Woman

Among what he considers defects in Wordsworth's poetry, Coleridge notices "an undue predilection for the *dramatic* form in certain poems." From it "two evils result": "either the thoughts and diction are different from that of the poet, and then there arises an incongruity of style"; or there is no differentiation, "and then it presents a species of ventriloquism, where two are represented as talking, while in truth one man only speaks." Coleridge shows little patience, in short, for Wordsworth's skills as a dramatic poet. Among the strengths of Wordsworth's poetry, however, Coleridge singles out the "meditative pathos," the "union of deep and subtle thought with sensibility; a sympathy with man as man [not as an individual]; the sympathy indeed of a contemplator, rather than a fellow-sufferer or co-mate, (spectator, haud particeps) [a spectator, not a participant]." Wordsworth and Goethe share "this peculiarity of utter non-sympathy with the subjects of their poetry. They are always, both of them, spectators *ab extra,* —feeling *for,* but never *with,* their characters."[1] As Coleridge would have it, Wordsworth executes best when he

1. *Biographia Literaria,* ed. James Engell and Walter Jackson Bate (Princeton and London: Princeton University Press and Routledge & Kegan Paul, 1983) 2:135, 2:150, and 2:150 n.1. (This is vol.7 in *The Collected Works of Samuel Taylor Coleridge,* ed. Kathleen Coburn.) For a defense of Wordsworth's dramatic skill in "The Thorn," see Steven Maxfield Parrish, "'The Thorn': Wordsworth's Dramatic Monologue," *English Literary History* 24 (1957) 153–63. I

writes in his own person from the stance of contemplative distance. Ventriloquism, as he finds it in Wordsworth's poetry, is anathema to Coleridge. By use of analogies to dreaming and the practice of ventriloquism, I hope to vindicate Wordsworth from Coleridge's charge. Nietzsche's insights into lyric poetry provide one means of reclaiming the ventriloquism in Wordsworth's tale of Margaret in *The Excursion* (1).[2]

On this question of Wordsworth's feeling for instead of with his characters, Nietzsche's *Birth of Tragedy* makes an analogous point in his analysis of the Apollonian and Dionysiac dimensions of lyric poetry. The poetry of Apollo renders "even the image of angry Achilles" as "no more . . . than an *image* whose irate countenance he enjoys with a dreamer's delight in appearance—so that this mirror of appearance protects him [Homer] from complete fusion with his characters." In the poetry of Dionysos, "the lyrical poet, on the other hand, himself becomes his images, his images are objectified versions of himself" (*BT* 39). Apollonian dream poetry, then, allows for delight in illusion or appearance; the Dionysiac fusion of the lyric poet with his subject is, in its tragic aspects, mediated by the Apollonian dream; the dream makes bearable the original suffering implicit in the Dionysiac vision. The argument in this chapter hinges upon the analogy between ventriloquism and dreaming: Wordsworth projects himself by a process of dream displacement into his abandoned women.

am indebted to Peter Manning, both for his generous reading of this chapter and for the stimulus of his psychoanalytic reading of *The Excursion* (1), "Wordsworth, Margaret, and the Pedlar," *Studies in Romanticism* 15 (1976) 195–220.

2. See Edward E. Bostetter, *The Romantic Ventriloquists: Wordsworth, Coleridge, Keats, Shelley, Byron* (1963; Seattle and London: University of Seattle Press, 1975) 4, 5, 306 for the poet as ventriloquist; see also Reeve Parker, "'Oh Could You Hear His Voice!': Wordsworth, Coleridge and Ventriloquism," *Romanticism and Language*, ed. Arden Reed (Ithaca: Cornell University Press, 1984) 130. Parker delineates Coleridge's bias against ventriloquism: "Regarded . . . negatively, ventriloquism leads us from the dummy back to the animator; and in his impatience with the perceived fault, Coleridge could even wish away the dummy altogether. As he said in *Table Talk*, 'I am always vexed that the authors do not say what they have to say at once in their own persons. . . . I have no admiration for the practice of ventriloquizing through another man's mouth.'" See also David S. Ferris, "Coleridge's Ventriloquy: The Abduction from the *Biographia*," *Studies in Romanticism* 24 (1985): 41–84.

The Erotic Dream in "Laodamia"

As a prelude to this enquiry, we must explore the implications of Wordsworth's treatment of abandoned women. It was Coleridge who first called attention to the masculine bias of Wordsworth's mind: "of all the men I ever knew, Wordsworth has the least femineity in his mind. He is *all* man. He is a man of whom it might have been said, 'It is good for him to be alone.'"[3] This remark carries special conviction because Coleridge himself is so contrary to Wordsworth in this respect. Virginia Woolf likewise singles out Wordsworth, along with Ben Jonson and Milton, as poets who have "a dash too much of the male in them."[4] John Jones extends the idea of solitary masculinity to imply metaphorically a stag or a bull presiding over its own territory: "The instinct to stand guard over its boundaries, to assert its distinctness, Coleridge considered the first indication of a masculine mind, and one supremely obvious in Wordsworth's."[5] But this remark piques our curiosity as to just what is being guarded *within* those boundaries, and what is being kept out and why. The solitary Wordsworth reflected from within the watchtower of his own absolute self (to borrow a phrase from Coleridge) explores the precarious limits of his quest for the philosophic mind. Solitary masculinity also marks his peculiar stance as a poet. But Wordsworth—the quintessential masculine poet—gravitates toward the abandoned woman as one of his recurrent subjects, and leads us to reconsider his excessive masculinity on the evidence of his poetry.

In "Laodamia" (1815), Wordsworth tells the story of the wife of Protesilaus, the Greek hero who died in accord with the Delphic oracle that the first enemy warrior to touch Trojan soil was fated to die. The poem begins with Laodamia's act of sacrifice, invoking her husband's shade from the underworld. She seeks in vain to embrace the bodiless ghost; her arms pass through the phantom form; later, she invites him to share her bed, "a second time a bride." The fates cast a "Stygian" pall upon his lips; he rebukes her "Rebellious passion: for the Gods approve /

---

3. *The Table Talk and Omniana of Samuel Taylor Coleridge,* ed. T. Ashe (London: Bell and Sons, 1909) 339.
4. Virginia Woolf, *A Room of One's Own* (New York: Harcourt Brace, 1957) 107.
5. John Jones, *The Egotistical Sublime: A History of Wordsworth's Imagination* (London: Chatto and Windus, 1954) 29.

The depth and not the tumult of the soul."[6] Although Virgil places Laodamia with Dido in the underworld in the *Aeneid,* it is Ovid's *Heroides* that provides the major source for "Laodamia." By fully developing Laodamia's fantasy life, Ovid adds to the reader's sympathy for her. Wordsworth reverses Ovid's anti-epic stance, however, by choosing to privilege the heroic over Laodamia's romantic love. For Lawrence Lipking, the conjuring of Protesilaus's ghost reveals Laodamia's reliance upon magic, upon the dreams of an abandoned woman, upon an incapacity to distinguish dream from reality: "That weakness makes her a woman; on this point at least Ovid and Wordsworth agree. But a far more disturbing implication follows: perhaps that weakness also makes her a poet. Wordsworth shrinks from this insinuation as if it were the plague."[7] Laodamia's passion serves to heighten Wordsworth's austere masculinity. In depriving Laodamia of her imaginative life as a dreamer or as a poet, Wordsworth adopts a masculine stance that elevates the male heroic life over female sexual passion.

Sara Coleridge (daughter of the poet) reacted strongly to Wordsworth's portrayal of Laodamia: "There is a great want of *feeling,* of *tenderness* and *delicacy,* of *truthfulness* in the representation of Laodamia herself." Sara felt that Wordsworth had depicted Laodamia merely on the level of sensuality, neglecting the more spiritual and active qualities of "a devoted and deeply loving wife." She had felt, in Wordsworth's relations with her, his animosity toward intellectual women and toward her literary efforts on behalf of her father's reputation. The main brunt of her criticism centers upon his bookish idea of women's love:

Mr. Wordsworth was never *in love,* properly speaking. I have heard him boast of it, in [the] presence of his wife, who smiled angelically, delighted that her husband should be so superior to common men. This superiority, however, entails a certain deficiency. He cannot sympathize with a certain class of feelings in consequence—he cannot realize them. He is always upon stilts when he enters these subjects.

---

6. *Poetical Works* 2:269.

7. Lawrence Lipking, *Abandoned Women and Poetic Tradition* (Chicago: University of Chicago Press, 1988) 143, also makes the point that Wordsworth deprives Laodamia of the dreaming imagination that she had in Ovid and that makes her more of a poet.

He stalks along with a portentous stride & then stamps his great
wooden foot down, in the clumsiest manner imaginable.[8]

Sara's reading of "Laodamia" rouses her ire, not merely for Wordsworth's judgmental rendering of Laodamia's sexual nature, but also
for what she considers the poet's widespread condescension toward
women. Writing three years prior to Wordsworth's death, Sara Coleridge supports with pointed testimony Lipking's reading of this poem.
The close of "Laodamia" bears out Sara's insights. Protesilaus rebukes
his wife as "strong in love," but "all too weak / In reason, in self-
government too slow." He warns her that sexual passion is beneath the
dignity of the land of the happy souls; he reminds her that earth destroys
the pleasures of sense; he admonishes her to sublimate her love by reason
to ensure their "blest re-union in the shades below." When his ghost
departs, Laodamia falls dead. The divine decree rules her death as tantamount to suicide; she

> By the just Gods whom no weak pity moved,
> Was doomed to wear out her appointed time,
> Apart from happy Ghosts, that gather flowers
> Of blissful quiet 'mid unfading bowers.
>
> (lines 160–63)

Unlike Ovid, Wordsworth reveals an unflinching masculinity in his
denial of the anti-heroic, domestic stance of Laodamia. Lipking's reading carries conviction: Wordsworth "deliberately contrives a poem that
distances the self—or the feminine side of the self—in every way."[9]

8. Cited in Bradford K. Mudge, *Sara Coleridge, A Victorian Daughter: Her Life and Essays*
(New Haven: Yale University Press, 1989) 136–37 [written by Sara in 1847]. I am indebted
to Mudge both for his lively discussion of Sara's review of "Laodamia," and also for
conversations about Wordsworth's patriarchal attitudes toward women.
9. Lipking, *Abandoned Women* 143. See also Marilyn Butler, *Romantics, Rebels and Reactionaries: English Literature and its Background 1760–1830* (Oxford: Oxford University Press,
1981) 136. Wordsworth goes "out of his way in his Greek-inspired *Laodamia* (1815) to
reprove unlicensed sexuality in a woman. Laodamia is struck down, apparently by the
gods, for her carnality; Wordsworth must have been pleased with so puritanical a pagan
story." For a different approach based upon an allusion to Sonnet 23 by Milton, see Edwin
Stein, *Wordsworth's Art of Allusion* (University Park and London: Pennsylvania State
University Press, 1988) 176. If the dead do not undergo ritual separation "from the living,"

Wordsworth consigns Laodamia to eternal gloom "apart from happy Ghosts," separated from her husband, unable to heed his warning to curb her unmastered desire. Although Wordsworth does play up the demeaning aspect of sexual passion, Lipking might have acknowledged how Wordsworth is imitating Virgil, who in the *Aeneid*, Book 6, places Laodamia in the underworld along with Dido among "those whom stern Love has consumed with cruel wasting," among the unhappy lovers.[10]

In his revisionary closure of "Laodamia," Wordsworth provides human sympathy for these blasted "mortal hopes." The tears of humankind are matched by nature. The trees growing out of Protesilaus's tomb—emblematic of the divine informing nature—wither as the level of their growth exposes them to the wall of Troy: "The trees' tall summits withered at the sight; / A constant interchange of growth and blight!"

In refashioning the story of Laodamia, Wordsworth exemplifies the masculine tendency to defend the hero's high-minded pursuit of glory against the abandoned woman's alien claims for the earthly body. For Wordsworth, this rejection of the domestic side of nature carries a strange bias against the rights of female passion. In this respect, he violates the androgynous profile delineated by Virginia Woolf as proper for the artistic mind: "Some collaboration has to take place in the mind between the woman and the man before the act of creation can be accomplished. Some marriage of opposites has to be consummated."[11] It

---

these ghosts "will haunt them or render them mad": "To perceive this is to perceive a further inverting relevance in Wordsworth's Miltonic allusions, for the phantasm which Laodamia has conjured, though it speaks with the voice of the blessed ("my late espousèd Saint"), is in reality a devil—the objectification of the madness of unsubmissive human desire."

10. Virgil, *Eclogues, Georgics, Aeneid I–VI*, trans. H. Rushton Fairclough (Cambridge: Harvard University Press, 1978) 1.536–37 (6.440–49). Laodamia's proximity to Dido in the underworld raises the question of suicide, but as R. G. Austin notes in his commentary on *Aeneid* (6) (Oxford: Clarendon Press, 1977) 161–62, the catalog of women around Dido is "strange and disturbing" because it includes "an incestuous woman, a notorious traitress, a woman of unnatural lust, a bizarre man-woman, a jealous and suspicious wife, a devoted wife, and a loving woman." The seven women are: Phaedra, Procris, Eriphyle, Pasiphae, Evadne, Laodamia, and Caenus. I am indebted to Rachel Jacoff for these details.
11. Virginia Woolf, *A Room of One's Own* 108.

is not that the masculine is bad and the feminine good, but that an overbalance of either can bias the artist's work. Fortunately for his poetry, Wordsworth does not always show an overbalance of what Nancy Chodorow calls masculine separation and detachment. His earlier poems about abandoned women—written mostly in the 1790s—disclose androgynous facets of his consciousness that run counter to Coleridge's remark about his notorious masculinity.

No small part of Wordsworth's keen sense of transience stems from the untimely deaths of his parents: his mother died when he was eight, his father when he was thirteen. Wordsworth records how, as an infant, "by intercourse of touch" he "held mute dialogues with . . . [his] mother's heart" (*The Prelude* 2.282–83). The infant's earliest imaginative connections with the world, according to Wordsworth's "best conjectures," are feminized by discovering and learning the names of objects filtered through its mother's love. The roots of its poetical spirit are nurtured by the maternal presence: within its "infant veins are interfused / The gravitation and the filial bond / Of Nature that connect him with the world." The maternal and the natural are virtually coeval, feminizing forces in the original growth of its mind. These feminine ties to the world are deliberately contrasted to the alienated adult consciousness: the infant is integrated with the universe, "No outcast he, bewildered and depressed" (*The Prelude* 2.238 and 261–64). Some unknown disturbance comes into Wordsworth's mind, perhaps as a result of his relation to nature; at least on the unconscious level, it is hard to imagine that the absence of his mother plays no part in his defensive construction of a separate identity:

> For now a trouble came into my mind
> From unknown causes. I was left alone
> Seeking the visible world, nor knowing why.
> The props of my affections were removed,
> And yet the building stood, as if sustained
> By its own spirit.
> (*The Prelude* 2.291–96)[12]

12. David Ellis, *Wordsworth and the Spots of Time* 43–44, following Raymond D. Havens, rejects reading the death of Wordsworth's mother into these lines, because of the phrase

Because children are prone to experience in their parents' death an ambivalent mixture of guilt and betrayal, as an orphan Wordsworth developed a hypersensitivity to the boundaries between life and death. Richard Onorato perceives Wordsworth's relation to nature as a maternal surrogate: "The 'ghostly language of the ancient earth' [*The Prelude* 2.328] heard in solitude in the windy darkness is a projection into Nature of a preconscious sense of a lost relationship, of the dialogue that the infant had with the mother's heart."[13] I am stressing the reverse of this insight: Wordsworth's finding in nature a surrogate mother also leads to his vulnerability to betrayal and to his finding in solitude the best society. Wordsworth's trope of betrayal—evident also in "Tintern Abbey" and "Elegiac Stanzas"—suggests that his parents' deaths might have provoked unconscious fears of an incipient betrayal by nature itself. Wordsworth insists, as a pivotal action in *The Prelude,* that love of nature leads to love of man.[14] But if loss of mother and father leads to love of nature, his predicament becomes the more precarious. The contrary argument that love of man leads to love of nature might carry more conviction. Difficulty in loving human beings increases the need for nature as compensation; concern for the indigent, for the abandoned, adds a deep sense of human vulnerability, a social dimension, to the imagination's reciprocity with nature.[15]

"from unknown causes" (1850 text) in relation to the source of the loss of "The Props of my affections." But see Richard J. Onorato, *The Character of the Poet* 25, 59–60, who relates the lost "Props" to the loss of both Wordsworth's parents, primarily the mother.

13. Onorato, *The Character of the Poet* 113. See also Manning, "Wordsworth, Margaret, and the Pedlar" 205.

14. For a different approach to Wordsworth's project here, see Jonathan Wordsworth, *The Music of Humanity* (New York and Evanston: Harper and Row, 1969) 228–31, who stresses the weakness in Wordsworth's argument that "Love of Nature Leads to Love of Man" in Book 8 of *The Prelude,* but aptly relates this possibility to the period of Wordsworth's adherence to "the One Life" at the time of "Tintern Abbey": "The fact that a presence of some kind is to be found in both the light of setting suns and the human mind means that Love of Nature is no longer essentially distinct from Love of Man" (231).

15. See James H. Averill, *Wordsworth and the Poetry of Human Suffering* (Ithaca: Cornell University Press, 1980) 141, for his perceptive use of the eighteenth-century tradition of sensibility, which informs Wordsworth's treatment of figures of human suffering. Of the "Addendum" to *The Ruined Cottage* he writes, "The model is not Love of Nature Leading to Love of Mankind, but sympathy for man leading to a sense of kindred with the external world."

Lyrical Ballads of Abandoned Women

"The Mad Mother" and "The Female Vagrant," two poems that do not employ the observer *ab extra,* both embody for Wordsworth the theme of betrayal and illustrate his androgynous relation to abandoned women. In "The Female Vagrant," a lyrical ballad the more trenchant for its sharp political edge, an abandoned woman follows her soldier husband to the American Revolutionary War in defense of empire. Wordsworth here portrays the victimization of a generic female vagrant, through the loss of her husband and children, as a by-product of the British Empire's struggle for its American territory. The Female Vagrant has pursued the wandering life that the husband Robert, in *The Excursion* (1), denies to his wife Margaret by surreptitious desertion. He departs for imperial wars to escape grinding poverty and to leave her his enlistment bonus. The Female Vagrant's life with children behind the battle lines protracts, as she relates it, "a curst existence, with the brood / That lap (their very nourishment!) their brother's blood," trudging "at the heels of war."[16] This political account of warfare, unlike the usual emphasis of Enlightenment thinkers, insists upon the domestic implications of the American revolutionary war. As the Female Vagrant retells her story aboard the ship that carries her home to poverty and social ostracism, the ocean appears distant "from man, and storms of mortal care"; a quiet invests the sea until it seems "to bring a joy to . . . [her] despair" (*LB,* lines 141–44). Nature here provides relief, a moment's peace, from the depression of abandonment. The facts of her destiny as a result of the American war speak for themselves:

> The pains and plagues that on our heads came down,
> Disease and famine, agony and fear,
> In wood or wilderness, in camp or town,
> It would thy brain unsettle even to hear.
> All perished—all, in one remorseless year,
> Husband and children! one by one, by sword
> And ravenous plague, all perished: every tear

---

16. *Wordsworth and Coleridge Lyrical Ballads 1798,* ed. H. Littledale (London: Oxford University Press, 1911) 76, lines 125–26. Quotations from this poem and "The Mad Mother" are taken from this *verbatim* reprint of the first edition (1798), and will be cited in the text as *LB.*

Dried up, despairing, desolate, on board
A British ship I waked, as from a trance restored.
(*LB*, lines 127–35)

Wordsworth here reveals himself as a man of the Enlightenment: the waste of human life tells against the imperial establishment engaged in an unjust war.[17] In "The Female Vagrant," he projects himself into a female voice, into the unvarnished monologue of a destitute woman, far removed from the heroic convention operative in "Laodamia." By projecting himself dramatically into a female character, Wordsworth here intuitively uses ventriloquism to render the psychology of a woman undone by fate.

Madame de Staël, writing in the period from 1787 to 1817, considered abandonment the dominant literary fate of women. She valued highly works such as Pope's *Abelard's Letters to Heloise* and the anonymous *Letter to a Portuguese Nun* that address primarily the feelings of passion endemic to deserted women: "Ceaselessly condemned, they might believe themselves alone in the world and might soon come to abhor their own character that isolates them from others, did not some impassioned and melancholy works enable them to hear a voice in the desert of life and to find in solitude some rays of happiness that elude them in society."[18] Although child rearing in Wordsworth's time was substantially different from that in our own, the proliferation of deserted females, both in the ballad tradition and in de Staël's historical account, anticipates Nancy Chodorow's modern psychoanalytic reading of female psychology. Chodorow traces gender differences back to their source in relation to mothering:

From the retention of preoedipal attachments to their mother, growing girls come to define and experience themselves as continuous with others; their experience of self contains more flexible or permeable

17. E. P. Thompson, "Disenchantment or Default? A Lay Sermon," *Power and Consciousness,* ed. Conor Cruise O'Brien and William Dean Vanech (London: University of London Press, 1969) 151, finds the prototype of Margaret in Southey's *Joan of Arc* and, also, Coleridge's Gothic verses on a widow dreaming about her "Husband's mangled corpse." These antiwar texts on abandoned women extend beyond Wordsworth's poems of the 1790s.

18. *Madame de Staël on Politics, Literature, and National Character,* trans. Morroe Berger (Garden City, NY: Doubleday and Company, 1964) 265.

ego boundaries. Boys come to define themselves as more separate and distinct, with a greater sense of rigid ego boundaries and differentiation. The basic feminine self is connected to the world, the basic masculine sense of self is separate.[19]

Although this theory—of "the basic masculine sense of self" as separate—remains controversial today because the preoedipal theory puts in question earlier formulations based on the Oedipal, Chodorow's insight corroborates the historical detail of de Staël's remarks on women in her time. The female who is more vulnerable to separation because of her dependency upon bonding—a bonding reinforced by her shared gender with the mother—suffers abandonment by the male, who desires to separate or to find another woman. De Staël's treatment of the condition of women reinforces the notion that "separation anxiety" applies to women in Wordsworth's time perhaps even more strongly than to those in our own. Wordsworth's Female Vagrant, a woman historically conditioned to value bonding as natural to the feminine gender, feels abandonment and separation from her husband the more acutely. Lipking finds "separation anxiety" a dominant factor in all female development—"a fear of being parted from others that is the female counterpart to the male fear of intimacy in Freud's Oedipus complex."[20] At a level deeper than consciousness, Wordsworth discloses his empathy for this female "separation anxiety"; this feminine dimension counters his masculine bias toward rigid identity. His psychic link

19. Nancy Chodorow, *The Reproduction of Mothering: Psychoanalysis and the Sociology of Gender* (Berkeley: University of California Press, 1978) 168–69, endorses, along with Helen A. Deutsch, the idea that "women's proneness to identification" is "a product of the continuing importance of the preoedipal stance of the ego." On the contrast between male and female in superego formation: "Denial of sense of connectedness and isolation of affect may be more characteristic of masculine development and may produce a more rigid and punitive superego, whereas feminine development, in which internal and external object-relations and affects connected to these are not so repressed, may lead to a superego more open to persuasion and the judgments of others, that is, not so independent of its emotional origins."

20. Lipking, *Abandoned Women* 224. Although he is not talking about Wordsworth here, his remarks upon Oedipus' parental abandonment speak to the poet's own condition: "A more extreme version of this theory [modern psychological theory such as Chodorow's] would claim that separation anxiety also dominates the infancy of men, as emblematized by the fact that all Oedipus' problems . . . stem from his original abandonment by his parents."

to the spirit of place reflects an extension of Chodorow's speculations on female preoedipal bonding to the world. In addition, his feminine need to bond with the human world is reflected in his treatment of abandoned mothers. But by cultivating this relation in solitude, he also becomes liable to a contrary masculine drive toward estrangement from human-kind. An androgynous balance, as suggested by Virginia Woolf, best serves the purpose of the artist.

Wordsworth's creative act in portraying abandoned women, unlike his disavowal of androgyny in "Laodamia," reveals a feminine aspect of himself. This process is analogous to accessing his unconscious in dreaming. Wordsworth's ventriloquizing abandoned women, as will later become clear, acts in part like the female figures in male dreams, as representations of his own inner life who give outward expression to the feminine aspect of his own psyche.[21]

In another ballad, "The Mad Mother," Wordsworth portrays femi-nine betrayal by means of a deserted woman speaking to her infant son. As he nurses at her breast, the baby frees the tension in her chest and, as she carries him high above "the sea rock's edge," she feels that his love preserves them from peril (LB, lines 36–48). In her wanderings about the sea cliffs in search of the child's father, she implores—afraid of its betrayal—her infant son to "still be true 'till I am dead" (LB, lines 57–58). The child here is father to the woman in that the parent/child roles are reversed: the infant son preserves the mother's precarious mental bal-

21. Wordsworth's dreamlike empathy with his female characters anticipates what Jung would later describe as a process by means of which the male dreamer reaches the feminine side of his unconscious, of his anima. C. G. Jung, *Memories, Dreams, Reflections*, ed. Aniela Jaffe, trans. Richard and Clara Winston (New York: Pantheon Books, Random House, 1973) 391, defines the anima in relation to dreams: "Anima and animus manifest themselves most typically in personified form as figures in dreams and fantasies ('dream girl,' 'dream lover')." Jung also defines these two terms as functions of gender: "The feminine nature of a man's unconscious and the masculine nature of a woman's." See also D. W. Winnicott, *Playing and Reality* (London: Tavistock Publications, 1971) 84, who takes therapeutic cognizance of male and female elements in both women and men, the male principle providing a basis for object relations, the female the basis for *being* in all of us, regardless of gender: he writes, "I associate impulse related to objects (also the passive voice of this) with the male element, whereas I find that the characteristic of the female element in the context of object-relating is identity, giving the child the basis for being, and then, later on, a basis for a sense of self."

ance.[22] When he finishes sucking, she sees a wild look on his face and imagines him moving apart from her. This mad look, she asserts, "never came from" her: the father's features in the son haunt his image and foreshadow separation and desertion (*LB*, lines 84–88).

Madame de Staël, who lamented the absence in the 1790s of an authentic woman's part in the literary canon, could have found an exception in Wordsworth's ballads. Focusing on female overinvestment in love, de Staël traces the central woman's story to melancholy abandonment: " 'How bitterly must a woman regret that she has ever loved.' The secret story of the greatest passions—the love almost unknown to men—is always abandonment."[23] Wordsworth's theme of the deserted woman is also identified by de Staël as the primary woman's story: a woman must endure the shame of rejected love. She avers that woman "has ever experienced that desolating sentiment, which, like the burning sands of Africa, parches the flower, blasts the stem, and leaves, a withered trunk, the tree which ought to spread its blossoms to the air, and shoot its branches to the sky!" Like Jane Austen, de Staël admonishes her female readers on the hazards of passionate love. She further deplores the solitude foisted upon the abandoned woman. She does not advocate the "solitary life" for any woman. Solitude is an affliction that befalls women "who cannot rely on their own strength to rescue them from the dominion of the passions which assail them in the world."[24] The bitter solitude of desertion holds little in common with Wordsworth's exaltation of solitary reflection. Wordsworth can also deploy passion in a spirit contrary to that of de Staël; the poet's meditation requires that "passion, which itself / Is highest reason in a soul sublime" (*The Prelude* [1850] 5.40–41).

22. Manning, "Wordsworth, Margaret, and the Pedlar" 199, employs a psychoanalytic insight to interpret this infant son sustaining its mother: "The mother saved by her son and retreating with him to live forever in nature probably corresponds with Wordsworth's desire to have saved his mother by the intensity of his love and thus to have maintained the intimacy recorded in the 'Blessed Babe' passage of Book (2) of *The Prelude* (written by 1799)."

23. Madame de Staël's *Treatise on the Passions*, cited by Lipking, *Abandoned Women* 223.

24. The Baroness Staël de Holstein, *A Treatise on the Influence of the Passions, upon the Happiness of Individuals and of Nations*, trans. anon. (London: George Cawthorn, British Library, 1798) 154 and 317.

In choosing a language suitable to the dramatic characters in such lyrics as "The Female Vagrant" and "The Mad Mother," Wordsworth enacts his belief that the poet must address the "passions the language of which, if selected truly and judiciously, must necessarily be dignified and variegated, and alive with metaphors and figures" (*LC* 48). It might be objected that Wordsworth does not address the woman's part in the passion of romantic love except in the negative example of "Laodamia" (1815) or in the Vaudracour and Julia episode in *The Prelude* (1805). Yet he does imply the aftermath of such romance in the condition of abandonment. Wordsworth uses the word "passion" in as broad a sense as de Staël, who often retains its root meaning of suffering. "Passion" must be taken, as Coleridge puts it, in "its general sense, as an excited state of the feelings and faculties."[25] If sexual passion, for both de Staël and Wordsworth, is the primary cause of abandonment, the word's implications extend for both beyond the ruin of women.

The homing instinct—as shown in detail in *Home at Grasmere*, written for *The Recluse*—is a pervasive theme in Wordsworth's poetry. The family takes on special meaning for Wordsworth in relation to his domestic experiment at Dove Cottage with Dorothy and later Mary. What Heinzelman calls the "cult of domesticity," includes "the belief that the household is the site of value not merely or even primarily because of what it produces in the economic sense but because it provides the place where the individual personality may grow and the occasion to discover in that growth a way of integrating self and society, family and polis." In this context, the abandoned woman—so pervasive in the contemporary culture—takes on political overtones. The betrayal of each woman becomes not merely a source of indigence found in all times, but also an act that undermines the moral center that Wordsworth advocated for every household. Milton provided Wordsworth with the model for his political sonnets of 1802: "Plain living and high thinking are no more." Heinzelman, who stresses "the analogy between patriotic and domestic love," points to Wordsworth's valuation of households on the basis of public finery versus genuine private "comfort."[26] If these moral stan-

25. *Biographia Literaria*, ed. Shawcross 2:56.
26. Kurt Heinzelman, "The Cult of Domesticity: Dorothy and William Wordsworth at Grasmere," in *Romanticism and Feminism*, ed. Anne K. Mellor (Bloomington and Indi-

dards serve to measure the viability of one household over another, how much more stringently do they apply to the figure of the abandoned woman, denied the comfort of home, whose condition was sometimes intensified by the imperial policy of the state? The theme of the deserted woman looms large on the contemporary scene in both broadside and traditional ballads. If Wordsworth's own psychic energy were not so strongly invested in the dynamics of desertion, he would not so frequently address subjects such as the demented mother, her fantasies of betrayal, and her need for nurture from her own child. Yet Wordsworth's decision to leave Annette Vallon and her daughter Caroline in order to marry Mary Hutchinson (1802) also cannot be irrelevant to his preoccupation with abandoned women in the poetry of the 1790s. Whether Annette's early letters to Wordsworth and Dorothy in 1793 are the "letters . . . of a girl who not only loves but knows herself beloved" or "the cries of a woman who is beginning to fear that she has been abandoned" remains a critical puzzle. What is of interest to our study of dreams emerges in a letter to Dorothy from Annette, who writes of her own dreamlike hallucinations of Wordsworth's appearance in her room: "His image follows me everywhere; often when I am alone in my room with his letters I think he has entered . . . emerging from my mistake as from a dream I see him not, the father of my child; he is very far from me. This scene is often repeated and throws me into extreme melancholy."[27] Annette's waking dream attests to Wordsworth's ambivalent relation to abandonment, not only as a victim himself, but as a victimizer, as a man who deserts the mother of his child.

---

anapolis: Indiana University Press, 1988) 53 and 64–65. The line, "Plain living . . ." is from one of Wordsworth's political sonnets. See also Karl Kroeber, "'Home at Grasmere': Ecological Holiness," *PMLA* 89 (1974) 132–41, for a pioneering ecological study of Grasmere as a feminized home: "The maternality of the vale is explicit, and much of the language of the poem works to feminize the landscape . . . and to emphasize the poet's dependence on it." Kroeber adds that Wordsworth "speaks for the pleasure of deliberately fitting oneself into a natural organization consciously discerned and appreciated" (135).

27. Stephen Gill, *William Wordsworth: A Life* (Oxford: The Clarendon Press, 1989) 66, also quotes an impassioned letter [March 20, 1793] from Annette to Wordsworth. The letter to Dorothy is written in the same month. Gill cites the translations of Annette's letters from Mary Moorman, *William Wordsworth a Biography: EY* 180–81. Moorman maintains that Annette is "beloved"; Gill skeptically conjectures that Annette's letter to Wordsworth may betray her fear of abandonment.

Ventriloquism in the Tale of Margaret

Considerable portions of the story of Margaret were written between 1797 and 1798 under such titles as *The Ruined Cottage, The Story of Margaret,* or *The Tale of a Woman,*[28] yet the latest version, *The Excursion* (1) (1814), reveals the political retrenchment that aroused Shelley in his *Preface to Alastor.* In the dialectic between solitary dream and suffering, Margaret's tale affords the best example of the poet's drive toward human relationship. Although the dream itself is marginal to Margaret's story, Wordsworth's projection into this feminine figure of abandonment moves us to ask what sort of fantasy—of daydream or wish fulfillment—is the source here of Wordsworth's "femininity." Because Margaret's tale also illustrates a salient rendering of the Wordsworthian "still sad music of humanity"—that cryptic phrase from "Tintern Abbey"—this narrative poem of poverty implies a historical context of societal responsibility for her pain. The Pedlar's story—in excess of 250 lines—thinly disguises an idealized version of Wordsworth's own childhood. The detached moral tone of the Wanderer, and the disparity between his intellect and his vocation as a peddler, have offended many critics, among them Francis Jeffrey, Hazlitt, Coleridge, and John Jones.[29] For them, the Pedlar is the primary example of Coleridge's qualms about ventriloquism, of Wordsworth's deficiency in dramatic skill, of his failure to write in his own person. From a psychoanalytic perspective, ventriloquism in *The Excursion* (1) no longer remains the pejorative term it became for Coleridge. Criticism tends to focus either on Margaret as an object of suffering, or on the joint consciousness of the Wanderer as teller and the poet as reader of her dilemma. If we consider ventriloquism as a form of dream displacement, neither side of this critical dualism will suffer neglect. Margaret's abandonment, then, discloses Wordsworth's Nietzschean, dreamlike projection of himself into her condition.

Wordsworth tried early on to combine the story of the Pedlar—also called the Wanderer in *The Excursion* (1)—and the tale of Margaret: later he tried to separate the two poems. *The Excursion* (1) represents his final

28. Jonathan Wordsworth, *The Music of Humanity* 9–22.
29. Francis Jeffrey, Review of *The Excursion, Edinburgh Review* 24:47 (November 1814): 30. *The Complete Works of William Hazlitt,* 21 vols., ed. P. P. Howe (London: J. M. Dent and Sons, 1932) 19:20; *Biographia Literaria,* ed. Engell and Bate 2:134–35; Jones 168.

attempt to weld the two actions into a single poem. Margaret's story begins after her death, with the Wanderer narrating it to the poet, who acts as an implied reader lodged within the narrative, mediating between the reader and the plight of Margaret. Her tragic end is known from the beginning: "the good die first," the Wanderer says, "And they whose hearts are dry as summer dust / Burn to the socket" (lines 500–2).[30] The heartless linger on, burning down in their endless lives, until their candle finally snuffs out in its holder. A poem contrived in the ventriloquist mode invites a psychoanalytic reading, as Edward E. Bostetter recognized: "To an increasing degree the poem has become the medium through which the ventriloquist poet attempts to release the unconscious, to give it voice and form apart from his conscious self."[31] Wordsworth, quintessentially the poet of the inner life, deploys the mode of ventriloquism to disclose unconscious psychic energies connected with his own abandonment. The Wanderer, whose stability allows him to suffer, constitutes a wishful, imaginary part of Wordsworth himself. The poet, on the other hand, reveals a radically different aspect of Wordsworth's self, one for whom the distress of Margaret over her husband's desertion is almost unbearable.

Leavis distinguished Wordsworthian from Shelleyan poetry by stressing Wordsworth's detachment as opposed to Shelley's "ecstatic dissipation." This distancing by Wordsworth derives from his formula for poetic creation, his "emotion recollected in tranquillity." Leavis defines the difference between these two poets: "Wordsworth seems static; poised above his own center, contemplating; Shelley always moving headlong—eagerly, breathlessly, committed to pursuing his center of gravity lest he should fall on his face." The process of distancing through imaginative memory, according to Leavis, allows Wordsworth to avoid the tendency toward ecstatic diction that mars Shelley's overwrought subjective poetry. By this standard, *The Excursion* (1), like *The Ruined Cottage*, "may be said to be *not* characteristic: its essential distinction is to have a disturbing immediacy that makes it, in its major way, unique."[32] The poet, as the

30. *Poetical Works* 5:25.
31. Bostetter, *Romantic Ventriloquists* 306.
32. See F. R. Leavis, *Revaluation* (New York: W. W. Norton, 1947; rpt. 1963) 213, for the phrase "ecstatic dissipation"; the other quotations are taken from F. R. Leavis, "Wordsworth the Creative Conditions," *Twentieth Century Literature in Retrospect*, ed. Reuben A. Brower (Cambridge: Harvard University Press, 1971) 325–26, and 333.

receptor of the Wanderer's tale, occupies the position of a tormented reader and becomes a part of a drama of one who feeds upon disquiet. Far from Wordsworth's usual formula for distancing, *The Excursion* (1) embodies a drama of emotion veering out of control in the poet's response to Margaret's story of undeserved distress. Ironically, Leavis's theory stresses detached control above the voice of personal feeling, yet it is the atypical Dionysiac voice of Wordsworth—disclosed through ventriloquism—that emerges in the poet's response to Margaret's plight. This voice paradoxically enhances the quality of the poetry that Leavis admires in spite of contradicting his theory of detachment. No doubt, the laconic restraint of the poet's anguished voice emerges the more powerfully because of the Apollonian voice of the Wanderer. This second ventriloquist voice preserves the poem from the very Shelleyan excess that Leavis deplores.

Wordsworth's ventriloquizing techniques are a part of his narrative strategy. The teller narrates the tale as an observer *ab extra*: this viewpoint—a stance that never allows the Pedlar to exercise more than a modicum of intervention—dramatizes the stark mechanism of the tale. In depicting the early, healthy facts of Robert's working in his garden after a long day at his loom, the Wanderer casts a dark shadow on the natural detail that stands as metonymy for the human action. Robert works "until the light / Had failed, and every leaf and flower were lost / In the dark hedges" (lines 530–32). Although at this point in the tale Robert has not yet succumbed to blighted harvests and poverty, a hint of menace lurks beneath this precise rendering of the external scene. The Pedlar stands slightly outside the action, armed with compassion, allowing the action to unfold with its own foreknown tragic destiny. Standing outside the circle of Margaret's fate, he unfolds a tale the tragic outcome of which is beyond his power to change. When, late in his history of Margaret, the Wanderer does not find her at home, he hears the neglected child inside the cottage:

> From within
> Her solitary infant cried aloud;
> Then, like a blast that dies away self-stilled,
> The voice was silent.
> (lines 735–38)

Presumably, the baby has been crying for some time, but the Wanderer never moves to pick it up. As the detached Apollonian observer, he allows the tale to reveal itself without tempering its starkness. The infant that cuts off its own cry prefigures the silence of its impending doom. The Wanderer presents Robert's derangement with the same matter-of-fact detail. Robert whistles snatches "of merry tunes / That had no mirth in them"; he mingles with "uneasy novelty" labors that are inappropriate to the season; he speaks with a "cruel tongue" of his babes; he tosses them "with a false unnatural joy: / And 'twas a rueful thing to see the looks / Of the poor innocent children" (lines 569–89). The Pedlar is either an eyewitness to these events or he filters them through Margaret's telling, yet he recounts Robert's unseemly story without direct comment. Unlike "The Female Vagrant" and "The Mad Mother," whose women tell their own stories, this tale of an abandoned woman intensifies its suffering through its detached narrative frame.

The Wanderer, as an embodiment of Wordsworth's hunger for consolation, ruminates upon his tendency to lapse into a trance as his "spirit clings" to Margaret's worth:

> And to myself I seem to muse on One
> By sorrow laid asleep; or borne away,
> A human being destined to awake
> To human life, or something very near
> To human life, when he shall come again
> For whom she suffered.
>
> (lines 778–90)

This recurrent reverie represents the wish to reunite Margaret and Robert in a timeless dream of an afterlife or better fate beyond her earthly lot of betrayal. This wishful impulse contravenes Wordsworth's own painful dream projection into Margaret. Where the Wanderer is driven to move beyond tragedy, Wordsworth, the poet, "who *is* in what he contemplates,"[33] projects an active Dionysiac life into Margaret's

---

33. Friedrich Nietzsche, *The Birth of Tragedy out of the Spirit of Music* in *Complete Works*, vol.3, trans. W. A. Haussmann (Edinburgh and London: T. N. Foulis, 1909) 45–46. For an application of this quotation from Nietzsche to the epic poet as compared to the "lyric-dramatic poet," see Langbaum, *The Poetry of Experience* 231–32.

desertion. If we apply Nietzsche's discourse on tragic theory to a lyric poet, the Wanderer acts as an Apollonian figure. For Wordsworth, who tends to mix genres, Nietzsche's category of the *lyric* extends to a wide range of his poetry, including *The Excursion* (1). The Apollonian Wanderer preserves his distance from Margaret with controlled compassion, but Wordsworth discloses his Dionysiac investment in her, much as he projects himself into other figures in his own dream. The Wanderer's trance, like the Apollonian dream that makes bearable the ruin of the tragic hero, plays off against Wordsworth's Dionysiac power to exist inside Margaret's skin. Far from the portrayal of a voyeur battening on Margaret's suffering, Wordsworth's ventriloquist drama meets Nietzsche's condition that the lyric poet does not indulge his narrow personality because he splits himself into all three characters. In this Dionysiac lyric portrayal of Margaret, Wordsworth, as in a dream, enters into her suffering through the indirection of his ventriloquism.

Wordsworth's identification with Margaret through his ventriloquizing voice provides an interesting analogy to Freud's gender-coded dream of a patient's infection. In Freud's dream, Irma, one of his widowed patients, appears in a hall where he and his wife are entertaining guests. He rebukes her for not accepting his diagnosis of her symptoms. She has pains in her throat, shoulder, and abdomen: Freud takes her aside and looks down her throat, an act which she resists but finally allows; he discovers excessive white and grey infections. When Dr. M. examines Irma's shoulder, he discovers an "infiltration." Freud, in his analysis of this dream imagery, had intuitively diagnosed Irma's infected shoulder—without removing her dress—before Dr. M. had. As his own dream interpreter, he reads his rheumatoid shoulder as projected on to Irma. In Freud's identification with Irma, the psychoanalytic critic Jim Swan detects

> a reversal of roles, as if unconsciously Freud realized that in order to discover the secret of dreams, he himself would have to undergo passively—like a woman—a probing, intrusive examination and analysis by masculine, scientific authorities. The dream is virtually a prediction and a demand for the ensuing self-analysis: the discovery of the secret of dreams obliges the dreamer to analyze his own dreams and the secrets they hold for him. It is a dream about creative recep-

tivity, an ability to be open to analysis and to the meaning of one's dreams as revealed by analysis.[34]

On the brink of his most creative discovery about the meaning of dreams, Freud takes on the passive role of woman, a trait that he attributes to the feminine gender and that he would have disdained in waking life. Freud is about to give birth to his most prized discovery, but he must first endure something analogous to the uncomfortable probing of the throat that he had impatiently forced upon Irma. Just as Freud fuses himself with the dream image of Irma, allowing himself to be "infiltrated" by and as the feminine, Wordsworth becomes Margaret through the agency of the dreamlike imagination. In both men, the assumption of feminine roles, of undergoing abjection, counters their inclination toward excessive masculinity and fertilizes their own creative invention. *The Prelude* as a whole reinforces this likeness between Freud and Wordsworth on the practice of self-analysis. The resemblance is further reinforced by Jonathan Bishop's insight into Wordsworth's psychic self-scrutiny: "We may even claim that *The Prelude* constitutes the record, half-concealed in a commonplace autobiographical structure, of a process, which in these days, we would call a self-analysis; the precipitate of an interior battle, a sequence of maneuvers against the incomprehensible, fought out in the public domain of verse."[35]

Wordsworth's dream connections with Freud and Margaret also include his more indirect ventriloquizing through the teller of her tale. The Wanderer in *The Excursion* (1), whose background is changed from that of the Pedlar in *The Ruined Cottage,* fits more squarely within "the

34. Jim Swan, "*Mater* and Nannie: Freud's Two Mothers and the Discovery of the Oedipus Complex," *American Imago* 31 (1974): 22–23. In this superb article, Swan also draws upon Erik H. Erikson, "The Specimen Dream of Psychoanalysis," in *Psychoanalytic Psychiatry and Psychology: Clinical and Theoretical Papers,* vol.1, ed. Robert P. Knight and Cyrus R. Friedman (New York: International Universities Press, 1954).
35. Jonathan Bishop, "Wordsworth and the 'Spots of Time,'" *English Literary History* 26 (March 1959) 60, compares Wordsworth's self-fashioning with dreams: "Can we suppose that we have, in Wordsworth, a mind with an extraordinary capacity to recreate, or have recreated for it, moments which embody the significance of its own life, as the ordinary mind can no longer do, once it has emerged from early childhood, except in the very much weaker and more ambiguous forms of dreams?"

traditional frame of paternalism, Anglican doctrine, fear of change."[36] What the Wanderer gains in aesthetic distance he loses in femininity, a lack that distinguishes him from the Wordsworth who portrays abandoned women. The Wanderer's change from the Pedlar of 1797 emerges most clearly in Wordsworth's political swerve from revolutionary to monarchist. Instead of an acolyte of nature, derived from an upbringing as a Cumbrian shepherd, the Wanderer now becomes a moral offspring of the Scottish kirk. This shift in his origin, according to Peter Manning, marks a "poignant illustration of Wordsworth's spiritual progress from the celebration of maternal nature to the patriarchal virtues of patience and fortitude enforced by his later poetry."[37] Nature itself, apart from the Wanderer's youth among the fells, becomes sterner in this poem, as if it is now mingled with a stoical acceptance of its rhythms, either for sustenance or for ruin. Although the Wanderer retains his education in nature in *The Excursion* (1), his feminine and maternal heritage now dwindles into a garrulous expansion of his former role in *The Ruined Cottage*. The Wanderer of 1814 advocates a state system of education for the growth of knowledge in the British Empire:

> this imperial Realm,
> While she exacts allegiance, shall admit
> An obligation, on her part, to teach
> Them who are born to serve her and obey . . .
> (*The Excursion* 9.295–98)

In contrast to his earlier affinity for Paine's *Rights of Man,* Wordsworth's sympathy for the international cause of French liberty has become a matter of duty and obedience to the British monarch. Book 9 of *The Excursion* thus adds a new dimension to the Wanderer of Book 1: it makes clear why Byron, Shelley, and Hazlitt reacted to the imperial theme with disdain. The education among the fells now merges with the Wanderer's allegiance to nationalism as a rebuff to earlier Enlightenment politics. The Wanderer attempts to comfort the poet, who feels the burden of

36. Edward P. Thompson, "Disenchantment or Default?" 176.
37. Manning, "Wordsworth, Margaret, and the Pedlar" 219. Apart from this quotation, Manning does not focus upon gender. I am indebted to his acute psychoanalytic insight in reclaiming *Excursion* (1) over *The Ruined Cottage* as the proper vehicle for Wordsworth's presentation of Margaret.

Margaret's affliction and requires the stability of the Wanderer to heal the poet's tendency to feed upon disquietude. The poet also stands for the part of Wordsworth that has confronted the betrayal of nature. In the character of the Wanderer, on the other hand, Wordsworth inclines toward the one-sided masculine values exemplified above in "Laodamia."[38]

In commenting upon Wordsworth's revision of *The Ruined Cottage* in *The Excursion* (1), William Galperin treats the Wanderer as a figure of innocence in comparison with the poet's experience. This criticism focuses upon lines attributed to the Wanderer for the first time in 1814: "He could *afford* to suffer / With those whom he saw suffer" (*The Excursion* 1.370–71). The Wanderer "has been protected from suffering altogether . . . and remains a virtual child."[39] This antiromantic reading stresses by contrast the poet's intensity of disillusionment, but it polarizes too sharply the differences between these two voices of Wordsworth. In fact, as a figure acquainted with pain, the Wanderer as peddler combines his solitary traveling with incursions into community. His Apollonian tendency to adopt an aesthetic stance toward Margaret's "common tale" does invite Galperin's criticism, yet he exists partly as foil to the alienated poet. The energy of the Wanderer's story casts such a pall upon the poet's imagination that "A heart-felt chillness crept along . . . [his] veins" (line 619). In words that may have suggested Keats's dilemma in distinguishing between poets and dreamers in *The Fall of Hyperion*, the Wanderer cautions against a "wantonness" that might "hold vain dalliance with the misery / Even of the dead"; he relies upon the moral value of gloomy thoughts; otherwise he fears he may have become a mere "dreamer

38. Leavis, *Revaluation* 178, writes powerfully about Wordsworth's need for the consolation of the idealized Wanderer. Leavis sums up the poet's own stance with a telling question: "How, in a world that has shown itself to be like this, is it possible to go on living?"
39. William Galperin, " 'Then the Voice Was Silent': 'The Wanderer' vs. *The Ruined Cottage*," *English Literary History* 51 (1984) 355. This bold reading underlies Galperin's admiration for an anti-Romantic Wordsworth: "What book 1 reveals is not the 'withdrawal' as Leavis has it, 'to a more reassuring environment,' but rather 'withdrawal' as the only livable option in a world without assurances, be they Christian, pantheistic, or subjective and humanistic" (346). For a different dimension see Susan J. Wolfson, *The Questioning Presence: Wordsworth, Keats, and the Interrogative Mode in Romantic Poetry* (Ithaca and London: Cornell University Press, 1986) 114, who sees in *Excursion* (1) (and especially in the later books) "the presence of an Author who alternately praises and resists the Wanderer's instruction."

among men, indeed / An idle dreamer" (lines 626–36). Even if he is such a dreamer, the mode of ventriloquism allows the tale of Margaret to speak for itself. The poet as alienated reader discloses his own urgency in trying to stomach the reality of unmitigated bleakness. If the Wanderer verges on the dreamer (in a pejorative sense), the poet enhances Margaret's story by proving it upon the pulses of his grief.

Unlike Laodamia, Margaret reveals an abundance of imagination in the very fertility of her hope, in her irrepressible fantasies of return. Her story of abandonment yields another instance of Wordsworth's depiction of obsessive female imagination: Margaret's uncanny fixation upon the return of her husband, Robert, erodes all other aspects of her life, including maternal love for her two children. Her imagination manifests the same unruliness of the lover, the same capacity to substitute illusion for reality.

Barbara Schapiro confronts the possibility that Wordsworth's hostile attitude toward the absent mother may underlie his treatment of abandoned women such as Margaret: "The mother is imaged as hostile and treacherous, in the form of a denying and rejecting Nature, and also as a suffering victim, in the figure of the deserted woman. The infant/poet's angry aggressive feelings toward the mother indeed make him feel as if he has betrayed her as well as she him."[40] This discussion of Wordsworth's ambivalence, coupling the dual betrayal by the mother and by nature with his own guilty betrayal, raises the issue of unconscious hostility toward women as a possible motive for the poet's choice of deserted and impoverished mothers. In Wordsworth's wavering between aggression and love for the mother, however, Schapiro finds an eventual predominance of the loving attitude. Aggressive feelings may operate subliminally in his choice of subject, yet his own empathy for Margaret, almost beyond his elastic limit, overshadows any latent enmity toward women. The poet's own desertion of Annette Vallon probably contributes to his choice of abandoned women as subjects for poems,

40. Schapiro, *The Romantic Mother* 125, also captures the positive side of the poet's ambivalence: "By suffering and confronting these feelings in the course of the poems, however, the poet emerges from his mourning with renewed faith in the essential goodness and love in the mother, in the self, and, by extension, in humanity." See also Barbara Johnson's comment on the women in Wordsworth's canon: "Even when Wordsworth speaks of or as a woman, the woman tends to be abused, mad, or dead," *A World of Difference* (Baltimore: Johns Hopkins University Press, 1987) 97.

and complicates his ambivalence about betrayal and betrayed. The Jungian anima would include these aggressive, dark, and daemonic aspects of the unconscious that take a feminine gender in the masculine personality. Wordsworth himself had experienced poverty and parental desertion; further, his conflicted response to the Wanderer's tale of Margaret authenticates his suffering.

Peter Manning reads Margaret's destiny as more generalized in Book I of *The Excursion* (1814): the poet's "pressing personal" problem in the 1790s is to transform "sadness into consolation"; "the story of Margaret that Wordsworth hears is his own story."[41] The urgent problem in Wordsworth's life that informs the contrast between the Wanderer and the poet belongs to the 1790s. His need for ventriloquism emerges more starkly in *The Ruined Cottage,* where the poet's pain is less unmitigated and the Pedlar's paternalism is merely incipient and not fully fleshed out. But in both versions the crucial completion of the ventriloquist triangle includes Wordsworth's own psychic investment in the imaginative obsession that embodies Margaret's love. The androgynous side of the poet emerges through his deep empathy with poverty and betrayal. The Wanderer, in contrast, stands for Wordsworth's calmer reflective attitude toward nature, for his hopes for the "philosophical mind" as depicted in the "Immortality Ode." Margaret is bound to her cottage and its spirit of place but, like the Leech-gatherer, her relation to nature is unselfconscious. She even falls victim to nature's predatory force. The poet reveals his own marginal political stance in bonding with the feminine, with what de Staël identifies as the distress endemic to the women of the time, the consequences of abandonment.

Why must Wordsworth's relation to deserted women make a difference on grounds of gender? Why would not his male solitaries—such as the Old Cumberland Beggar, the Discharged Soldier, or the Blind

41. Manning, "Wordsworth, Margaret, and the Pedlar" 207. Leavis, "Wordsworth the Creative Conditions" 332, along with Manning, maintains that *Excursion* (1), rather than *The Ruined Cottage*, is the form in which the tale of Margaret ought to be read. See also Carol T. Christ, "Visionary Dreariness and the Female Solitary in Wordsworth's Poetry," Paper at MLA meeting, San Francisco, December 27, 1987 3, mentions the Grisson Gypsy in *Descriptive Sketches* and the female vagrant in *An Evening Walk* "who indeed threaten the coherence and the project" of their respective poems, "less because of the pathetic suffering they embody than because of the way in which they provide a dark mirror of the poet himself." What Christ says about these two abandoned women applies also to Margaret.

Beggar in London—create the same effect upon the poet? In the sublime mode, characters such as the abandoned women of Wordsworth can act as blocking agents, in which the loss of self that initiates the sublime in the poet rebounds as sublime energy that rushes in to fill the gap. Or as Carol Christ puts it, "a sense of the self as solitary, misplaced, and desolate is transformed into the bliss of solitude." By an act of imagination, the poet appropriates the blockage: "Because the vagrant woman, usually with some troubled connection to a child, so frequently functions as that blocking image for Wordsworth, her treatment indicates how he recuperates the threat she represents." Paradoxically, the poet encounters these women in solitude; yet, by overcoming the blockages of his distressed females, he achieves a negative epiphany that returns him to relationship with society. He salvages a social connection—in the sense of responding to human otherness, of emerging from solitude to relation—from a blockage that his abandoned women are unable to surmount for themselves.[42]

In poems such as "The Female Vagrant" and "The Mad Mother," the poet's recuperation occurs at a distance, primarily on the aesthetic level. With Margaret, on the other hand, the poet who cannot afford to suffer responds to her tragedy as a highly threatened reader/auditor who struggles to comprehend a message that is all too close to home. Because Wordsworth's relation of ventriloquism to Margaret includes contact— as in dreams—with his own anima, the gender of these women is essential to his project as a poet. The male solitaries also produce a blockage that releases the sublime epiphany, but the abandoned women relate to Wordsworth on a different psychic wavelength. The component of desertion does not appear in the male solitaries in the same way. Because these abandoned women usually have children, the shattered potential family undermines Wordsworth's idea of the family as a moral building block of the polis. In the poems of the 1790s, Wordsworth discloses an androgyny that undercuts his tendency toward excessive masculinity.

The treatment of deserted mothers affords insight into the feminizing

42. Christ, "Visionary Dreariness and the Female Solitary in Wordsworth's Poetry" 5, 6, and 8, bases her argument about blockage in Wordsworth upon Neil Hertz, "The Notion of Blockage in the Literature of the Sublime," *The End of the Line: Essays on Psychoanalysis and the Sublime* (New York: Columbia University Press, 1985) 40–60.

underside of Wordsworth's masculine need for identity in solitude. While recognizing how arbitrary definitions of gender may be, it is tempting to speculate upon the ambivalence, stemming from desertion, of this poet's identity. Leo Bersani finds in artists such as Keats and Baudelaire a feminine prostitution of the self by the extremity of its openness to otherness. "The constant in Baudelaire's thought," Bersani says, is "the idea of a connection between art and the loss of virility." The artist, moreover, "loses his virile identity *through* an obscene openness to external reality which makes him an artist but which also makes him—a woman."[43] Wordsworth's poetry of "the egotistical sublime" would seem to resist comparison with these negatively capable poets. But these contradictions are not irreducible: just as Keats recasts *Hyperion* into an egotistically sublime dream vision in *The Fall of Hyperion,* so Wordsworth yields to "wise passiveness" and to self-destroying encounters with outer forces. In the boat-stealing incident of *The Prelude,* Book 1, and in the "Fallings from us, vanishings; / Blank misgivings of a Creature / Moving about in worlds not realized" of the "Immortality Ode" Wordsworth records a feminine tendency, as Bersani defines it, to penetration by otherness.

Wordsworth's taking part in the separation anxiety of the abandoned mother augments our hearing, beyond the frequencies of sound, of the "still, sad music of humanity." In "Tintern Abbey," the reader must infer the meaning of this phrase, but in Wordsworth's tale of Margaret in *The Excursion* it receives embodiment. It is this acquaintance with grief that subtends the "philosophic mind." Wordsworth has earned his affinity for the outcasts through his Dionysiac ventriloquy. John Jones, who reinforces Coleridge's dictum upon Wordsworth of "extreme masculinity," glosses this stance forcefully: "He is a striking exception to the classical type of bi-sexual genius; and there is from the start something incomplete about his 'self-sufficing power of solitude.'"[44] This judgment carries conviction for Wordsworth as he grows more conservative, yet it misses the mark for the poet of the deserted female. His best poetry includes a dialectic between solitude and relation: even his solitary epiphany implies a social sharing with his reader. *The Excursion* (I), far

43. Leo Bersani, "Artists in Love," *Literature and Psychoanalysis,* ed. Edith Kurzweil and William Phillips (New York: Columbia University Press, 1983) 351.
44. Jones, *The Egotistical Sublime* 49.

from a failure of ventriloquism, includes both the Wanderer as a detached observer, and, along with Margaret, a dramatic projection of the ventriloquist voice. No one has wished the Wanderer's own story longer, yet the tale of Margaret takes on added psychic energy from Wordsworth's ventriloquy. It is the more remarkable that he should achieve a precarious balance between solitude and community, even as his femininity of mind is on the verge of abandoning him. Through Margaret's undeserved pain, it is Wordsworth we mourn for.

The Dark Interpreter in dream and reverie
reveals the worlds of pain and agony and woe possible to man
—possible even to the innocent spirit of a child.

De Quincey, *Suspiria de Profundis*

CHAPTER FOUR

Carnage & Its Consequences: Reveries of Power

Two passages from Wordsworth offer insight into the relationship between the literary use of reverie and the language of power: the episode of human sacrifice by the Druids on Sarum Plain (*The Prelude* [12]) and the episode of the Discharged Soldier (*The Prelude* [4]). These reveries illustrate two levels of trance: the first operates beyond the conscious will, the second acts in its absence. In *The Prelude* (5), Wordsworth explored the language of power in his discussion of books, and in Book 12 he precedes the lurid reverie on Sarum Plain with the hope that his own poetry, "Enduring and creative, might become / A power like one of Nature's" (12.311–12). Here the language of dream contains power as one of the matrices of his creativity: this energy works, as we saw in chapter 1, through his typical strategy of memory. I shall now investigate Wordsworth's crisis over French revolutionary betrayal: his own false imagination—linked with France's political failure—and its restoration to ensure his survival as a poet. Here reverie becomes the vehicle of destructive power as it emerges through the poet's ancient British heritage and, by the displacement native to dreams, also epitomizes the French revolutionary bloodbath. In writing an epic on the growth of his imagination—an agonistic imitation of his precursor, Milton—Wordsworth stages for himself a vast psychic conflict, one that acts as a microcosm of the French revolutionary combat with hereditary power.[1]

1. Ronald Paulson, *Representations of Revolution 1789–1820* (New Haven: Yale University Press, 1983) 272–73.

III

Reverie on Sarum Plain

Wordsworth's reverie on Sarum Plain, on the barbaric power of human sacrifice, leads me to consider a number of critical responses to his poetry. New historicist critics, such as Marjorie Levinson, Jerome McGann, and Clifford Siskin, react skeptically to Wordsworth's visionary bent. Jerome McGann represents Romantic ideology as "transhistorical—eternal truths which wake to perish never":

> The very belief that transcendental categories can provide a permanent ground for culture becomes, in the Romantic age, an ideological formation—another illusion raised up to hold back an awareness of the contradictions inherent in contemporary social structures and the relations they support. As far as Romantic poetry is concerned, this General Ideology informs all its work as an implied and assumed premise which takes various forms specific to the particular writers and their circumstances.[2]

Given the variety of Romantic poetry, such sweeping generalities ("this General Ideology informs all its work") require scrutiny in relation to the specifics of the poetry they seek to govern. Because reveries might be perfect conduits for exactly such ideological evasion of historical contradiction, they afford a means of testing this theory of ideology. Long before the new historicists, Hazlitt, Shelley, and Byron offered various critiques of Wordsworthian practice. This chapter will consider valid objections to Wordsworth's excesses of imagination, including his own self-criticism.

Although Wordsworth does not resemble Keats in making dreams an alternate term for imagination, he creates a precedent for Keats by using dream to tap subliminal sources of energy. In *The Prelude*, Wordsworth is beguiled by the very kind of power that he turns out to abjure in the

2. Jerome McGann, *The Romantic Ideology* 134. See also Clifford Siskin, "Revision Romanticized: A Study in Literary Change," *Romanticism Past and Present* 7 *(1983)*: 1–16, who writes of the "Immortality Ode," "The poet becomes philosophic hero as change felt as loss is transformed by revision into intimations of the unchanging . . . the apotheosis of the 'Poets' entails the repression of history under the weight of transcendent continuities." See also William J. Galperin, *Revision and Authority in Wordsworth* 2, who traces a process of self-correction in Wordsworth whereby he demystifies his own transcendence: "Wordsworth does not 'become' an orthodox Christian in his later phase. Instead, his orthodoxy cancels the authority it supersedes so as to cancel *all* authority, including, of course, the authority of orthodoxy itself."

French Revolution. Wordsworth's reverie on Sarum Plain, his evocation of an image of human sacrifice among the ancient Druids, represents an example of imagination's ambiguous relation to power. This vision, radically unlike Gaston Bachelard's "benign reverie," which remains under the full control of the will, reaches a deeper hypnagogic level of trance. In dreaming, some other will emerges from Wordsworth's unconscious. In an essay on *Coriolanus* written in 1816, Hazlitt notices how "the language of poetry naturally falls in with the language of power. The imagination is an exaggerating and exclusive faculty: it takes from one thing to add to another: it accumulates circumstances together to give the greatest possible effect to a favorite object." Imagination, in Hazlitt's view, is aristocratic, the understanding, republican; imagination finds its identity in passion, while the understanding seeks "the greatest quantity of ultimate good, by justice and proportion."

Paradoxically for our discussion of Wordsworth, Hazlitt (perhaps exercising his love of contradiction by tending to overstate a polemical stance) pronounces on "the principle of poetry" as "a very anti-levelling" one. Both before and after his *Coriolanus* essay, because Hazlitt describes Wordsworth's muse as "a levelling one," we are confronted with a discrepancy in the critic's own discourse. This inconsistency is obviated if, on the other hand, "levelling" merely means "prosy" or "anti-Poetic." Hazlitt's ambivalence is emblematic of a problem close to Wordsworth: the imagination's susceptibility to distortion by power. Hazlitt does not disguise his subtle critique of Coriolanus' tyrannical impulses, but neither does he exempt himself (as in his sympathy for Napoleon) from admiring the awesome energy of Coriolanus, a figure who attracts the theater audience even as he denigrates the mob. Hazlitt depicts imagination in a way that reminds us of its flirtation with brute force: poetry "has its altars and its victims, sacrifices, human sacrifices. . . . 'Carnage is its daughter.' Poetry is right-royal. It puts the individual for the species; the one above the infinite many, might before right."[3]

Because Hazlitt frequently uses imagination in much more conventional senses, we must recognize that *Coriolanus* affords him an oppor-

<hr />

3. *The Complete Works of William Hazlitt* 4: 214–15. Hazlitt's political bias boldly emerges from his dismantling of Coriolanus's logic in denying the legitimate suffering of the commoners because of their ignorance: "This is the logic of the imagination and the passions; which seek to aggrandize what excites admiration and to heap contempt on misery, to raise power into tyranny, and to make tyranny absolute" (216).

CARNAGE AND ITS CONSEQUENCES

tunity to reflect upon power. John Kinnaird remarks upon Hazlitt's tendency "to distrust the adequacy of" an "honorific account of the function of imagination in politics." Kinnaird proceeds to describe this stage in Hazlitt's critical thought on the imagination's relationship to politics as his "mature theory."[4] Although Hazlitt is writing about *Coriolanus*, his remarks disclose their relevance to Wordsworth's affinity for power. His phrase "Carnage is its daughter" alludes to the poet's "Thanksgiving Ode" (1816), to the derivation of the lineage of a personified Carnage from God:

> But Thy most dreaded instrument,
> In working out a pure intent,
> Is Man—arrayed for mutual slaughter,
> —Yea, Carnage is thy daughter![5]

In constituting carnage as God's daughter, a notoriously bold paradox, Wordsworth sounds like an Old Testament prophet. His ode begins with retrospect, with his imagination roving in unsatisfied desire that can find no fulfillment in reality until the heroic British victory over Napoleon. In writing about Coriolanus, Hazlitt displaces God to imagination. He thus casts an invidious glance at Wordsworth's chauvinistic entrancement in 1816, with English martial power confidently underwritten as part of the divine plan working through "mutual slaughter."

In 1845 Wordsworth excised from the poem the last two quoted lines with their reference to carnage as God's daughter, perhaps in response to Lord Byron who, in his unseemly siege of Ismael, had turned these lines to sardonic purpose in *Don Juan*:

> "Carnage" (so Wordsworth tells you) "is God's daughter:"
> If *he* speak truth, she is Christ's sister, and
> Just now behaved as in the Holy Land.   (8.9)

Byron's jibe adds point to Hazlitt's awareness of the political liabilities of imagination. Byron even added a note to reinforce his logical deduction of the Wordsworthian "sisterhood" of Christ: "this is perhaps as pretty a

---

4. John Kinnaird, *William Hazlitt: Critic of Power* (New York: Columbia University Press, 1978) 110. See also David Bromwich, *Hazlitt: The Mind of a Critic* (New York: Oxford University Press, 1983) 320–21, who suggests that power as sublime energy of mind can override morality for Hazlitt, but this fact does not mitigate my claim that Hazlitt uses Coriolanus's tyrannical proclivities to attack Wordsworth's politics.
5. *Poetical Works* 3:155.

pedigree for murder as ever was found out by Garter King at Arms.—
What would have been said, had any freespoken people discovered such
a lineage?"[6] Byron transfers his perspective to the people, as opposed to a
monarch, in hypothetically giving them a divine sanction to power,
unthinkable from the point of view of the royal establishment. Shelley
further complicates the issue by adapting, in *Peter Bell the Third,* Wordsworth's cancelled lines as part of Peter's ode to the devil:

> "May Carnage and Slaughter,
> Thy niece and thy daughter,
> May Rapine and Famine,
> Thy gorge ever cramming,
> Glut thee with living and dead!"
>
> (6.36–37)

In addressing Peter Bell's "meek" ode to the devil, Shelley makes "Carnage" the daughter of Satan instead of God. Shelley and Byron had
received added provocation for these sardonic allusions from Wordsworth's own preface to his 1816 volume containing the "Thanksgiving
Ode." Apart from his encomium to British martial power in this preface,
Wordsworth adopts a high moral tone incompatible with his earlier
partisan espousal of French liberty. Wordsworth is proud of his revul-
sion towards Napoleon, and he hopes that his poem will "counteract, in
unsophisticated minds, the pernicious and degrading tendency of those
views and doctrines that lead to the idolatry of power, as power, and, in
that false splendour to lose sight of its real nature."[7] Napoleon, no less
than the *ancien regime,* can betray freedom by the corrupting magnetism
of power. Wordsworth has good reasons for his apostasy, but the fervor
of his tone belies his own guilt over an earlier seduction by power.[8] The
ardent nationalism of his "Thanksgiving Ode," contested by Byron and

---

6. Lord Byron, *Don Juan,* ed. Leslie A. Marchand (Boston: Houghton Mifflin, 1958) 248,
and 479 n.

7. From the Fenwick note to the "Thanksgiving Ode," *Poetical Works* 3:464; Shelley's
passage from *Peter Bell the Third* is quoted in *Poetical Works* 3:461.

8. Alan Liu, *Wordsworth: The Sense of History* 426, cites Carl Woodring's question in *Politics
in English Romantic Poetry* (Cambridge: Harvard University Press, 1970) 24–48, "How
could . . . [Romantics such as Wordsworth] swing from 'romantic revolt' to Romantic
'Facism?'" See also Liu's discussion of Wordsworth's depth of political animus against
Napoleon, including his own project for imagination as a rival adversary to Napoleonic
empire.

Shelley, also illustrates his enchantment with British reactionary power against the Napoleonic empire.

In the light of Hazlitt's remarks on poetry and its affinity with blood-shed, the reverie on Sarum Plain now requires study.[9] Wordsworth portrays his own attempt to invoke a language of power by means of a reverie: walking along the Plain of Sarum among the Druid circles, he feels the morose pressure of his solitude helping to conjure up a vision of the ancient past. He hears the shock of arms, spear, and stone axe, and sees a "Briton in his wolf-skin vest." He invokes the darkness as it is about to obscure all present objects from his sight. Just as the "barbaric majesty" of this primitive battle holds him in awe, his dream-trance binds him to a spectacle of human sacrifice, to an immense wicker basket that imprisons its victims upon the "dismal flames":

> It is the sacrificial altar, fed
> With living men—how deep the groans!—the voice
> Of those in the gigantic wicker thrills
> Throughout the region far and near, pervades
> The monumental hillocks; and the pomp
> Is for both worlds, the living and the dead.
> (*The Prelude* 12.331–36)

In dreaming the language of power, Wordsworth discloses a proclivity for violence that informs scenes such as this one of barbaric sacrifice, yet also infuses human nature from Stonehenge to the French Revolution. Wordsworth employs the language of dream in trying to summon an energy like nature's enduring force. Nature reveals itself not in the external world but in human nature, where its violence transgresses the boundaries of the benign. The external gives way to the internal, as Wordsworth anticipates a psychoanalytic reading of inner space.

De Quincey's Dark Interpreter—the pre-Freudian dream interpreter closest to Wordsworth in time and culture—reveals himself through dreams as an accessible power and discloses within Wordsworth's reverie an image of the unconscious. "This apparition is but a reflex of yourself," de Quincey explains, "and in uttering your secret feelings to *him*, you make this phantom the dark symbolic mirror for reflecting to the day-

---

9. Kenneth R. Johnston, *Wordsworth and 'The Recluse'* (New Haven: Yale University Press, 1984) 204, offers support for my argument by asserting that Wordsworth "neither blinks nor mollifies the horror" of his vision of human sacrifice.

light what else must be hidden forever."[10] The uncanny recall of barbaric power in Wordsworth's Sarum Plain reverie releases his "secret feelings" (in de Quincey's terms) through the language of dream: "the pomp" of sacrificial ceremony is not only for the historic dead and living but also for his own imagination's attraction to savage power. Amid what Freud would call the "dream condensation" of his reverie, Wordsworth reveals none of the guilt that so often accompanies his moods of visionary dreariness.

Wordsworth had earlier planned to conclude his Five-Book *Prelude* by elaborating the kindred emotions provoked by power in nature and books; thus, the reverie on Sarum Plain invites a decoding of its discourse of power. De Quincey makes a distinction, adopted from Wordsworth, that bears upon this question: "All that is literature seeks to communicate power; all that is not literature, to communicate knowledge." De Quincey elaborates this difference between the discourses of knowledge and power: "The function of the first is to *teach*; of the second is to *move*. The first speaks to the *mere* discursive understanding; the second speaks ultimately to the higher understanding or reason, but always *through* the affections of pleasure and sympathy."

Wordsworth finds in Milton a supreme example of the language of power; he exercises and expands our "latent capacity of sympathy with the infinite, where every pulse and each separate influx is a step upwards."[11] Yet Wordsworth's sublime explication of power to de Quincey (in conversation) leaves out of account what Hazlitt saw as a potential distortion or amorality of imagination. Typical of a disclosure of repressed energy, the sacrificial victims are merely presented—without authorial comment upon the episode's meaning. This discourse of power comes from beyond the conscious will, with the poet's imagination hovering over a spectacle of violent death.

In *The Birth of Tragedy,* Nietzsche affords a different perspective from which to view Wordsworth's fixation upon human sacrifice. Just as we

10. Thomas de Quincey, "Apparition of the Brocken," *Blackwood's Magazine* 57 (June 1845) 749.
11. Quoted in *Wordsworth: The Prelude or the Growth of a Poet's Mind (1805),* ed. Ernest de Selincourt and Stephen Gill (New York: Oxford University Press, 1970) 265. De Quincey records this distinction between the literature of knowledge and the literature of power from his conversations with Wordsworth. De Quincey had also written "The Literature of Knowledge and the Literature of Power," as part of a critical essay on Pope, *North British Review* (August 1848).

come away from staring at the sun with lingering dark spots on our eyes, so "the luminous images of the Sophoclean heroes" provoke their contraries, and "are the necessary productions of a deep look into the horror of nature; luminous spots, as it were, designed to cure an eye hurt by the ghastly night" (*BT* 59–60). Wordsworth on Sarum Plain, like Nietzsche, takes that deep look into "the horror of nature" and exemplifies the Dionysiac world of turbulent disintegration as part of the essential configuration of power. Sophoclean tragedy allows the audience to witness the hero—the embodiment of Dionysiac suffering and dismemberment—under the auspices of dream interpreter Apollo, who makes the pain endurable by fostering the illusionary world of art. This paradoxical merging of Dionysos and Apollo constitutes that rare fusion of dream and reality that forms the criterion for Nietzschean tragedy.

Wordsworth's own reverie includes not only human sacrifice in wicker baskets, but also its Apollonian equivalent—"bearded teachers" with their "white wands" pointing to the constellations. As in his spots of time, Wordsworth here moves from uncanny turbulence toward the mollifying presence of these ancient priests and their soothing music. Like Nietzsche, he seeks to yoke the suffering depth with pleasing appearance modulated through dream, but with a different purpose, to lodge turbulent memories within a context of human order. Wordsworth thus reveals the estranged within the ordinary, "the mind's power to defamiliarize and reperceive objects so fully that the borders between mind and nature, nature and the supernatural, begin to blur."[12] For the poet, this unsettling energy tends to counteract a contrary bondage to habit; the poet's creativity requires this infusion of energy to resist the pressures of adult rigidity. The private imagination implicit in Wordsworth's reverie discloses, through his specter of barbarity, a public world with its own infectious dynamics of power. Wordsworth's dark interpreter need not be limited, through a reductive Freudian interpretation, to the private psyche, because the political may also emerge in dreams.[13]

12. Lawrence Kramer, "That Other Will" 312, in limiting *imagination* to the Apollonian idealizing function of uplifting (*Aufhebung*), ascribes to the *daemonic* what I prefer to include as a Dionysiac attribute of imagination.
13. V. N. Vološinov, *Freudianism: A Critical Sketch,* trans. I. R. Titunik, ed. Neal H. Bruss (Bloomington: Indiana University Press, 1976; rpt. 1987) 90, attacks the private and sexual in Freud's decadent society: "All periods of social decline and disintegration are characterized by *overestimation of the sexual* in life and in ideology, and what is more, of the sexual in an extreme unidimensional conception; its *asocial* aspect, taken in isolation, is advanced to

In his early revolutionary sympathy, Wordsworth partly reacted to "the clamorous friends / Of ancient Institutions," who provoked his hostility by disgracing their reactionary cause. "A strong shock / Was given to old opinions; all men's minds / Had felt its power, and mine was both let loose, / Let loose and goaded" (*The Prelude* [1850] 11.260–73). Born in Cockermouth, a town in the northwest of the Lake District, Wordsworth claimed rarely to have seen anyone privileged by rank or wealth. Later, as a student at Cambridge, "wealth and titles" counted for less, in this model of a republic, than "talents and successful industry" (*The Prelude* 9.227–36). But his father was an attorney and lived in one of the town's finest houses (provided by Sir James Lowther), and Cambridge scarcely barred its gates against rank and privilege. Wordsworth's remarks here need not be taken at face value. Yet, for all that, we have no cause to doubt the integrity of his early Enlightenment politics, as when in *Lyrical Ballads* he demonstrates the inspiration of his leveling muse. Yet the semantic bias of "imagination" as an exclusive and aristocratic faculty, as a gift primarily accessible to solitary genius, is already beginning to emerge in the Simplon Pass and the Mt. Snowdon episodes of the 1805 *Prelude*. Hazlitt's objection to this faculty's exclusivity hinges upon imagination as a solipsistic drive that tends to produce an antisocial poet. In his *Lectures on the English Poets* (1818), Hazlitt, partly as a political move, makes his case against Wordsworth on the grounds "of art against nature and sociability against egotism."[14] Rather than urging public political action, *The Excursion,* for example, aims to correct *individual* despondency, in the melancholy aftermath of Napoleon's defection from the French revolutionary cause of freedom.

The Personal as Political: Imagination Impaired

In telling his revolutionary story of "youthful errors," Wordsworth had already anticipated Hazlitt. Wordsworth bases his own story of political change upon the tendency of his fancy and imagination to overreach. In a passage deliberately couched in the past tense, he recalls his youthful

---

the forefront. The sexual aims at becoming a surrogate for the social." If one substitutes *solipsistic* for *sexual* in this passage, one sees a danger that Wordsworth could fall into. Yet Wordsworth's reveries in this chapter often embrace the political and, hence, the social.

14. Cited by Marilyn Butler, *Romantics, Rebels and Reactionaries: English Literature and its Background 1760–1830* (Oxford and New York: Oxford University Press, 1981) 171.

exuberance over the changes in France: "Bliss was it in that dawn to be alive, / But to be young was very heaven!" (*The Prelude* 10.692–93) At that stage in human life when "plain imagination and severe" is no longer a mute influence in the psyche, books and works of art provoke the fancy to exceed itself, vaunting in its new pride: "There came among these shapes of human life / A wilfulness of fancy and conceit / Which gave them new importance to the mind" (*The Prelude* 8.511–22). Whetted by mimetic rivalry with books and art, fancy upstages imagination and proceeds to play "fantastic tricks." Under the auspices of this overweening power nothing remains unscathed: the elder tree next to the "charnel-house" acquires "a dismal look"; the yew tree begets its ghost; a natural death becomes "the tragic super-tragic." The upstart fancy, here uncurbed, hyperbolically mimics the normal authority of imagination. If Wordsworth happens to see a widow walking once or twice in sorrow toward her husband's grave,

> The fact was caught at greedily, and there
> She was a visitant the whole year through,
> Wetting the turf with never-ending tears,
> And all the storms of heaven must beat on her.
> (*The Prelude* 8.538–41)

Wordsworth adduces several more instances of the fancy's playing "fantastic tricks" with reality, akin to Hazlitt's description of the imagination as an "exaggerating and exclusive faculty" working beyond the strict confines of reason. Yet more important for Wordsworth (and bringing him even closer to Hazlitt), imagination itself does not go untainted by this mad work of the fancy: "Thus sometimes were the shapes / Of wilful fancy grafted upon feelings / Of the imagination, and they rose / In worth accordingly" (*The Prelude* 8.583–86). The antecedent of *they*, as required by logic, must refer to *shapes* of fancy and not to the *feelings* of imagination. As revealed by his later revision in the 1850 text, Wordsworth intended to reverse his elevation of the fancy by imagination and to show the imagination as contaminated by the fancy. In revision, the fancy subverts imagination by diverting it to "human passions, then / Least understood" (*The Prelude* [1850] 8.421–26). Coleridge, as Nicholas Roe points out, had traced Robespierre's failure during the Reign of Terror to a "'horrible misapplication' of imagination."[15] Wordsworth

15. Nicholas Roe, *Wordsworth and Coleridge: The Radical Years* (Oxford: Clarendon Press,

here ironically includes himself in a similar betrayal by false imagination, an error that Coleridge had applied to one of Wordsworth's most ingrained political enemies. Because Wordsworth is likely to have read Coleridge's piece on Robespierre, the degree of Wordsworth's self-incrimination takes on added point.[16] These mental vagaries forebode a deeper consequence, Wordsworth's own imaginative seduction by a French revolutionary cause that deserted its own ideals. These extravagant hopes for the cause of liberty later betray Wordsworth into sacrificing his "exactness of a comprehensive mind / To scrupulous and microscopic views," and this act in turn leads him into a "false imagination" that sweeps him beyond the boundaries "of experience and of truth" (*The Prelude* 10.844–48).[17] This entire process of psychic distortion, woven into *The Prelude* in such detail, illustrates Hazlitt's historical speculation upon power's proclivity to dazzle imagination.

1988) 217. See also Brooke Hopkins, "Representing Robespierre," in *History and Myth: Essays on English Romantic Literature,* ed. Stephen C. Behrendt (Detroit: Wayne State University Press, 1990) 120, who discloses the psychological insight that Robespierre is the double of a daemonic aspect of the poet himself: in the figure of the child who runs with its pinwheel against the wind (a trope for revolutionary violence), "Wordsworth and Robespierre are united in the figure of this child, that is at this moment in the poem they are revealed to be *doubles* of one another, with equal capacities for creation and destruction." Robespierre represents a part of Wordsworth, "the destructive—ultimately, the self-destructive—part of his psyche" (126).

16. Jonathan Wordsworth, *The Borders of Vision* 235, 242, 244, 260, 269, 272, and 275, takes the view that Wordsworth never really lost his imagination, that he was trying to develop an epic parallel to the fall in Milton's *Paradise Lost* and, therefore, did not deeply feel his need to restore imagination: "Again and again Wordsworth brings himself to a point in his autobiography when he seems to be about to show some significant deterioration [in imagination]; and then he steps back and says no, I can't, I won't, it wasn't so" (235). As early as the Five-Book *Prelude,* Jonathan Wordsworth sees the poet as unsuccessfully trying to build a fall into his poem, based upon his experience at Cambridge University. The point about Cambridge carries conviction, but Jonathan Wordsworth ignores the theme of false imagination and its link to the failure of Wordsworth's revolutionary hopes. See also Don H. Bialostosky, *Making Tales* 173, for a position opposite to Jonathan Wordsworth on Wordsworth's imaginative loss in *The Prelude* (4): "The loss which the narrator sees in his younger self is a serious one, because it involves the whole imaginative mode in which he apprehended man, nature, and himself."

17. Stephen M. Parrish, "'The Thorn': Wordsworth's Dramatic Monologue," *Wordsworth: A Collection of Critical Essays,* ed. M. H. Abrams (Englewood Cliffs, NJ: Prentice Hall, 1972) 75–84, makes a strong case for the dramatic distortion of the narrator of "The Thorn," who exemplifies imagination carried away on a tide of superstition.

The fact that Wordsworth sees false imagination as the cause of his personal crisis should not blind us to other factors in his moral collapse. Even though he selectively limits his complex relation to the French Revolution by consigning it mainly to imagination, we recognize this connection as coming from his primary theme, the growth of a poet's mind. On turning against his own country in support of the French cause, Wordsworth portrays the revolution within his own psyche through the simile of a wildflower uprooted from his own native rock:

> As a light
> And pliant harebell, swinging in the breeze
> On some grey rock—its birth-place—so had I
> Wantoned, fast rooted on the ancient tower
> Of my beloved country, wishing not
> A happier fortune than to wither there:
> Now was I from that pleasant station torn
> And tossed about in whirlwind.
>
> (*The Prelude* [1850] 10.276–83)

This organic metaphor of the flower, torn asunder by the wind, aptly captures the onset of deracination and despondency.

The conflict is not merely private but also social: his own uprooting occurs from "the ancient tower" of his "beloved country." As he triumphs over the defeat of English soldiers in France, Wordsworth suffers the consequences of violating the continuity of his own imagination clinging, like the harebell, on the grey rocks of Cumberland. James Chandler connects Wordsworth as microcosm with the macrocosm of England: "If the personal dimension of Wordsworth's 'personal epic' invites us to read the poem as a 'crisis-autobiography,' then its epic dimension invites us to see its crisis as national in scope." For Chandler, the crisis comes from Wordsworth's painful rupture, the gap between his traditional English nurturing and his international loyalty to the French Revolution. The poet's breakdown stems from his severance from his roots in the Cumbrian fells to a slippery allegiance with French rationalism.[18] This reading dovetails with my own tracing of false imagination, for healthy imagination depends upon nothing so much as its temporal

---

18. James Chandler, *Wordsworth's Second Nature: A Study of the Poetry and Politics* (Chicago: University of Chicago Press, 1984) 203. I am indebted to this excellent historical reading of Wordsworth, especially chapter 8, "The Discipline of an English Poet's Mind" 184–215.

and spatial ties with memories of childhood, in this case, Wordsworth's link with spirit of place in the English Lake District. Rejection of English ancestral memory in favor of French revolutionary theory creates an intolerable pressure upon Wordsworth's psyche and causes Freudian "melancholia," that is, depression.

In his days of strong commitment to the French revolutionary struggle, Wordsworth had "Exulted in the triumph of . . . [his] soul / When Englishmen by thousands were o'erthrown"; he had gloated over their inglorious fall and their ignominious retreat. Although these details give him pain to record in retrospect, he further recounts his alienation among the congregation under "a village steeple" amid prayers for English victory. He alone among "the simple worshippers" sat "like an uninvited guest" in silence, feeding "on the day of vengeance yet to come" (*The Prelude* 10.260–74).[19] In a strangely convoluted metaphor, reaching back to John the Baptist, Wordsworth writes of "patriotic love" giving way to the coming of Christ: "Like the precursor when the deity / Is come, whose harbinger he is." Yet this hope is false: "apostacy [*sic*] from ancient faith" merely seems a "conversion to a higher creed" (*The Prelude* 10.280–5). In the conflict between French revolutionary betrayal in the present and his previous youthful ardor, binaries such as patriot and traitor dismantle themselves. According to Samuel Johnson, *patriot* in eighteenth-century parlance also means "a factious disturber of the government." Although Wordsworth most likely did not intend this pun, it defines the parameters of his political dilemma. Wordsworth's own patriotism ironically blurs into its opposite: as an adult looking back upon his disloyalty to Britain, youthful revolt transforms into false faith. When the Revolution becomes a bloodbath, and Wordsworth finds himself indulging in "the worst desires," he yet persuades himself

That throwing off oppression must be work
As well of license as of liberty;

19. Alan Liu, "Wordsworth and Subversion, 1793–1804: Trying Cultural Criticism," *Yale Journal of Criticism* 2 (1989): 58, 62, connects this incident—in which Wordsworth (in an alien congregation) prays silently for a French victory over the British, with Wales: "The place, as Mary Moorman suggests, is North Wales, where Wordsworth was visiting his recently ordained college friend Robert Jones and where patriotic sermons were symptomatic of the gathering Welsh counter-Revolution led by Anglican churchmen (58)." See also Mary Moorman, *William Wordsworth—A Biography: EY* 224, who says the English defeat, "When Englishmen by thousands were o'erthrown," was at "Hondeschoote on September 8th 1793."

And above all (for this was more than all),
Not caring if the wind did now and then
Blow keen upon an eminence that gave
Prospect so large into futurity. . . .
(*The Prelude* 10.738–51)

As evidenced by the indirection of his language, Wordsworth allows his boundless hopes for "liberty" to connive at a world of blatant force. The very aesthetic concealment of his trope—a sporadic wind blowing upon a promontory—reveals an insidious encroachment of power and implies a bloodbath. Included within "the pardonable 'license'" represented by this apparently innocent metaphor are such actions as, to use Gene Ruoff's catalog, "the riotous bloodshed following the outbreak of the revolution, the suppression of religious orders, the early terror of the Paris commune, and the execution of Louis XVI."[20] Wordsworth's imagination, its good inextricably mingled with ill, meets Nietzsche's standard of Dionysiac suffering and horror through its liaison with French power.

Book 10 of *The Prelude* tells of the recurrent nightmares in France that throw light upon his reverie on Sarum Plain. Wordsworth confesses to sleep troubled with "ghastly visions . . . of despair"; with dreams of

tyranny, and implements of death;
And innocent victims sinking under fear,
And momentary hope, and worn-out prayer,
Each in his separate cell, or penned in crowds
For *sacrifice,* and struggling with forced mirth
And levity in dungeons, where the dust
Was laid with tears.
(*The Prelude* [1850] 10.401–9; my italics)

Wordsworth finds himself struggling with feverish brain and faltering voice to defend himself before "unjust tribunals," with "a sense / Death-

20. Gene W. Ruoff, "Religious Implications of Wordsworth's Imagination," *Studies in Romanticism* 12 (Summer 1973) 681, asserts that for Wordsworth's imagination to become enthralled by a political cause "that in the end brought international destruction and deep personal embitterment argues strongly that it is not an organ for the perception of absolute truth" (679). Hazlitt's remarks in his essay on *Coriolanus* support this conclusion.

like, of treacherous desertion, felt / In the last place of refuge— . . . [his] own soul" (*The Prelude* [1850] 10.409–15). Freudian displacement helps to account for the connection between Wordsworth's own dark conjuring of ancient sacrificial victims in wicker baskets and these revolutionary victims of atrocity as marked for slaughter. In *The Prelude* (10), his own repressed guilt emerges in his vain attempt to plead his cause before lawless judges; in the Sarum Plain reverie, his personal involvement with sacrifice issues from his unconscious in the uncanny disguise of ancient Druids who empower his discourse in the language of his dream. The greater distortion of the reverie on Sarum Plain, as compared with his nightmares in Paris, would indicate that the Druid fantasy emerges from a deeper level of the self. The disguise of Wordsworth's reverie leads us to understand the poet's sore need to temper human sacrifice by inclining toward "the bearded teachers" with their astronomical wisdom and their musical accompaniment to their public function, presiding over violence and the sacred. But we should not forget that "these same inspired sages are responsible for the 'dismal flames' and the deep groans of dying men which lend terror to the midnight darkness of the desert."[21] The link between ancient priests and burning men in wicker baskets ought to give us pause before reading this episode as a Wordsworthian consolation.

Because Wordsworth had already written his scene of human sacrifice in *Salisbury Plain* (1793–94), one might challenge my connection of Sarum Plain in *The Prelude* (1805) with French revolutionary atrocities, rather than with abuses of British power. The circumstances of his composing *Salisbury Plain* help to explain the connection. In a gloomy foreboding, Wordsworth heard cannon from the English ships off the Isle of Wight. He was separated from William Calvert, who had ridden away on their only horse after a carriage accident, leaving the poet alone to hike back across the plain of Stonehenge. In *Salisbury Plain*, the vision of primitive warfare and human sacrifice is triply displaced: instead of a

21. Enid Welsford, *Salisbury Plain: A Study in the Development of Wordsworth's Mind and Art* (New York: Barnes and Noble, 1966) 11. For a different reading of the Sarum Plain episode, see Chandler, *Wordsworth's Second Nature* 139, "As for the Druidic markings—'Lines, circles, mounts, a mystery of shapes' (*The Prelude* [12] 340)—their mystery is now an occasion of the poet's enchantment." Wordsworth does uplift these uncanny moments by lodging them within contrasting contexts, yet the turbulence of the uncanny center is what he chiefly values, just as he prizes above all the "Fallings from us, vanishings" of the "Immortality Ode."

reverie by Wordsworth himself, the incident is seen by a local swain who tells it to an old man who, in turn, tells it to a Female Vagrant. As a victim of the American revolutionary war, her poverty and alienation offer concrete evidence of Wordsworth's outrage against British authority on the eve of declaring war against France. Although *Salisbury Plain* presents the scene of human sacrifice in a context indicting English power, this fact in no way undercuts its association with abuses of French power in *The Prelude*.[22] Wordsworth's nightmares in France, of course, precede the time of either poem. Both contexts depend upon excesses of power: by changing the sacrificial reverie to a personal experience in *The Prelude,* Wordsworth intensifies the political dilemma that threatens to unhinge his imagination. The reader's awareness of the poet's double bind—inferred from these British and French perversions of authority—reinforces disclosure of his psychic trauma.

Actually, Wordsworth's reverie of the Druids began as early as *The Vale of Esthwaite* (1787) and validates *The Prelude*'s stance in ascribing the Druid dream to the poet's own experience. Yet in *Esthwaite,* Wordsworth makes himself the victim: "Why roll on me your glaring eyes? / Why fix on me for sacrifice?" These Druids emerge clearly as forces of darkness, "Where brooding Superstition frown'd" (*PW* lines 33–34, and 27).[23] And again, in *Salisbury Plain,* where the poet envisages a renovated future, he distances himself from the Druids: "not a trace / Be left on earth of Superstition's reign / Save that eternal pile which frowns on Sarum's Plain."[24] In these early poems, as Enid Welsford shows, the Druids symbolize "the sinister ambiguity of human authority and human justice, and of the barbarism surviving in contemporary society." By making these Druids stand for destructive barbarity safely relegated to the primitive past, Wordsworth diminishes Stonehenge; it is "no longer the grim rendezvous of the ghosts of the past and the outcasts of the present."[25] In *The Prelude,* Wordsworth no longer excludes himself from

---

22. Gayatri Chakravorty Spivak, "Sex and History in *The Prelude* (1805): Books Nine to Thirteen," *Texas Studies in Language and Literature* 23 (Fall 1981) 348, connects the image of human sacrifice with revolutionary violence in France: "At last the carnage of the French Revolution is reconstructed into a mere image of generalized 'history' on the occasion of a highly deconstructive and self-deconstructed Imagination."

23. *Poetical Works* 1:270.

24. *The Salisbury Plain Poems of William Wordsworth,* ed. Stephen Gill (Ithaca: Cornell University Press, 1975) 38, lines 547–49.

25. Enid Welsford, *Salisbury Plain* 11 and 20.

barbaric superstition: he merely presents human sacrifice in his dream as part of the human condition. Even if we concede the liabilities of his relation to violence, Wordsworth remains sincere in numbering himself among "the ghosts of the past and the outcasts of the present," among the hostages of power.

In thus confronting this ceremony of sacrificial death, Wordsworth abides Hazlitt's criticism of the imagination subverted by power. Yet he goes beyond Hazlitt, in some respects, by discovering and correcting his own false imagination in *The Prelude*. Hazlitt could not have read the unpublished *Prelude,* and it is uncertain whether Wordsworth had read Hazlitt on *Coriolanus.* Wordsworth's own critique of errant imagination, written prior to Hazlitt's, shows that both were aware of the danger of imagination's seduction by power and keenly alert to its distorting bias. Conversely, both knew how thin the dividing line was between the errancy and the potency of this faculty. If Wordsworth often finds his own imagination flagging in its attempts to carry out its social tasks (one of the telling points of Hazlitt's criticism), his language of dream on Sarum Plain engages political life at the deepest level. For Marjorie Levinson, the history that Wordsworth tries to assimilate "to Nature" returns as the "revenge of History—the repressed—under the aspect of Mind."[26] Where Levinson sees Wordsworth retreating into private subjectivity and resorting to nature as an evasion of history, I see his dream language as revealing a political conflict that informs both conscious and unconscious struggle. Perhaps the great period poems that Levinson discusses—"Tintern Abbey," *Michael,* the "Immortality Ode," and "Elegiac Stanzas"—are not comparable to *The Prelude,* yet history, which Wordsworth engages in the Enlightenment coding of *Lyrical Ballads,* is by no means confined to the return of the repressed. The public is not excluded in favor of private escape, as Levinson would have it; on the contrary, the private engages itself on the scene of political conflict emergent through dream. McGann's Romantic typology of transcendence also ignores the discourse of the political unconscious and distorts the dream language of the body in its very attempt to categorize all Romanticism as transcendent. Freudian displacement discloses Wordsworth's own attraction to and repulsion from atrocities in France reborn upon the heath of Stonehenge.

26. Marjorie Levinson, *Wordsworth's Great Period Poems: Four Essays* (Cambridge and New York: Cambridge University Press, 1986) 126.

Reverie on the Discharged Soldier

Among the social outcasts in the age of Wordsworth are victims of British military power such as the Discharged Soldier. No longer feeling empathy for aristocratic power, as they had for Hazlitt's Coriolanus, readers view the commoner as discarded by imperial neglect. Wordsworth's encounter with the soldier in *The Prelude* (4) emerges "like dreams" and functions as a spot of time fraught with visionary dreariness. Unlike Bachelard's reverie that only permits an optimistic form of creative play, Wordsworth's episode tests the waking dream for its capacity to include human distress and tragedy. In the 1805 text, Wordsworth meets the spectral Soldier on a nocturnal walk during the long summer vacation from Cambridge. In the 1850 version, much watered down, he attends the sailboat races on Winander (followed by a party that lingers until a late hour), and then meets the wraithlike man on his return home. Although his exultant dedication to poetry appears shortly before both versions of this incident, in neither version does he meet the Soldier on the same night as the dedication. Contrasts are revealed, however, by juxtaposing the two incidents. The scene of solitary encounter follows— in the act of reading—a festive night of dancing and the epiphany of a brilliant sunrise that consecrates Wordsworth's sense of vocation as a poet. The addition of the redundant Winander party in the 1850 edition, with its typical disparaging of social manners, "spirits overwrought / Were making night do penance for a day / Spent in a round of strenuous idleness" (4.375–77), detracts from the disquieting encounter with the Soldier, first written in a more direct style fifty-two years before *The Prelude*'s publication in 1850.[27]

In the 1805 version, the episode—whose voice comes to the poet like the language of dream—is preceded by Wordsworth's describing himself as the exhausted traveller, locked in nocturnal solitude, moving along the watery track that extends itself like a river. The recurrent topos of the traveller and the river provide a fit prelude to an imaginative confrontation. The solitude speaks not to his eye, "but it was heard and felt." The sound of the stream helps to instigate a liberation from ordinary sensation, as the narrator's mind changes into a revitalizing dream state, curative of his earlier "listless" weariness. The stillness is

27. Don H. Bialostosky, *Making Tales: The Poetics of Wordsworth's Narrative Experiments* (Chicago and London: University of Chicago Press, 1984) 180–84.

infectious: he drinks from it "A restoration like the calm of sleep, / But sweeter far." A pattern of harmonious imagery rises "As from some distant region of . . . [his] soul / And came along like dreams" (*The Prelude* 4.381–95). Until his body materializes, the Soldier seems like an imaginary construct. Yet despite this tranquil preamble to the narrator's discovery of the Discharged Soldier, his meeting with him remains precarious:

> While thus I wandered, step by step led on,
> It chanced a sudden turning of the road
> Presented to my view an uncouth shape,
> So near that, slipping back into the shade
> Of a thick hawthorn, I could mark him well,
> Myself unseen. He was of stature tall,
> A foot above man's common measure tall,
> Stiff in his form, and upright, lank and lean—
> A man more meagre, as it seemed to me,
> Was never seen abroad by night or day.
> His arms were long, and bare his hands; his mouth
> Shewed ghastly in the moonlight; from behind,
> A milestone propped him, and his figure seemed
> Half sitting, and half standing. I could mark
> That he was clad in military garb,
> Though faded yet entire. He was alone,
> Had no attendant, neither dog, nor staff,
> Nor knapsack; in his very dress appeared
> A desolation, a simplicity
> That seemed akin to solitude.
> (*The Prelude* 4.400–419)

The narrator's walk, blending in with the river, gives way to his matter-of-fact discovery of the Soldier. The reverie, as preamble to the encounter, absorbs the lean figure as the road transforms to stream, giving the natural a surreal cast. Propped against a milestone, the uncanny figure utters "scarcely audible" moans of indigent "complaint." This "uncouth" figure, like a revenant, startles Wordsworth, causing him to slip back into the shade and to remain hidden. The word *uncouth* evokes the meaning, still current in his time, of "unseemly, shocking, repellent" (*OED*). The uncommonly tall Discharged Soldier, gaunt from poverty, reveals "ghastly" lips in the moonlight. Not only does this ghostly figure induce fear in the beholder, but he also generates guilt in Wordsworth for infringing stealthily upon his pain. Wordsworth blames himself for thus prolonging his vigil, and at length overcomes his "heart's specious cowardice" in order to make his presence known. This incident is similar, in some respects, to the death of Lucy in "A Slumber Did My Spirit Seal": the poet moves in both situations from a dream state to an awareness of death. The eeriness of the Soldier's shape, although he later proves not to be a ghost, nonetheless turns Wordsworth's dream into visionary dreariness. The solipsism of the mental traveler's vision moves from the prior disclosure of his vatic calling after the party, followed by an indeterminate space of time, to solitary dream and then to discovery of a suffering human being.

This movement from solitude to relation merges the life-affirming visionary imagination with the ominous presence of mortality that invades his dream before he actually talks to the Soldier. David Ellis believes "that the sharp visual awareness" marking Wordsworth's vision of the Soldier "indicates that his previous trance-like state was at that point over."[28] It is difficult to say just when Wordsworth wakes from his reverie. But, because this visual sharpness includes an uncanny dimension, the trance may extend into the poet's prolonged, concealed scrutinizing of the enigmatic figure of the Soldier. At such a moment of heightened imagination, "sensual tyranny," sometimes produced by the eye's fixation, does not interrupt the visionary dreariness of Wordsworth's state of mind.

This encounter between the dreaming poet and the Discharged Soldier discloses a number of central Wordsworthian dilemmas about values. On the one hand is "the still, sad music of humanity" and, on the other, the solitary poet, potentially isolated from society by his dream. Edward E. Bostetter bridles at the serene closure of the incident in which Wordsworth leaves the Soldier safely lodged for the night and departs for home "with quiet heart": "The turmoil aroused by the tale is not resolved or reconciled dramatically into a higher serenity, as in a tragedy, but simply *pronounced* resolved." From a modern standpoint, one might well prefer Wordsworth to have sought "his distant home" (clearly too far away for him to take the Soldier) with an "*un*quiet heart." Bostetter

28. Ellis, *Wordsworth, Freud and the Spots of Time* 53.

also finds it hard to accept the "quiet heart" as anything other than "the complacency growing out of a purely personal sense of well-being. And in the Wordsworth of 1804 it becomes a sign of moral and artistic rationalization by which any evil can be justified and contemplated with equanimity."[29] Clearly, Bostetter is accurate in describing Wordsworth's downgrading of the strong implication of social injustice, as embodied in the Soldier, and eliding the issue of social injustice to focus upon his own role as a visionary.[30] As Bostetter further points out, the 1850 revision elaborates the incident in the uninspired mannerism "of the older Wordsworth":

> When from our better selves we have too long
> Been parted by the hurrying world, and droop,
> Sick of its business, of its pleasures tired,
> How gracious, how benign is solitude. . . .
> (*The Prelude* [1850] 4.353–56)

The Soldier becomes the "appropriate human center" of "Solitude" and "the soul of that great Power" (lines 359, 356, and 365). In sum, Bostetter's "Wordsworth has achieved the 'esthetic' distance that enables him to contemplate his Soldier undisturbed, without pain, as the embodiment of the gracious and benign soul of solitude." Although this argument justly describes the detachment in Wordsworth's revision for the 1850 edition, the Soldier's eerie presence more darkly dominates the trance in 1805, and the specter in the earlier version is much closer to Wordsworth

29. Bostetter, *Romantic Ventriloquists* 58 and 60. For a different opinion, see Bialostosky, *Making Tales* 176–7, who sees a providential design in Wordsworth's seeking his "distant home" with a "quiet heart" after performing an "act of charity" in finding a night's lodging for the Soldier: the narrator's "'transient and loose' thoughts have not been regrets only at his departure from his former 'glory' or from his incipient vocation or even from Nature alone but from a Divine plan which manifests itself in Nature and man."

30. Bostetter, *Romantic Ventriloquists* 58. But see Bialostosky, *Making Tales* 165, "The soldier's reply interprets the narrator's act as part of a reliable providential order in which benefactor and beneficiary can participate without embarrassment at giving or receiving aid." See also Meisenhelder, *Wordsworth's Informed Reader* 65–66, who provides an alternative to Bostetter's reading of Wordsworth's self-aggrandizing solipsism. Although she does not react to the uncanniness of the episode, she focuses upon the immaturity of the poet, who has not yet learned to feel the sublime of human suffering in the aspect of the soldier. Yet the reader can intuit beyond the boy's impercipience the proper meaning of the Soldier's sublime suffering.

in his reverie than in his waking distancing through departure. In the dream encounter, the Soldier serves as cautionary figure for what Wordsworth could become. In that part of the incident, solitude is anything but "benign." Only after the turbulent merging of the two figures in the trance has been anxiously prolonged for the reader does the telling of the incident move toward composure. By thus prolonging the ghostly dreariness of this encounter with the Soldier, Wordsworth implies, if not foregrounds, issues of social poverty, as Bostetter would wish.[31]

At issue again is Coleridge's contention that Wordsworth's most appropriate stance is to remain the observer *ab extra*. The attempt in 1850 to make the Soldier pervade the poet's own solitude, as chancy as the move remains, raises a tantalizing issue at the very center of Wordsworth's work. Does Wordsworth use the abandoned mothers, the Leech-gatherer, the Blind Beggar, Margaret, and the Discharged Soldier—all marginal figures—for his own aggrandizement? Does he objectify these characters for his own visionary convenience? Or does he maintain objective empathy? However these questions are answered, Wordsworth's moving attempt to connect human suffering and solitude, deftly achieved in the reverie on Sarum Plain, reemerges here as skewed. Whereas in "Elegiac Stanzas" Wordsworth rebukes himself for his dreamlike proclivity for solitude at the price of ignoring the suffering of humankind, in the Discharged Soldier episode of *The Prelude* (1850) he attempts to embrace human pain within the private circle of solitude.

Unlike in "Elegiac Stanzas," the poet remains at greater distance from his subject the soldier, as if the visionary encounter with human misery is fraught. The radical political context that Wordsworth portrays so starkly in his early poems doubtless suffers from his leaving the Soldier with "quiet heart," yet in the wider context, in which his poems read each other, an alien human presence erupts from his unconscious. Typically, Wordsworth shocks the reader in his closure of the episode. His departure from the Soldier in tranquillity echoes the consolation at the end of *Excursion* (i), as the disturbed poet turns away from the ruined cottage and the tragedy of Margaret and walks "along . . . [his] road in happi-

31. Bostetter, *Romantic Ventriloquists* 60. Jones, *The Egotistical Sublime* 61, mentions Wordsworth's tendency to skirt tragedy in the portrayal of his solitaries, as if unwilling, as in *Michael,* to sound the tragic note. Leavis, *Revaluation* 177–79, makes a similar point with respect to *Excursion* (i).

ness." The "Thanksgiving Ode" also ends in a shocking metaphor, making carnage a daughter of God.

Various critics of the Discharged Soldier episode focus upon the pitfalls of solipsism. Charles Rzepka, who writes about the danger of Wordsworth's absorption in his own dream, raises further misgivings about the narrator's selfish leave-taking from the Soldier: "The poet is more moved by his having done the right thing than by the sufferings of his beneficiary." The poet begins this episode with the weariness of an unimaginative mind bound in its cage of habitual sense, a mind unconsciously desiring the dream encounter of "a world elsewhere" (Coriolanus' phrase). The present reverie satisfies this desire. The act of receiving thanks from the Soldier thereby confirms Wordsworth's recognition by an other and breaks the prison of solipsism. Wordsworth deploys encounters with border figures like the Soldier, figures on the margins between life and death, to confirm his own identity, his bodily existence in relation to human otherness: "Like Jacob wrestling with his angel, Wordsworth has struggled with this ghost [i.e., the Soldier] making it familiar by obtaining its blessing and, in so doing, making his idea of himself a reality."[32] This reading does justice to Wordsworth's problem of grounding visionary space back in the physical world. Unlike Rzepka, I believe that Wordsworth's reverie of the Discharged Soldier moves into a dream metamorphosis that is not only private and solipsistic, but also public and concerned (if not in an entirely disinterested way) with victims of political upheaval. In this period, such unemployed and impoverished soldiers were no uncommon sight.[33] If Wordsworth projects himself upon the Discharged Soldier, as he did with the Leech-gatherer, the solitary world of the poet's mind constitutes for itself, during this visionary encounter, a community of two. Paradoxically, the way up to reverie is the way down to unconscious fusion with the Soldier. The Soldier appears to Wordsworth like a revenant, like a providential gift from his imagination, indeed, like a dream image of himself. As the Soldier gradually emerges out of reverie, he relates his tale: as a figure of bare survival, of humanity at its lowest common denominator, his appeal to Wordsworth's unconscious is undeniable.

32. Rzepka, *The Self as Mind* 62.
33. Woodring, *Politics in English Romantic Poetry* 87, writes "From the beginning of the war with the Colonies, such figures had been seen on the roads with increasing frequency."

Because Wordsworth shares the generic condition of this soldier, the critical appeal to solipsism is untenable. A more convincing reading is James Chandler's, in which he claims that the Burkean psychological underpinning of Wordsworth's inner life involves a public heritage. Although Chandler does not apply this reading to the Soldier, it seems tailor-made for the poet's reverie on his condition. What Wordsworth discovers during this poetic self-scrutiny, this gaze into "the disciplined mind of man" is, according to Chandler, "not a substitute for tradition . . . but rather tradition itself, in its psychological recapitulation."[34] Such a version of history, at a deeper level than mere ideology, generalizes the poet's roots as outgrowths, like this soldier, of his native Lake District.

This communal inner resonance, amplified in the life of Wordsworth, enriches his reveries beyond mere private fantasy. The reveries of human sacrifice on Sarum Plain and of the ghostly Discharged Soldier are not indulgent mind games. On the contrary, they release a dimension of feeling, a benchmark of imagination, that makes the private psyche of the poet reflect an English cultural psychology that transcends solipsism. The visionary dreariness, the haunting shock that invades Wordsworth's reverie, is what fixates the spot in his memory. That baffling enigma poses the primary task for the reader: to prevent the problematic closure of the incident from upstaging its uncanny center. Within the poetics of reverie, Wordsworth invigorates his own language of poetry by invoking daemonic power on Sarum Plain. Within the same poetics, he tempers his exultation over his previous dedication to poetry by juxtaposing it with the Discharged Soldier. The Soldier's poverty darkens the poet's vision as he melds with human otherness.[35] Like the Leech-gatherer, the poet projects himself into the limits of human possibility by entering, through the medium of dream, the solitary figure of the Soldier. For my

34. Chandler, *Wordsworth's Second Nature* 198.
35. Wordsworth, *The Borders of Vision* 11–12, discriminates between a "self-enclosed, all repelling" solipsism typified by Blake's Urizen and Wordsworth's "open and creative" state of mind as he encounters the Discharged Soldier. Jonathan Wordsworth, without exploring the psychological aspects, also sees the Soldier as a part of the poet: "Turning a sudden symbolic corner in the road . . . [Wordsworth] comes upon a curious version of himself." See also Paul Magnuson, *Coleridge and Wordsworth: A Lyrical Dialogue* (Princeton: Princeton University Press, 1988) 91, who first sees the shadow of the soldier as his double, "by the shadow's becoming his double. . . . But when the figure appears by Wordsworth's side, it becomes Wordsworth's double as well."

readings of the Leech-gatherer, Margaret, and the Discharged Soldier, Nietzsche furnishes the paradigm by which lyric poets move beyond their subjectivity and merge with their fictive creations. There is a paradox here: what seems like egotistical sublimity is actually a mental fusion with alterity. By absorbing the Soldier into his dream, Wordsworth becomes the other, absorbing the nightmare aspects of menace in the Soldier's penury. The episode on Sarum Plain and the encounter with the Discharged Soldier contain the very disorder and contradiction supposedly evaded by McGann's "Romantic Ideology."

William Blake. *L'Allegro,* plate 6: *The Youthful Poet's Dream.* About 1816. Department of Special Collections, Stanford University Libraries. The Youthful Poet, sleeping on a bank by the Haunted Stream by Sun Set, sees in his dream the more bright Sun of Imagination under the auspices of Shakespeare and Jonson, in which is Hymen at a Marriage & the Antique Pageantry attending it.

> What I saw
> Appeared like something in myself, a dream,
> A prospect in my mind.
>
> Wordsworth, *The Prelude*

CHAPTER FIVE

The Dream Prospect: Imagination Regained

Imagination and dream often merge, not only in their interaction, but also in their common resistance to sensual tyranny. Wordsworth uses *sensual tyranny* in a special sense, to denote a fixation upon a particular sense, such as sight, that obstructs the mental activity of imagination. The term implies connotations of the sensuous as well as the sexual. Before we examine Wordsworth's faculty psychology, his relation to Milton as precursor—tantamount to a subtext within *The Prelude*—requires comment. The work of both Wordsworth and Coleridge builds upon Milton's Renaissance conception of the mental faculties. Both poets deploy a seventeenth-century sense of reason, validated by Milton. Moreover, the spots of time, explored for their bearings upon the uncanny in chapter 1, will here subtend an argument on the liberated imagination. This chapter explores the link between dream and imagination and traces the return to health of diseased imagination.

The Miltonic Dream

Like Blake in *Milton*, Wordsworth oscillates in *The Prelude* between the outdoing topos and direct inspiration from his revolutionary precursor. Ronald Paulson discovers in revolution a paradigm for writing an epic on the poet's mind, "which is a struggle with (as Harold Bloom would put it) his poetic father John Milton reflecting in microcosm the oedipal

137

conflict of the Revolution itself."[1] Although Paulson does not develop in textual detail his contention that Wordsworth wins this combat with his father figure, he provides in the microcosm/macrocosm a suggestive analogy between the personal and political roles of Wordsworth. Milton had chosen, by portraying the inner action of the Fall, to write an argument that would outdo his classical forerunners, focusing elsewhere than on the physical details of warfare:

> Sad task! Yet argument
> Not less but more Heroic than the wrath
> Of stern *Achilles* on his Foe pursued
> Thrice Fugitive about *Troy* Wall; or rage
> Of *Turnus* for *Lavinia* disespous'd;
> Or *Neptune's* ire, or *Juno's,* that so long
> Perplexed the Greek and Cytherea's Son . . .
> (*Paradise Lost* 9.13–19)

In *Paradise Lost,* Milton had proposed to sing "the better fortitude / Of Patience and Heroic Martyrdom," hitherto overlooked, a fortitude also reflected in the essentially internal action of *Samson Agonistes.*

In his rivalry with Milton, Wordsworth also aims to intensify internal action beyond the bounds of his precursor. To carry out his perilous mission, he needs the aid of either Milton's Urania "or a greater Muse":

> Not Chaos, not
> The darkest pit of lowest Erebus,
> Nor aught of blinder vacancy, scooped out
> By help of dreams—can breed such fear and awe
> As fall upon us often when we look
> Into our Minds, in the Mind of Man—
> My haunt, and the main region of my song.[2]
> (*Home at Grasmere,* 788–94)

Where Milton strives to outdo Homer and Virgil, Wordsworth seeks to outdo Milton by looking into the abyss of the mind. Rhetorically dismissing Milton's Chaos—by comparing it to the fearful pit of Erebus and the blinder vacancy of dreams—Wordsworth implies the nightmare

1. Paulson, *Representations of Revolution* 273.
2. *Poetical Works* 5:4, lines 35–41.

nature of his "haunt." By transferring the epithet "blinder" from sight to the "vacancy" of dreams, he keeps at bay the prophetic insight of his blind adversary. But poetic influence need not take the form of an Oedipal combat, as it does in Wordsworth's impassioned "Prospectus to *The Recluse*." The connection with Milton may also take the quieter form—a type of "sacramental" imitation—of carrying over the vital heritage of the past, of putting on the armor of Miltonic thought as a means of solving one's present problem.

The "help of dreams" in scooping out vacancies—part of the competitive catalog with Milton—gestures toward Wordsworth's marked affinity for Milton's own dream lore. Eve's dream toward the end of Book 4 of *Paradise Lost,* as well as Adam's interpretation of it at the beginning of Book 5, best illustrates this seminal literary exchange. Adam's interpretation relates to potential errancies of imagination that bear upon Wordsworth's account, as elaborated in the previous chapter, of his own distortions of fancy and imagination. Milton presents Satan, "squat like a toad," at the ear of the sleeping Eve, insinuating the first dream of discord into the human race. Unchecked by interference from the critical reason, the imagination projects its images upon the screen of the dreaming brain. What makes this prophetic dream so productive for Wordsworth and Coleridge is the link between dream and imagination.

Dream prophecy, anathema to Freud but congenial to Milton and to the ancients, derives in Wordsworth from the "virtue of imagination" operating upon "life and nature." He speaks of a place—a "there"— where memory and prophecy merge: a place where "the instinctive wisdom of antiquity" unites with "the meditative wisdom of later ages" to produce an "accord of sublimated humanity, which is at once a history of the remote past and a prophetic enunciation of the remotest future." In that generative place, Wordsworth concludes, "the Poet must reconcile himself for a season to few and scattered hearers" (*Essay, Supplementary to the Preface, LC* 186). Dream for Wordsworth merges with imagination and, hence, shares in the act of prophecy.

Milton's prophetic dreams, according to Geoffrey Hartman, invite comparison with Wordsworth's because the earlier poet's "respect for the mind's natural powers anticipates that of Wordsworth." Like Dante in *The Purgatorio,* Milton illuminates the *alta fantasia*—the inspired imagination—in Adam's prophetic dreaming: "Before Adam is allowed to see Eden in actual sight, as before he is allowed to look at Eve, both are anticipated in dream, because the reality is too great to bear without the adumbration of a dream, or because Adam's spirit must be gently raised toward the truth that is to meet him. By these repeated dream-awakenings divine light kindles rather than darkens the natural light in man."[3] Just as Dante the pilgrim rises beyond the limits of his "natural" reason upon the wings of divinely infused dream elevation, Milton's Adam dreams prophetically of "truth" beyond his embryonic right reason. Milton not only inspires Keats, in works such as *Endymion,* and provides him with the paradigm of Adam's dream as a prototype for imagination, but he also affords Wordsworth a hint of the dream prophecy in which the shell foretells deluge upon "the children of the earth" in the Arab dream (*The Prelude* 5.96–99). If Adam dreams of truths that later transpire, Milton's Eve dreams, by her satanically distorted fancy (here synonymous with imagination), of an unnatural flight. Eve's dream not only prophesies the Fall of humankind but also provides, for Wordsworth and Coleridge, a text that signifies their kinship with Milton's Renaissance psychology.

Milton demonstrates how a dream based upon faulty logic emerges to inflame the unruly imagination with delusions of grandeur. By clouding Eve's imagination, Satan instills self-fulfilling prophecies into her dreaming consciousness. Adam's interpretation of Eve's dream prefigures liabilities of both imagination and dreaming that will inform the poetry of Wordsworth and Keats. Under the aegis of Satan, Eve inclines toward desiring the forbidden fruit. The rich scent of the fruit whets her instinctive appetite, addressed to the sense of smell, to question the paternal hierarchy. Satan projects into Eve's dream an angelic figure who urges tasting the fruit as the key to her rising up the scale of being to become a goddess among the gods. This prophecy is ironically fulfilled in Book 9, as Adam and Eve taste the fruit, become intoxicated, and *fancy* "Divinity within them breeding wings / Wherewith to scorn the Earth" (9.1008–10). Henceforth, by infecting her "animal spirits," Satan infects her unconscious energy, distorting female aspiration into a source of subversion. Just as the Freudian dream frequently undermines the Oedipal authority of waking life, Eve's elevation to a great height discloses her latent desire to slough off her role of inferiority to Adam.

Milton epitomizes the hierarchy of Renaissance psychology in

3. Hartman, *Wordsworth's Poetry* 52–53.

Adam's reading, on the following morning, of Eve's satanic dream. This hierarchy emerges from an analogy of the individual mind as a microcosm of the macrocosmic state: reason as queen presides over fancy, the next in command, who in turn governs the five senses, the commoners in this miniature kingdom of the faculties:

> But know that in the Soul
> Are many lesser Faculties that serve
> Reason as chief; among these Fancy next
> Her office holds; of all external things,
> Which the five watchful Senses represent,
> She forms Imaginations, Aery shapes,
> Which Reason joining or disjoining, frames
> All what we affirm or what deny, and call
> Our knowledge or opinion; then retires
> Into her private Cell when Nature rests.
> Oft in her absence mimic Fancy wakes
> To imitate her; but misjoining shapes,
> Wild work produces oft, and most in dreams,
> Ill matching words and deeds long past or late.
> (*Paradise Lost* 5.100–13)

Eve's sleeping reason gives free reign to the upstart fancy. Normally, in the waking state, reason checks the message from the eye, as when a straight stick appears bent in water, by overruling this false opinion produced by the sense of sight. By the same token, "mimic" fancy (here more or less synonymous with imagination) is more vulnerable than the absent reason to Satan's dream manipulations. Like Wordsworth's own distortions of fancy and imagination, Eve's fancy provokes stirrings against the gradations of the Great Chain of Being, against patriarchal authority.[4]

Satan's possession of Eve's dreaming brain, however, undermines the restorative activity of her normal dream thought. Eve's eating of the forbidden fruit launches an ironic motif—one that appears four times—

---

4. Hobson, *The Dreaming Brain* 51. A modern neurophysiologist, Hobson depicts dream activity in language that parallels Milton's suspension in the dreamer's mind of the faculties reason and will during sleep: "dreaming is the result of a reorganization of brain and mental activity, with intensifications of some faculties mirrored by reduced activity of others, and both serving purposes yet unclear but as likely to be productive as protective."

relating to her new clarity of vision, presumably gained from eating the fruit. Satan, in serpent form, insinuates this matter as follows:

> he [God] knows that in the day
> Ye eat thereof, your eyes that seem so clear,
> Yet art but dim, shall perfectly be then
> Op'n'd and clear'd, and ye shall be as gods.
>
> (9.705–8)

Satan, his sugary words tempting Eve's ear, also appeals to the other four of her senses to stimulate her appetite with the fruit's aroma, to arrest her attention with its seductive appearance, and to whet her desire to touch and taste. Thus, Milton's version of sensual tyranny makes an idol of the fatal fruit. To Adam she praises the fruit, not as a prelude to evil and death, "but of Divine effect / To open Eyes, and make them Gods who taste" (9.865–66).[5] Yet, unlike Blake—who would cleanse the doors of perception to see "with not through the eye"—Adam and Eve, misled by the illusion of their sensory intoxication, have diminished their powers of perception. Wordsworth, who imitates Milton so pervasively in *The Prelude,* furnishes his own analogous motif of sensual tyranny, including a more modern idolatry. Where Milton focuses upon fallen perception in its ironic arrogance, Wordsworth portrays the tyranny of the senses as a blockage to imagination. Both views imply distortions by sensory power.

Dream helps to explain Wordsworth's concept of sensual tyranny, a matter that (as will later become clear) Coleridge had expounded in his science of method. In the 1805 *Prelude,* Wordsworth relies increasingly upon the imagination and moves closer to Coleridge in striving to become a philosophical poet. As his perceptual powers recede with aging, Wordsworth relies more upon imagination to fill the gap created by the diminishing vigor of his sensory response. A trace of defensiveness even appears in his disparagement of the senses.[6] He protests too much over the very faculties that had always been his greatest strength— the faculties of perception. In seeking to become a prophet of imagina-

5. Milton, *Paradise Lost* 398, for further references to the motif of "open'd eyes" see also 9.983–87 and 9.1067–72.
6. See Empson, "Sense in *The Prelude,*" 641, who writes "The word [sense], I maintain, means both the process of sensing and the supreme act of imagination." It is only in the adult stage that Wordsworth becomes anxious about the unruliness of the senses.

tion, Wordsworth adopts his friend's Platonic resistance to bondage by the senses. The senses unleavened by imagination, according to Coleridge, can weaken the mind's initiative in favor of a mental passivity, enthralled by external impressions. Imagination itself, as we saw in chapter 4, can err when beguiled by fancy or by power. The senses, in turn, can enslave the mind by upsetting the balance between imagination and the outer world. Both poets look back to Milton's depiction of the play of faculties at work in Eve's dream for an awareness of the imagination's capacity to err. Coleridge even adapts the Miltonic microcosm of the human faculties as the basis for his own science of method. His hierarchy of the mind helps to illuminate Wordsworth's anxiety in *The Prelude* about the need for imagination to preserve its mental mastery over those rebellious commoners, the senses.

Conquering Sensual Tyranny: Imagination Restored

Coleridge adapts the Platonic analogy—the human faculties as a microcosm of an ideal state—to his own account of human psychology. Like the ideal state, the Coleridgean hierarchy of mental powers ought to function as an integral whole, not as divisive entities unproductive in their isolation. For Coleridge, Hamlet and the Nurse in *Romeo and Juliet* typify opposite poles of the mental spectrum. In trying to remember Juliet's age, the Nurse, with characteristic total recall, tells all that happened on a day eleven years before when an earthquake struck and she, as wet nurse, was weaning Juliet by putting wormwood on her nipple. Whereas this Nurse, through her inability to give one event importance above another, is virtually a passive victim of her senses—a hostage to sensual tyranny—Hamlet veers in the opposite direction. He recounts to Horatio his escape from Rosencrantz and Guildenstern aboard ship either in tones of playful satire or in generalizations upon the event. Hamlet becomes so absorbed in his inner world that Horatio must finally check his onrush of words to discover one crucial fact: how Hamlet resealed the royal packet that was to send Rosencrantz and Guildenstern to their deaths in England. Neither the garrulous Nurse nor the contemplative Hamlet achieves the ideal balance of the well-governed state in the economy of the individual mind.

In order to liberate himself from bondage to sense, Coleridge resorts to the dream as a fiction-making power. Yet, he does not deny the senses.

In accordance with his theory of method, they are enhanced insofar as they become infused with the mental initiative of imagination. In rejecting the Lockean or Hartleian philosophy of mind derived from sensory experience, Coleridge aims at an "Idealism necessarily perfecting itself in Realism, & Realism refining itself into Idealism."[7]

In *The Prelude,* perversions of fancy, imagination, and Coleridgean sensory misgivings are not the whole story: by disciplining these erring faculties, Wordsworth also heals diseased imagination. This reversal in the action of *The Prelude* also depends upon the relationship between dream and the senses. As a prelude to Wordsworth's renewal, the motif of sensual tyranny, akin to imagination's truancy, functions as an essential preamble. In his period of moral crisis over the disturbing course of the French Revolution, Wordsworth writes in *The Prelude* of his perverted modes of pleasure, "disliking here, and there / Liking, by rules of mimic art transferred / To things above all art." His precarious mental state here includes a tyranny of the sense of sight: "the bodily eye, in every stage of life / The most despotic of our senses, gained / Such strength in *me* as often held my mind / In absolute dominion" (*The Prelude* [1850] 12.110–12 and 128–31).

Yet nature can thwart such sensual tyranny by setting the senses against each other, thus preserving a healthy balance of power in the microcosmic kingdom of the self. Typically, Wordsworth employs the language of dream to describe those moments that baffle the individual senses, particularly the eye, with its tendency to overreach. The ear can also hinder imaginative activity. For Wordsworth to discover the "one life" that informs "all things," he hears a song beyond the ken of ordinary hearing:

One song they [all things] sang, and it was audible—
Most audible then when the fleshly ear,

7. *Collected Letters of Samuel Taylor Coleridge,* ed. Earle L. Griggs (Oxford: Clarendon Press, 1959) 4:575. Although Coleridge did not publish his "Essays on the Principles of Method" until the 1818 *Friend,* his thinking on the senses began early in his life. The following passage in a letter to Wordsworth, May 30, 1815, seems partly to react against *Observations on Man* by David Hartley, who includes sections on each of the senses: "I supposed you first to have meditated the faculties of Man in the abstract, in their correspondence with his Sphere of action, and first, in the Feeling, Touch, and Taste, then in the Eye, & last in the Ear, to have laid a solid and immoveable foundation for the Edifice by removing the sandy sophisms of Locke, and the Mechanic Dogmatists, and demonstrating that the Senses were living growths and developements [*sic*] of the Mind & Spirit in a much juster as well as higher sense, than the mind can be said to be formed by the Senses" (574).

O'ercome by grosser prelude of that strain,
Forgot its functions, and slept undisturbed.
(*The Prelude* 2.428–34)

Wordsworth begins by listening to sound, but then the ear yields its normal function to an "expression through sense of something beyond sense."[8] Yet the sense of hearing can help overcome a fixation upon the sense of sight: "Visionary power is associated with the transcendence of the image and in particular with the 'power in sound'; yet it depends upon a resistance within that transcendence of sight for sound."[9] The sublimity of vision depends partly upon the poet's surmounting a blockage fixated on the visual image by the liberating force of sound. Paradoxically, although dream images empower the visual, dreaming liberates the dreamer from the tyranny of the eye. As a youth, Wordsworth would rise before the sun and climb among the crags to look out over the Vale of Esthwaite in its utter solitude: he "forgot / That . . . [he] had bodily eyes, and what . . . [he] saw / Appeared like something in . . . [himself], a *dream,* / A prospect in . . . [his] mind" (*The Prelude* 2.359–71, my emphasis). Wordsworth maintains his "first creative sensibility" untrammeled by "the regular action of the world." In this state of "wise passiveness," his imagination—working upon sensory experience—transcends the separate senses and is in touch with an unconscious force analogous to dreaming.[10]

8. A. C. Bradley, *Oxford Lectures on Poetry* (London: Macmillan, 1926) 132. See also Frederick Burwick, *The Damnation of Newton: Goethe's Color Theory and Romantic Perception* (Berlin and New York: Walter de Gruyter, 1986) 176–209, for a study on the scientific depth behind Wordsworth's thinking on sensory perception, including Newton, Kepler, and Sir Humphry Davy. Burwick traces Wordsworth's intricate pondering of the relation between the senses and imagination in *The Excursion*. Wordsworth is concerned with "how the mind informed the senses," and in a poem called "The Power of Sound" is again aware of the pitfalls of sense: "Somehow judgment must arbitrate, the poet implores in lines of optative urgency, over 'the cozenage of sense,' the 'voluptuous influence,' the 'sick Fancy,' the suicidal despair that may otherwise wield a compelling sway over the vulnerable senses" (196–97).

9. Thomas Weiskel, *The Romantic Sublime: Studies in the Structure and Psychology of Transcendence* (Baltimore: Johns Hopkins University Press, 1976) 175.

10. Peter Malekin, "Wordsworth and the Mind of Man" 3–11, offers a philosophic discussion of the mystical element in Wordsworth, coupled with readings on visionary sight, such as the paradox of "an eye made quiet," common to St. Teresa and Wordsworth, where his "eyes continued to function during the physiological quietness when the body was 'laid asleep,'" (8). See also Paul Hamilton, *Coleridge's Poetics* (Oxford: Basil Blackwell, 1983)

If Coleridge's science of method aims at a balance between mind and sense, Wordsworth aims, in his own idiosyncratic way, at defying bondage to sense. He departs from Coleridge by depicting this process with the help of dreams. In his "Reply to 'Mathetes,'" however, he writes in a language that taps into Coleridgean terminology. Wordsworth urges the youthful mind (whom he addresses as his intended reader) to "feed upon that beauty which unfolds itself, *not* to his eye as it sees carelessly the things which cannot possibly go unseen, and are remembered or not as accident shall decide, but to the thinking mind; which searches, discovers, and treasures up,—infusing by meditation into the objects with which it converses an intellectual life; whereby they remain implanted in the memory, now, and for ever" (*LC* 88). *Meditation* is a technical term, opposed by Coleridge to *observation,* which implies the act of reflection in which sensory objects are richly informed by mental initiative. Reason elaborates the germ of the ideas by governing the relations of things, using what the mind brings to its experience. The senses are not passive onlookers but active builders of perception. Wordsworth avoids such sensuous passivity by brooding on images until they are enlivened, as it were, into the intensity of dreams. He describes the Wanderer's recollection in *The Excursion* (1) as filtering sensory percepts through the habit of sublimity that lingers in his memory:

> he thence attained
> An active power to fasten images
> Upon his brain; and on their pictured lines
> Intensely brooded, even till they acquired
> The liveliness of dreams.
>
> (lines 144–48)

26–35. In a section on "The Tyranny of the Eye," Hamilton traces Coleridge's and Blake's reactions against the visual basis in the language of Locke and Hume. By employing the sympathetic imagination, Coleridge "develops an eighteenth-century attempt to emancipate theories of imagination from the 'despotism of the eye'" (29). See also Stephen Bygrave, *Coleridge and the Self: Romantic Egotism* (London: Macmillan, 1986) 61–62, who cites Coleridge's *Biographia Literaria* 1:107, "Metaphysical systems, for the most part, become popular not for their truth but in proportion as they attribute to causes a susceptibility of being *seen,* if only our visual organs were sufficiently powerful." In his section on "The Despotism of the Eye," Bygrave notes a moral slant to such tyranny: "The despotism or tyranny of egotism is a danger analogous to 'that Slavery of the Mind to the Eye' (*PL*, p.434). (The words are often used in the eighteenth century to denote a mastering of the moral impulse by the passions.)"

At stake here is an infusion of mind into acts of sensory response. Memories of sublime greatness become "almost indistinguishably mixed / With things of bodily sense."[11] This quotation from an unused passage was replaced by "great objects" that lie "Upon his mind like substances, whose presence / Perplexed the bodily sense." By probing such perplexity between sensation and mind, Wordsworth develops a phenomenology in which the border between imagination and sense breaks down. Thralldom to sense is averted when mind and sensation become so fused together that they cannot be separated. Mental images come to seem less the product of "ordinary sensation" than "images specially constructed by the mind itself," what A. O. Wlecke calls "psychic entities" that resemble "the intense subjectivity of the act of dreaming."[12] According to eighteenth-century association theory, dreams reveal a more intense form of affiliation, which makes them "more purely associational than the activity of the mind when awake."[13] Imagination and dream merge to vanquish sensual tyranny and to reveal Wordsworth's phenomenological mode of thought. Imagination acquires a dreamlike power of meditation to draw upon a residue of sublimity that informs the temporal and spatial memory.

In order to clarify Wordsworth's quandary over the proper role of the senses in *The Prelude,* we must now consider the intricate ninth stanza of the "Immortality Ode." In these lines, Wordsworth reserves his ultimate gratitude not for the delight, liberty, and hope of childhood,

> But for those obstinate questionings
> Of sense and outward things,
> Fallings from us, vanishings;
> Blank misgivings of a Creature

11. *Poetical Works* 5:12–13. De Selincourt and Darbisher (who print the final version of *The Excursion* 1850, rather than the text of 1814) include this passage from (MSS E, M 1814–20?), an earlier revision by Wordsworth. In 1845 Wordsworth made another telling unused revision: "Great objects on his mind, with portraiture / And Colour so distinct, that on his mind / They lay like substances, *and almost seemed / To haunt the bodily sense*" [my italics].
12. Albert O. Wlecke, *Wordsworth and the Sublime* (Berkeley: University of California Press, 1973) 64. I am indebted to Wlecke's discussion of sublime visionary seeing in relation to the senses. In his note to this quotation, he usefully cites de Selincourt on the vividness of dream images for Wordsworth, "It is generally stated that the images of dreams are vague and indistinct and lack colour. Wordsworth's experience was the opposite" (*Poetical Works* 5.411).
13. David D. Perkins, "The Imaginative Vision of *Kubla Khan*" 104.

Moving about in worlds not realized,
High instincts before which our mortal Nature
Did tremble like a guilty Thing surprised.[14]

Lionel Trilling equated these self-destroying moments with the dream-like investment in sensory objects, with the visionary gleam perceived by the child. Helen Vendler, in contrast, sees the "obstinate questionings" and the "fallings from us, vanishings" as strong moves against the bondage of sense. She cites the following passage from a canceled draft of the ode: "The difficulty of our attempt to liberate ourselves from 'the spell / Of that strong frame of sense in which we dwell.'" Far from inviting any equation with the visionary gleam of childhood, Words-worth's "blank misgivings" of unreality are valued because they go counter to a dangerous enchantment by sense: "Of course one would rather recall the "splendour in the objects of sense" than this mistrust of the "strong frame of sense," but Wordsworth was able to complete the Ode only by at last recalling the first motions of the *non*-sensuous instincts as the most valuable of his childhood experiences."[15] Words-worth's "fallings from us, vanishings," then, were not only disquieting to him as a child, but also appeal directly to intellect and imagination by reaching beyond ordinary sensory experience. The poet was struggling with the paradox that to move beyond the prison-house of the senses was also to liberate the senses by making them instruments of mind rather than passive representations of nature.

14. *Poetical Works* 4:283, lines 142–48.
15. Helen Vendler, "Lionel Trilling and the *Immortality Ode*," 81–83. The canceled lines cited by Vendler do not occur in the passage on "vanishings" and "blank misgivings," as one might expect. Their full context follows: "But for those first affections, / Those shadowy recollections, / Which, be they what they may, / Are yet the fountain light of all our day, / Are yet a master light of all our seeing; / *Throw off from us, or mitigate, the spell* / *Of that strong frame of sense in which we dwell*; / Uphold us, cherish, and have power to make / Our Noisy years seem moments in the being / Of the eternal Silence . . ." (lines 149–58, my italics). With the italicized canceled passage placed in context, these lines strengthen the argument for reading this passage in apposition with the one preceding it on "the obstinate questionings." This point is reinforced by the parallel syntax of the openings of both passages: "But for those obstinate questionings . . . [and] "But for those first affec-tions . . ." Both passages oppose the bondage of sense (*Poetical Works* 4:283–84; the canceled lines appear in MS L). See also Lionel Trilling, "The Immortality Ode," *The Liberal Imagination* 138.

In *The Prelude* (1), after the episode of stealing the boat, Wordsworth describes a similar experience of "blank desertion," where his normal sensory experience is violated:

> There, in her mooring-place, I left my bark
> And through the meadows homeward went with grave
> And serious thoughts; and after I had seen
> That spectacle, for many days my brain
> Worked with a dim and undetermined sense
> Of unknown modes of being. In my thoughts
> There was a darkness—call it solitude
> Or blank desertion—no familiar shapes
> Of hourly objects, images of trees,
> Of sea or sky, no colours of green fields,
> But huge and mighty forms that do not live
> Like living men moved slowly through my mind
> By day, and were the trouble of my dreams.
> (*The Prelude* 1.415–26)

These "unknown modes of being" disorient his common sensory response to nature and invade his dreams with their uncanny potency. As a child, Wordsworth found these fearful questionings of the boundaries of the self disquieting, but as an adult poet he found that sense could tyrannize and baffle imagination. The visionary dreariness of his spots of time also permeates the ninth stanza of the "Immortality Ode" and the boat-stealing episode. Such dreariness now pervades the senses themselves and makes them instruments of mind, rather than permitting mind to become a passive victim of sensation.

With their kinship to dreaming, Wordsworth's spots of time act as his primary mode of resistance to blockage by sensual tyranny. They become his "passages of life." The power that "lurks" in them—in hidden ways—gives "Profoundest knowledge to what point, and how, / The mind is lord and master—outward sense / The obedient servant of her will" (*The Prelude* [1850] 12.19–230). This mastery of imagination is reiterated in his reflection upon Mt. Snowdon, where such minds maintain a balance between sensory input and mental initiative: "in a world of life they live, / By sensible impressions not enthralled" (*The Prelude* 13.102–3).

William Galperin has impugned this resistance to sensual tyranny, deploring Wordsworth's prejudice against the overweening sense of sight. The power in the spots of time to renovate an impoverished present—or for 'the inner faculties' to overcome the blockage of 'outward sense' and to transport one into 'a state of grace'—seems to Galperin a mere mystification. For him, Wordsworth's attempt to yoke visionary dreariness with renovative powers of memory results in the poet's refusal "to reenter the 'gulph' that 'parted' the 'Man to come' from 'him who had been.'" This failure, Galperin argues, produces a crisis of sincerity: the poet substitutes the comfortable ease of transcendence for the conflict that marks his best poetry, such as "Tintern Abbey."[16] But a reading of these spots as a vehicle of the uncanny (akin to a return of the traumatic in dreaming) authenticates their visionary dreariness as engaging Wordsworth at a far deeper level than the rhetoric of transcendence. Because the spots are often precariously yoked with more tranquil overlays of memory, these different layers of time provide an essential lodging for the Dionysiac within the continuity of everyday life. Like the reverie on Sarum Plain, the spots, in their ambivalence between the numinous and the turbulent, in their frequent sublime conjunction of death and sacral space, constitute the leaven of imagination.

Two episodes, both hinging upon a prospect of visionary dreariness, illustrate Wordsworth's tendency to confront death by merging it with a temporal spot of landscape as an imaginative hedge against sensual tyranny. Because the senses can obstruct imaginative power, the spots of time liberate the poet by their transfiguring of sensory activity. In the first episode, before he was six years old, the poet becomes separated from his guide and encounters a gibbet where a murderer had been hung, his name inscribed in the plucked turf. Wordsworth's fear impregnates the site of execution with uncanny potency. A girl with a pitcher on her head, "her garments vex'd and toss'd / By the strong wind," epitomizes the eerie bleakness on the moor beside a "naked pool" (*The Prelude* 11.303–7). Later, the energy lodged in this spot is overlaid by memories of wandering across the same terrain with Dorothy and his future wife during the stages of their courtship. The shades of death inherent in this spot balance, in their "visionary dreariness," a life-affirming beauty in the

16. See William Galperin, " 'Turns and Counter-Turns': The Crisis of Sincerity in the Final Books of *The Prelude*," *Modern Language Quarterly* 40 (1979): 262. See also Douglas Wilson, "Wordsworth and the Uncanny" 92–98.

commonplace. To the child of six, the turbulence of this encounter with the gibbet is disorienting and terrifying. Yet for the adult, these memories reinforce the deep bonds of continuity and a renovative contact with power. A singular indifference to the role death plays in his most cherished memories would seem to account for his return to health.[17] In my reading of this spot and the episode containing his father's death, the cause is not exactly "indifference," but rather Wordsworth's stance that allows him to derive energy from a detached confrontation with death. The adult mind can enter the gulf between past and present identity, can engage death displaced on to the scene, and can reaffirm the lodgings of imaginative power.

The second spot of time also illustrates how memory continually alters its reservoir of images as the growing mind reflects back from its changed perspective in time. In the episode in which he waits for the horses, a scene invested with visionary dreariness, Wordsworth rebukes himself for his extravagant desires. Wordsworth's guilt, his rebuked desire, strangely does not inhibit his impulsive return to these "spectacles and sounds" from which he "drinks as at a fountain" (*The Prelude* II.382–85).

By using a phenomenological approach, David Simpson finds vitality in Wordsworth's multiple figurings of reality, in the poet's overlaying the time spot of his early trauma with later memories of revisiting the scene with Mary and Dorothy. In both spots, as Simpson correctly argues, Wordsworth is restored by a variety of figurings: "The whole cycle of 'transgression' and punishment now becomes restorative, and continually restorative, as the fountain both quenches the thirst of the moment and yet continues to flow. The confidence which accrues from this [process] seems to consist in the insight that the mind can contain and survive such antithetical events, and put them to the service of a continually evolving identity." Diverse layers of perceptual consciousness prevent the tyranny of any single sense or the danger of a reified single perception, and they validate the imaginative mind, buttressed against its liability for errancy. Although Simpson does not focus upon sensual tyranny, his idea of multiple perceptions correcting each other includes a balancing of imagination and sensation: "There is no privileged figuring of the real, which becomes an objective standard of normalcy; there is

17. Weiskel, *The Romantic Sublime* 176.

only a *series* of figurings, wherein a whole set of positions will be taken up from time to time, rising to vanish like clouds in the sky, and living on in the modified figures of the imaginative memory."[18]

Part of Wordsworth's "figuring" includes the visionary dreariness that clings to the objects as he views them in the mist from the crag looking down upon the two roads. The uncanny potency within this spot of time invests the actual scene with the vividness of dreams, not as in some transcendent vision, but as implicit in the bleak detail of the boy watching over the misty fork in two roads. The uncanny works through but transforms sense; imagination can thus fruitfully augment the perception of objects in addition to overcoming its capacity for distortion. Thus freed from tyranny, the senses become vital extensions of mind.

"Reason in Her Most Exalted Mood"

We have seen how dream and reverie can free imagination from the tyranny of the eye: it remains to explore the philosophic implications that subtend Wordsworth's restorative design in *The Prelude*. Immanuel Kant's "Analytic of the Sublime," within his *Critique of Judgement,* offers another perspective on the sensory function in the play of faculties within the unique context of sublime experience. For Kant, the sublime consists of an overwhelming of the senses and of the experiential imagination: at first, these faculties are baffled by a sensory experience that overtaxes them, leaving the ordinary categories unstrung. But later, the mind recoils from its astonishment and rebounds to match, by a mental expansion, the vast torrent of outward impressions that had previously overwhelmed the sensory imagination. This experience of the sublime illustrates the reason's "dominion over sensibility," during which "the imagination" is "regarded as an instrument of reason." In the sublime mode, the imagination paradoxically loses its apparent freedom of operation in its more comfortable realm of imaging sensory experience. In acting in accordance with the unknowable ideas of the reason, the imagination obeys a law different from that of ordinary experience: "It thus acquires an extension and a might greater than it sacrifices—the

18. David Simpson, *Wordsworth and the Figurings of the Real* (Atlantic Highlands, NJ: Humanities Press, 1982) 65, 66.

ground of which, however, is concealed from itself—while yet it *feels* the sacrifice or the deprivation and, at the same time, the cause to which it is subjected." Although the imagination cannot grasp the unknowable ideas of the reason, its very failure to do so intimates—under the auspices of the sublime—the existence of these transcendent though unattainable ideas. The paradox resolves itself for Kant as the mind escapes the determinism of the sensory imagination (analogous to Wordsworth's sensual tyranny), which had merely *appeared* to be freedom, through sublime experience that links imagination with the actual freedom of reason.[19] In the reverie upon Sarum Plain, as in his spots of time, Wordsworth encounters a visionary dreariness that divests the senses of their power to dominate by an infusion of sublime energy, abetted by the spots' proximity to death.

Kantian sublimity empowers the faculty of imagination, which is infused by and operates on the ideas of reason rather than the data provided by the senses. The dreaming brain, with its tendency toward the irrational and the bizarre, also focuses upon the mind's inner images; unlike the sublime that empowers, however, the dream may condense psychic insight and/or disclose a potency for distortion. Wordsworth's awareness of the imagination's propensity to err leads to respect for the mistakes it must make as part of its schooling.[20] In his "Reply to 'Mathetes,'" written for Coleridge's *The Friend,* Wordsworth extends this insight into prescriptions for the education of imagination. He is sensitive to the danger of a teacher's undermining imaginative integrity and self-confidence: an incautious remark from a teacher may "wither" the "generous sympathy" native to a young mind and destroy the pleasures of joy and love. Such insidious teaching lodges in "the ingenuous mind misgivings, a mistrust of its own evidence, dispositions to affect to feel where there can be no real feeling, indecisive judgments, a super-

19. *Critique of Judgement by Immanuel Kant,* trans. J. H. Bernard (London: Hafner Press, Macmillan, 1951) 108–10.

20. For a different opinion on Wordsworth's impaired imagination, see Jonathan Wordsworth, *The Borders of Vision* 260, "Once again there is the conflict between Wordsworth's obstinate sense that nothing had ever gone wrong, and the structural needs of his poem that require him to show imagination (his own imaginative response to Nature) as having been impaired." This pattern of false imagination is not only directed toward nature, but also to his "extravagant hopes" and to political betrayal by the French Revolution.

structure of opinions that has no base to support it, and words uttered by rote with the impertinence of a parrot."[21] For one schooled like Wordsworth by beauty and fear, imagination must be allowed to flirt with errancy and excess, to make its own mistakes. Although in his conservative certitude he ignores the fact that youth may seize the truth and age give way to folly, Wordsworth puts his trust in unfettered youth above the rigidities of elder educators. Craven deference to authority, whether to teacher or parent, can impede the growth of authentic feeling that is essential to the judgments of imagination. The betrayal of the French Revolution was a crisis that struck near the heart: for this reason, Wordsworth's inflamed imagination unhinged his politics while internecine violence ran rampant, and a war of liberation became transformed into a war for Napoleonic empire.

The education of imagination becomes more important in the light of all the "annoyances" (Keats's word) that oppose this faculty even in the best of times. In a fragment written for the Five-Book *Prelude* in March 1804, Wordsworth catalogs these adversaries to the imaginative faculty:

> The unremitting warfare from the first
> Waged with this faculty, its various foes
> Which for the most continue to increase
> With growing life and burthens which it brings
> Of petty duties and degrading cares,
> Labour and penury, disease and grief,
> Which to one object chain the impoverished mind
> Enfeebled and [?], vexing strife
> At home, and want of pleasure and repose,
> And all that eats away the genial spirits,
> May be fit matter for another song.
> (lines 1–11)[22]

This battle of the imaginative power with its opposing forces extends through Book 5 of *The Prelude,* as Wordsworth defends the school of

21. *The Friend,* ed. Barbara E. Rooke (Princeton and London: Princeton University Press and Routledge & Kegan Paul, 1969) 1.403–4. (This is vol.4 in *The Collected Works of Samuel Taylor Coleridge,* ed. Kathleen Coburn).
22. The Norton *Prelude* 499–500.

freedom and error against current educational ideology, tainted by post-revolutionary French educational theory.[23] He defends the right of the imagination to make its own mistakes, to rise again stronger in the broken places. Against the weight of pettiness in everyday life, he attempts to forge a stronger link between imagination and reason, rejecting the imagination's merely passive determination by the senses. Whether he arrived at this philosophic stance by his own lights or through conversations with Coleridge, Wordsworth shares with Kant the idea of inter-animating imagination and reason while recognizing imagination's more common role, that of working upon sensory experience.

Coleridge's free adaptation of Kant's *Critique of Judgement,* with its "Analytic of the Sublime" on the productive power of imagination to build upon the ideas of reason, finds a concrete analogue in Wordsworth's *Prelude.* Where Kant considers the ideas of reason to be "regulative," Coleridge regards them as "constitutive" and more accessible to imagination than does Kant. At the culmination of an evolving tradition, Wordsworth boldly proceeds beyond Kant's carefully nuanced connection between imagination and reason and even beyond Coleridge's customary practice of assigning a subordinate role to imagination in relation to reason. In the final book of *The Prelude,* Wordsworth's account of spiritual love inverts the normal hierarchy by elevating imagination above reason. Only in its highest form does reason rise to equality with imagination:

> This love more intellectual cannot be
> Without imagination, which in truth
> Is but another name for absolute strength
> And clearest insight, amplitude of mind,
> And reason in her most exalted mood.
> (*The Prelude* 13.166–70)

The blockage of sensual tyranny and the motif of false imagination both

23. See Chandler, *Wordsworth's Second Nature* 216–34, for a strong argument that the educational policy, endorsed by the French government, was in danger of infecting Britain with the disease of unsound ideology. This ideology, apart from Rousseau's *Emile* (1762) and the Irish Maria Edgeworth's *Practical Education* (1798), is the real target of Wordsworth's ironic attack on modern education in Book 5 of *The Prelude.*

give way: what had been a tale "of traumatic separation and loss" yields to "a story of reunion and re-integration."[24] In stressing analytic reason, "which insists upon the primacy of the 'eye' only," leading "always to discontinuity," and by neglecting reason in the nonanalytic sense, Galperin ignores this precarious merger between reason and imagination.[25] For reason, as a previous agent of discontinuity, here becomes a paradox of integration. Wordsworth directly invokes, as a foundation for his restored faith, Miltonic reason as

discursive or *intuitive*;
Hence sovereignty within and peace at will,
Emotion which best foresight need not fear,
Most worthy then of trust when most intense . . .
(*The Prelude* 13.113–16, my emphasis)

In the 1850 *Prelude,* Wordsworth makes even clearer that he considers this refinement of imagination—buttressed by its connection with reason—a counterpoise to the moral collapse of his revolutionary hopes. Against "ills that vex and wrongs that crush / Our hearts," he invokes "that peace / Which passeth understanding, that repose / In moral judgments which from this pure source / Must come, or will by man be sought in vain" (*The Prelude* [1850] 14.124–29).

Just as Wordsworth invokes his precursor, Milton, in the passage above, so Coleridge also adopts this practice. In the following passage from *Paradise Lost,* Raphael is conversing with Adam on the difference between angelic and human, unfallen intelligence. As plants move from lower to higher on the scale of being, so humans incorporate the lower faculties of sense that lead up to "fancy and understanding":

whence the Soul
Reason receives, and reason is her being,
Discursive, or Intuitive; discourse

24. James A. W. Heffernan, "The Presence of the Absent Mother in Wordsworth's *Prelude*," *Studies in Romanticism* 27 (1988): 266, in a subtle psychoanalytic argument, sees Wordsworth's loss and separation from his mother as leading to his restored reunion and renewal with the mother figures, Dorothy and Mary Hutchinson. I think this personal loss also overlaps with his political trauma.
25. Galperin, " 'Turns and Counter-Turns' " 263.

Is oftest yours, the latter most is ours,
Differing but in degree, of kind the same.
(*Paradise Lost* 5.482–90)

Discursive reason exercises itself against the experiential world in making judgments, yet human reason also shares with the angelic an unmediated connection with the divine order of reason that also operates
in nature. This passage from Milton is attractive to Coleridge, who
quotes it in at least three instances: in his letter to Wordsworth on his
disappointment with *The Excursion,* in *The Statesman's Manual,* and
again in *Biographia Literaria.*[26] By alluding to this passage, Coleridge,
like Wordsworth, draws upon the seventeenth-century meaning of reason. In Milton's discourse, the word *reason* packs a strong charge of
religious and emotional commitment: this dimension of feeling carries
over for Wordsworth and Coleridge in their attempts to revitalize the
word *analytic* against the contemporary tendency, abetted by the rise of
modern science, to use it in the sense of analytic reason.

Wordsworth carefully discriminates between reason and reason in
touch with logos:

There comes a time when reason—not the grand
And simple reason, but that humbler power
Which carries on its no inglorious work
By logic and minute analysis—
Is of all idols that which pleases most
The growing mind.   (*The Prelude* 11.123–28)

Despite his praise for its dissective and critical value, Wordsworth rejects
analytic reason as idol worship. One thinks of the idolatry of Milton's
Eve as she does reverence to the forbidden fruit before tempting Adam
to share her fatal choice (*Paradise Lost* 9.834–38). Wordsworth disavows
his own brief liaison with analytic reason; his return to Miltonic reason
deliberately repudiates this proclivity for "logic and minute analysis" as
an idolatry endemic to his own youth. He recognizes that analytic
reason, in its proper place, fulfills a necessary function as forerunner to

26. Coleridge, *Letters* 4:575 (30 May 1815); *The Complete Works of Samuel Taylor Coleridge,* 7
vols., ed. W. G. T. Shedd (New York: Harper, 1853) 1:460; Coleridge, *Biographia Literaria,*
ed. Engell and Bate 1: 173–74.

technological reason. The danger lies in elevating it beyond its proper sphere.

In rejecting his own overemphasis on analytic reason, Wordsworth implicitly strengthens the linkage between dream and imagination. Wordsworth and Coleridge not only draw upon the preeminent role of reason in Milton's microcosmic kingdom of the mind, but also find in it a vital source for generating new philosophical meanings latent in the changing currency of imagination in its relation to reason.[27] The visionary imagination averts a thralldom to sense by drawing upon the faculty of reason as well as upon its kinship to the language of dream. Yet Wordsworth does not merely imitate Milton's Christian humanist adaptation of classical reason. The paradoxical equation of reason and imagination merges opposites in a precarious balance, unlike the Miltonic subordination of fancy/imagination to the government of reason.

The postmodern crisis-of-reason thinkers, reacting to the Frankfurt School on the meaning of reason, offer a lively comparison to Wordsworth in that they also react to the word in relation to science and technology. For them, Wordsworth's paradoxical merging of reason and imagination might seem too invested in hierarchy ("reason in her most exalted mood") and in the ideology of idealism. Writing about the crisis of reason as perceived by the Frankfurt School and by Italian intellectuals such as Giuseppi Sertoli and Franco Rella, who epitomize their own generation, John Paul Russo observes that

> in modernity, so it was said, there could be no culture-as-synthesis whatsoever, no psychological "wholeness," no "totality" of an "integrated civilization," not under existing modes of industrialism and the technocratic state. Instead, there is only the continuous flux of the fragmentary, the precarious, the transitory, and the unbidden: Montale's "vestigia / che il vuoto non ringhiotte" ("vestiges / which the void does not swallow").[28]

27. John Bullitt and Walter Jackson Bate, "Distinctions Between Fancy and Imagination in Eighteenth Century English Criticism," *Modern Language Notes* 60 (1945): 8–15, provide insight into the changing meaning of these two terms, especially into the image-making aspect of imagination that made it seem more reliable than the more whimsical subjective fancy.

28. John Paul Russo, "Logos and Transience in Franco Rella" 188. I am indebted to Russo for sending me this article about postmodern Italian thinkers on reason. I follow his

Although this thinking through negation is foreign to Wordsworth's discourse on the sublimity of reason in conjunction with imagination, his reason-imagination paradox in some ways anticipates the postmoderns. Wordsworth tends to include the irrational as rational: the bastions of truth and meditation, he writes, of the "works of bard and sage" are the fruits of "passion . . . which itself / Is highest reason in a soul sublime" (*The Prelude* [1850] 5.40–42).

Rella epitomizes the common ground of the ten postmodern crisis-of-reason critics in *Crisi della ragione*, by defining their sense of the word *reason*: "On their view, classical reason should be supplemented by Freudian condensation, displacement, the overdetermined, and opposition, with the 'logic of the double,' with the 'atemporal' and 'silent' unconscious, with the free-association technique of psychoanalysis" (*CF* 36; *CR* 151–53; Russo 190). Although Wordsworth's crisis of reason is different from that of these modern Germans and Italians, they are all reacting against reason as preempted by science since Descartes's *Discourse on Method*. The presence of the uncanny in Wordsworth and his skirmish with analytic reason reveal the depth of his pre-Freudian insights into the vitality of the irrational, of his merging reason and passion. The Cartesian break with the past, as Rella summarizes it, was anti-authoritarian: "The new science does not consider knowledge a going back to the past, a recollection of *priscia philosophia*, but a rupture with this past, and an increase and progress precisely because of this rupture" (*M* 25). Ironically, the new science reclaimed classical reason by "a tearing it from the senses' (*MF* 13), that is, from the body and the body's memory with its idiosyncratic notions of space and time. The body was a 'victim condemned to non-existence' (*M* 15) and denied the right to plead its case."[29]

Wordsworth shares with the new science a distrust of the senses, but his defiance of science's authority over the meaning of reason cuts against the Cartesian split between subjectivity and objectivity. Where

---

practice of using abbreviations for Franco Rella's works: *CF,* "Introduzione," "Ipotese per une descrizione di una battaglia," *La critica freudiana,* ed. Franco Rella (Milan: Feltrinelli, 1977); *CS, Critica e storia: materiali su Benjamin,* ed. Franco Rella (Venezia: Cluva, 1980); *M, Metamorfosi: immagini del pensiero* (Milan: Feltrinelli, 1984); *MF, Miti e figure del moderno* (Parma: Practiche Editrice, 1981); and *CR* for *Crisi della ragione,* ed. Aldo G. Gargani (Torino: Enaudi, 1979).
29. Cited by Russo in "Logos and Transience in Franco Rella" 203.

the crisis-of-reason critics redefine reason against tradition under the auspices of technology, Wordsworth denies the appropriation of reason to science's own uses by invoking the discourse of Milton. Whereas the crisis-of-reason critics validate a plurality of reasons in the wake of technology and post-Freudian culture, Wordsworth attempts to resist the anarchizing force of technological science. In connecting the imagination with dreaming, Wordsworth liberates the senses from tyranny and valorizes the unconscious power of the body. As Wordsworth's daemonic moments supplement classical reason with the discourse of the unconscious, they supplement through imagination his own use of reason. Wordsworth thus, in part, abides the test of the psychoanalytic strictures of these postmodern Italians.

By subordinating analytic reason to Miltonic reason, Wordsworth tries to heal the split represented by Cartesian dualism and the modern scientific revolution. Historically, the dualism of Descartes is epitomized for science by Galileo, who

> revealed that, in scientific observations based upon measurable or calculable properties of substances, it was necessary to distinguish between what he called "primary" and "secondary" qualities. Thus number, size, weight or mass, motion, and time were *primary* qualities and colour, sound, smell, taste (and anything involving sensation) were *secondary* qualities in as much as they had no objectivity since they were bound up with feelings and were, therefore, subjective and unreal.[30]

If Galileo (a leading exponent of the empirical mind) located the major threat to the science of his time in the obstructions of those addicted to fantasy, Wordsworth saw a major adversary in the misuse of analytic reason (fostered by science) that could impair genuine feeling. Galileo's scientific distrust of the subjectivity of the senses might appear to share common ground with Wordsworth's tyranny of the senses.

The imagination (as shown in chapter 4) is prone to distortions of subjectivity. Yet, part of the poet's project in restoring imagination is to expand the scope of the senses by making them subserve the governance of healthy imagination and reason. For Wordsworth, especially in his

30. R. H. Barfield, "Darwinism," *Evolution of Consciousness: Studies in Polarity,* ed. Shirley Sugerman (Middletown: Wesleyan University Press, 1976) 77.

youth, the senses remain a source of abiding power. In the attempt to heal the split between mind and matter, Wordsworth's return to Miltonic reason unites feeling and thought. Reason is the divinely sanctioned faculty that entertains the laws of nature as ideas. Before 1800, Wordsworth seldom predicates God as underlying the marriage of mind and nature. In the final book of *The Prelude,* however, Wordsworth draws closer to Coleridge on this point. Coleridge depicts a relationship between nature and God shared by both poets:

> The human mind is the compass, in which the laws and actuations of all outward essences are revealed as the dips and declinations. (The application of Geometry to the forces and movements of the material world is both proof and instance.) The fact, therefore, that the mind of man in its own primary and constituent forms represents the laws of nature, is a mystery which of itself should suffice to make us religious: for it is a problem of which God is the only solution, God, the one before all, and of all, and through all![31]

The return by Wordsworth (and Coleridge) to the discursive and intuitive reason of Milton, woven into the very texture of *The Prelude,* earns a firm place in the history of ideas by making imagination—in its now disciplined state—the faculty that can redeem the senses and deny the Cartesian split between mind and nature.

Liabilities of Closure in The Prelude

Wordsworth's strategy for restoring imagination in the later books of *The Prelude* has distressed feminist critics. His move to restore the prophetic imagination suggests another look at the poet's endangered androgyny. In the final book of *The Prelude* (1805), Wordsworth uses Dorothy as a mediator to assuage his proclivity for sublime terror in nature and to embrace a newly discovered tenderness through the feminine:

> And he whose soul hath risen
> Up to the height of feeling intellect
> Shall want no humbler tenderness, his heart
> Be tender as a nursing mother's heart;

---

31. *Coleridge, The Statesman's Manual* 1:465.

Of female softness shall his life be full,
Of little loves and delicate desires,
Mild interests and gentlest sympathies.
(*The Prelude* 13.204–10)

Although the intimate confessional tone of this tribute must have
warmly pleased Dorothy, modern feminists question this passage and its
role in the closure of *The Prelude*. Wordsworth leaves himself open to the
charge that he mediates through Dorothy to regain an androgynous
state, that he restores imagination only at the price of excluding women.
Gayatri Spivak detects, for example, a marginalizing of women in the
process of restoring imagination in the final book of *The Prelude*: the
poet's mediating through Dorothy is "his own oedipal accession to the
Law, Imagination as the androgyny of Nature and Man—woman shut
out." This "androgyny" that excludes women in favor of nature and man
results in a defeminized imagination. According to Spivak, Wordsworth's suppression of the paternity of his own child by Annette Vallon,
displaced and transformed into the Vaudracour and Julia episode (1805),
underlies the poet's guilty relationship to "Nature as mother and lover."
Spivak sees the pattern here as "the sexual-political program of the Great
Tradition."[32] From the standpoint of twentieth-century cultural perspectives, Spivak discovers what she calls Wordsworth's patriarchal assumptions and his tendency to marginalize the feminine. This postmodern look at the privileged canon is subversive in its scrutiny of the
patrilineal implications of Wordsworth's project for reclaiming his back-
sliding imagination. As Wordsworth becomes more vatic in singing
himself and Coleridge as poet prophets, Dorothy *is* excluded.[33]

32. Spivak, "Sex and History in *The Prelude* (1805)" 333, 336. Mary Jacobus, "Genre Theory
and *The Prelude*," *diacritics* (1984) 54, supports Spivak's conclusions here that Dorothy's
mediation "allows Wordsworth to play at Mothers and Fathers, thereby acceding to an
androgyny which finally excludes women in the interests of a restored imagination."
33. Susan Levin, *Dorothy Wordsworth and Romanticism* (New Brunswick: Rutgers University Press, 1987) 172, expands upon the differences between female Romantics and their
male counterparts in a way that sheds light upon Wordsworth's exclusion of Dorothy from
the poet prophets in *The Prelude*'s closure: "Writing the story of the feminine self, the
women of romanticism could never be totally integrated into the communities of writing
where men concerned themselves with what have generally been seen as the Great Romantic Issues: depictions of the self-made Promethean and Byronic hero and the power and
agony self-fashioning engenders, the demonstration of man's mind as 'A thousand times
more beautiful than the earth / On which he dwells,' the vision of the poets as 'the
unacknowledged legislators of the world'" (168).

In "Tintern Abbey," however, Dorothy had shared with Wordsworth, virtually as a second self, the mind's endangered covenant with
nature. If anything, she exceeds the poet in perceptual power, in the
visionary generosity of the senses. She belongs more to the earlier
dispensation of sense than to the confidence in the creative faculty that
marks the ending of *The Prelude*. As Wordsworth moves away from his
vision of the one life in "Tintern Abbey," Dorothy and his own femininity recede, notwithstanding his invocation of androgyny through her
offices.

The question of Vaudracour and Julia, offered by Spivak as a displacement of Wordsworth's own lingering guilt over Annette, unfolds salient
personal and political implications. Vaudracour is a projection of Wordsworth, guilty in the same ways he is. This episode of defiance toward
Vaudracour's father mirrors Wordsworth's own relationship to love and
war: "Used to represent the paternal/contractual tyranny of the ancien
régime about which Paine and others wrote," the episode, as Ronald
Paulson makes clear, "is a displaced paradigm of Wordsworth's experience of the Revolution": "he falls in love with the alien woman (alien by
class and nationality), challenges his father, runs away with her, but
eventually succumbs to the external, paternal pressures. The act of loving
with this slightly alien woman *is* the act of revolution—and in fact
corresponds to it in Wordsworth's experience as well as in his poetry—
and the total story of the Revolution is played out in their failed relationship."[34] By deciding not to include Vaudracour and Julia in the 1850
Prelude, and by publishing the episode separately in 1820, Wordsworth
suppresses the antipaternal action and its revolutionary politics in relation to his own life. Paulson's linking of the episode to the public and
private roles of Wordsworth supports Spivak's feminist argument that,
in his return to Miltonic reason and his renovation of imagination,
Wordsworth denies the feminine.

Before resolving the question of Wordsworth's precarious androgyny
in the closure of *The Prelude,* it is necessary to consider the proposed
ending of the Five-Book *Prelude.* Rather than end as the longer versions
do, "the last book of the five-book poem was to have *begun* with
Snowdon and *ended* with the spots of time."[35] The change from the
proposed ending to the 1805 version amounts to a shift from the femi-

34. Paulson, *Representations of Revolution* 268–69.
35. Liu, *Wordsworth: The Sense of History* 396.

nized, personal voice of the spots (explored in chapter 3) to a more public, universal utterance of a manifesto for the imaginative mind. The Mount Snowdon vision of the moon presiding over the misty gulf above the Irish sea becomes a "perfect image of a mighty mind" that is also a paradigm of the human imagination properly governing the unruly senses. Such minds can make their own imaginative transformations, analogous to the vision given to Wordsworth as he breaks out of the oppressive cloud layer to discover the full moon shaping the Snowdon scene into unity:

> They from their native selves can send abroad
> Like transformation, for themselves create
> A like existence, and, when'er it is
> Created for them, catch it by an instinct.
> Them the enduring and the transient both
> Serve to exalt. They build up greatest things
> From least suggestions, ever on the watch,
> Willing to work and to be wrought upon.
> They need not extraordinary calls
> To rouze them—in a world of life they live,
> *By sensible impressions not enthralled,*
> But quickened, rouzed, and made thereby more fit
> To hold communion with the invisible world.
> (*The Prelude* 13.93–105, my emphasis)

One can understand Wordsworth's decision to place the spots of time before rather than after Mount Snowdon, as he had originally intended to conclude the Five-Book *Prelude*. Had he concluded with the spots of time, their uncanny, personal aspect would not have served his final, universalizing purpose—to write an epic on a mental journey into the depths of his own mind. Here he generalizes the motif of sensual tyranny by recapitulating that motif in abstract terms, sermonizing to his reader in the white heat of his message. This kind of prophetic discourse, no matter how tightly it ties in with his theme of restored imagination, does not carry the androgynous weight that marked either the spots or the passages ventriloquizing the abandoned woman. Wordsworth's dream of androgyny does not inform *The Prelude*'s closure as it does, for example, his projection into Margaret's desertion in *The Excursion* (1).

Alan Liu's focus upon Wordsworth's aesthetic reasons for closing *The*

Prelude in a manner contrary to the poet's earlier intentions for the Five-Book *Prelude,* invites a political reading. Liu's solution to the "puzzle of revisionary structure" pertains to the closures of the 1805 and the 1850 versions of *The Prelude*:

> The motive for reordering the close of *The Prelude,* I suggest, lies in the fact that only a prior moment of autobiographical self-correction can allow the Imagination to become like, but not too like, Napoleon. Only prior atonement for the Imagination's complicity in imperialism, that is, can justify its final ascent to empire as an act *antithetical* to Napoleonic imperialism—as an imperial restoration that is also true restoration.[36]

This critical solution accords nicely with my discussion in chapter 4 of Wordsworth's imagination beguiled by power. Wordsworth, as Liu puts it, must atone for his excessive desires, for his betrayal by false imagination, for his seduction by the French Revolution that later succumbs to Napoleonic imperialism. In the blasted hawthorn spot of time, Liu finds that the personal correction Wordsworth endured as penance before daring to assert his own imagination is a just rival to the corrupt empire of Napoleon. Wordsworth corrects his "anxiety of hope" and his "trite reflections of morality": "in the deepest passion, I bow'd low / To God, who thus corrected my desires" (*The Prelude* 11.371–74). This reading makes sense of the cryptic "desires" that all but come clear. They must be seen not as the "desires" of a boy of thirteen at the time of his father's death but as those of the adult poet at the time of composition. These desires become a code word for the entire motif that I have developed as false imagination's extravagant hopes for France. History, as Liu justly argues, not only explains the difficult crux of desire, but also prepares for the crescendo of Wordsworth's ending. It is history that situates Wordsworth's self-correction in the second spot of time before Mount Snowdon, before the episode that is to become the apotheosis of the inner empire of imagination. This is Wordsworth's epic voice speaking for "the mind of man" on inner terrain, not on the earth soaked with blood by Napoleon:

> Prophets of Nature, we to them will speak
> A lasting inspiration, sanctified

36. Liu, *Wordsworth: The Sense of History* 447–48.

By reason and by truth; what we have loved
Others will love, and we may teach them how:
Instruct them how the mind of man becomes
A thousand times more beautiful than the earth
On which he dwells, above this frame of things
(Which, 'mid all revolutions in the hopes
And fears of men, doth still remain unchanged)
In beauty exalted, as it is itself
Of substance and of fabric more divine.

(*The Prelude* 13.442–52)

This chapter began with Milton, who rivaled Homer and Virgil by writing an epic of a more inward action than their clashes of arms. Wordsworth—who contrives an inner epic, a tour of his own mind— outdoes Milton on this score, on this inner quest into the abyss of his own psyche. Speaking in Book 3 of "the awful . . . might of souls" in childhood, when the "yoke of earth is new to them," Wordsworth called this theme "in truth heroic argument" (*The Prelude* 3.178–82). In the final epic elevation of his theme, the revolutions, both public and private, across the span of Wordsworth's poem come inextricably to inform each other.

Unlike the consummate skill Milton demonstrates in fashioning the closure of *Paradise Lost,* however, Wordsworth strikes some sour notes in the final cadenza of his prophetic strain. By emulating Milton, he gains the epic stature of his heroic song, but the price of prophecy is the exclusion of women and the betrayal of the earlier androgynous dream worked out in his "spots of time" and in his tale of Margaret.

When Wordsworth rescripts imagination "as but another name" for "reason in her most exalted mood," however, he not only bridges the gap in Cartesian dualism, but also reconstitutes reason as feminine. In this move, he echoes Milton, who, in his dream of Eve, makes reason feminine in accord with its Latin gender (*ratio, -onis*). In his "Reply to 'Mathetes,'" Wordsworth repeats this pattern, dismantling the dualism between thinking and emotion even as he feminizes reason: *she* "gives much spontaneously, but she seeks for more; she works by thought, through feeling, yet in thoughts she begins and ends" (*LC* 86). In a dismantling of the male/female polarity, Wordsworthian reason is troped as a female working, through feeling, to leaven masculine discourse—a representation that gives the lie to T. S. Eliot's later formulation, the "dissociation of sensibility," which had supposedly set in during the seventeenth century. The feminization of reason pits the Miltonic against the scientific brand of reason that Wordsworth had earlier singled out for idolatry. We might have expected Wordsworth in the closure of *The Prelude* to derive his credentials as a prophet from the dream matrices of his own unconscious. After the high point of merging imagination and reason (with its hint of androgyny), Wordsworth resorts in his ending to the rhetoric of prophecy rather than the hazards of dream.

The divorce between reason and dreaming that occurs at the end of *The Prelude* is illuminated by comparison with Keats's *Lamia*, where the dream of love and poetry (Lamia) collides with the incompatible figure of analytic reason (Apollonius). There is an inevitable conflict between these two mutually exclusive poles because, as Andrew Cooper puts it, "dream and reason eventually repel each other as negations rather than uniting as contraries."[37] By closing *The Prelude* with his epic manifesto on imagination rather than his spots of time, Wordsworth separates his authentic prophetic voice from its uncanny source in the language of dream. His final comfortable assumption of prophetic status risks losing contact with these Dionysiac roots. Keats's separation of dream and reason into two discrete negations—indeed, his embodiment of the conflict—polarizes this matter more sharply than does Wordsworth's closure of *The Prelude,* where the prophetic claim lacks poise in direct proportion to its elevated rhetoric. If less is more, more is also less. Wordsworth's uncertainties about genre help to account for his difficulties in closing. Although he had deserted his epic aspirations to restore the lyric voice of imagination in Books 12 and 13, he tries to swerve back to epic elevation in his finale. This poetry violates Wordsworth's earlier leveling muse and his focus upon the commonplace. The next chapter will consider the apocalyptic nightmare of the Arab, where reason cohabits with dream. In the Arab Dream, however, contraries unite rather than exist, as in *Lamia,* as incompatible negations.

37. Andrew M. Cooper, *Doubt and Identity in Romantic Poetry* (New Haven: Yale University Press, 1988) 105.

Full often, taking from the world of sleep
This Arab phantom, which I thus beheld,
This semi-Quixote, I to him have given
A substance, fancied him a living man,
A gentle dweller in the desert, crazed
By love and feeling, and internal thought
Protracted among endless solitudes;
Have shaped him wandering upon this quest!

Wordsworth, *The Prelude*

CHAPTER SIX

Wordsworth's Self-Analysis: The Arab Dream

Reading *The Prelude* as "the precipitate of an interior battle, a sequence of maneuvers against the incomprehensible, fought out in the public domain of verse," Jonathan Bishop observes that the poem "constitutes the record, half-concealed in a commonplace autobiographical structure, of a process which, in these days, we would call a self-analysis."[1] It is this process, enlightened by Freud's self-analysis, that I address in my closing chapter. How does self-analysis, which for Freud implied a confrontation with death, empower creativity? Unlike Freud, who conducts his self-analysis primarily through dreams, Wordsworth proceeds more indirectly, working through memory as well as trances, reveries, and dreams. Wordsworth's approach, more impersonal than Freud's introspective dream analysis, is carried on unobtrusively throughout *The Prelude*. The Arab dream, however, emerges as an epitome of the poet's self-analysis.

The Freudian typology of dream contraries lends itself to an inter-

1. Jonathan Bishop, "Wordsworth and the 'Spots of Time'" 60.

168

pretation of the Arab dream within the context of *The Prelude* (5). These opposites exist together in dreams—not canceling each other out, but sometimes merging into each other—linking the texts of *Don Quixote* and *The Prelude,* especially in the narrativity of dreaming. Because *Don Quixote* embodies to an hallucinatory degree the very biases that Wordsworth ascribes to wayward fancy and false imagination, Cervantes's presence in *The Prelude* may now serve to complete the circle of this study of dreams.

Wordsworth situates his apocalyptic dream of the Arab at the beginning of *The Prelude* (5). This dream follows the poet's rebound from a fallow time at Cambridge, a period that led to the epiphany of his dedication to poetry and ended with his providential encounter with the Discharged Soldier. The Arab dream precedes the greater lapse of imagination and the fall of the poet's hopes for revolutionary France. The dream, then, affirms the perennial rebirth of poetry in contradistinction to a nightmare portending its destruction. This nightmare signals its debt to its two forerunners, Cervantes and Descartes. Paradoxically, in commandeering one of Descartes's dreams, and by making himself the dreamer in the 1850 version, Wordsworth clarifies his own anxiety about the extinction of poetry.[2] This adopted dream, very like Wordsworth's own, resonates with the discourse of the unconscious that subtends *The Prelude.*

The Dream of the Book

Because Wordsworth is responsible for altering a reported dream of Descartes to include Cervantes's Arab/Quixote figure, the fifth book of *The Prelude,* devoted to Wordsworth's own reading, makes the *Quixote* a logical choice to enforce this subject.[3] In his critique of the Romantics as

2. See Thomas, *Dreams of Authority* 50, who writes of the Arab's obsession to save the stone and shell, seeking to bury them, which would merely substitute "one form of erasure for another": "These seemingly contradictory impulses within the dream parallel Wordsworth's contending attitudes toward authority: he intends to tell his own story in the poem and yet he desires to submit his own powers to the voice that nature sends him in his dreams."

3. Edward Dudley, "Cervantes and Wordsworth: Literary History as Literature and Literature as Literary History," *Cervantes: Su obra y su mundo, Actas del Primer Congreso Internacional sobre Cervantes* (Madrid: EDI-6, 1981) 1098, points out that the stone and shell were "a *Dictionnaire* and a *Corpus Poetarum*" in Descartes's dream and that the Arab/Quixote figure—"added by Wordsworth"—replaces "a more shadowy figure in the original."

readers of *Don Quixote,* Anthony Close debunks their sympathy for the mad knight as an archetypal figuring of the imagination: whereas "the seventeenth and eighteenth centuries could see an excess of the imaginative faculty as a blight, the Romantics could only see it as a sublime merit."[4] Close's anti-Romantic stance fails to recognize that the Romantics provide their own critique of errant imagination. Although Wordsworth follows the Romantic pattern of empathy for the questing Arab, he also recognizes, as we have seen, the pitfalls that lie in wait for imagination. What might easily qualify as a liability of imagination—the madness of the questing rider—redeems itself in the attempt to save poetry and geometry from the waters of the deep. The embodiment of holocaust as an irresistible force renders the Arab Dream, like Sarum Plain, a stark type of the Kantian sublime. Whereas Cervantes allegedly had set out to destroy "that ill-founded edifice of the books of chivalry" (Prologue to *Don Quixote*), Wordsworth employs a doomed quest for a contrary intent—to preserve the frail vessels of literature. Notwithstanding the different intentions of these authors in their handling of books, the figure of Quixote—who freely merges with the Arab in Wordsworth's dream—acts as a bond with tradition in both works. Where Quixote enacts imaginary chivalric ideals in an anachronistic world, Wordsworth's Arab (who lacks the comic dimension of his prototype) desperately seeks to preserve imagination from the onrush of deluge.

The Cervantine episode of the Cave of Montesinos,[5] an antiromantic reverie countering the ideology of love in the outmoded romances of chivalry, offers a bookish counterpart to Wordsworth's dream of a salvific Arab. By staging the anti-heroic deflation of Durandarte and Belerma, as well as the banal exposure of Dulcinea, Cervantes discloses Don Quixote's unconscious awareness that his knight-errantry is a mere construct of an inflamed imagination. Belerma's reputed epic beauty has decayed into "great, dark circles around her eyes" and a "sickly complexion." Dulcinea and her two companions appear in peasant garb, in a

---

4. Anthony Close, *The Romantic Approach to 'Don Quixote'* (Cambridge: Cambridge University Press, 1978) 53.

5. For references to *Don Quixote* see Miguel de Cervantes Saavedra, *El ingenioso hidalgo Don Quixote de la Mancha,* ed. Luis Andrés Murillo, 2 vols. (Madrid: Clásicos Castalia, 1978) 2.23. Because of the many editions now in use, I refer to passages or incidents in *Don Quixote* by part and chapter number in parenthesis. Unless otherwise stated, translations are by Diana Wilson.

dream from the day's residue, as the country girls whom Sancho had earlier "invented." Although Dulcinea flees at her lover's approach, one of her simpering companions comes to beg for six *reales,* offering a cotton petticoat as security on the loan. Caught with only four *reales,* Quixote discovers that he cannot, so to speak, afford Dulcinea. This dream dismantles the chivalric romance codes, exposing romantic love as the product of a sick imagination.

Whereas Cervantes deflates romantic love in the Cave of Montesinos, Wordsworth excludes it from his Arab dream altogether. Books that were for Quixote so dangerous, for Wordsworth become endangered. The poet's purpose, however, resembles Cervantes's: both use the dream to embrace literature and its interpretation by multiple narrators. To what degree Don Quixote's reverie in the Cave of Montesinos is a subtext of Wordsworth's Arab dream remains arguable; however, these two dream texts, united by the common theme of books, manifest a deep psychic kinship. Enchanted by the landscape of chivalric desire and living in a world constructed out of his reading, Don Quixote nonetheless dreams a story that will dismantle his delusion of romance. Wordsworth, however, transfixed by nightmare before a rising tide of destruction, awakens from his dream to an unscathed imagination, indeed, an imagination energized by its dream skirmish with annihilation. Don Quixote is charmed by an ironic dream, one disclosing his unconscious awareness that Dulcinea is a pernicious fiction. The trajectory of Wordsworth's dream and waking reverses the drift of Don Quixote's. Where Cervantes moves from desire to its disenchantment, Wordsworth moves from ruin to reenchantment.

The Dreamer as Author

Another generative subtext for Wordsworth's Arab dream derives from Descartes. In the third of three dreams, Descartes discovers a dictionary that appears mysteriously, ravishes him with delight, and implies a blessing upon his vocation—philosophy:

> Almost immediately he chanced on a second book, without knowing how it too had come to be there. This second one was a collection of poetry, entitled *Corpus Poëtarum.* As he was leafing through this volume, a man whom he did not know appeared and began to converse with him. The man presented to him a poem by Ausonius

entitled "Est et Non," as being of great worth, and Descartes in turn searched the volume of poetry first for that poem and then for another poem of Ausonius entitled "Quod vitae sectabor iter," which he had already seen in the volume. The random conversation, the confused search for the two poems, the inexplicable appearance, disappearance, and reappearance of the Dictionary, the ultimate vanishing of the man and the books—all these happenings bear the marks of an authentic dream.[6]

Instead of an Arab fleeing from a deluge, here a strange figure emerges in an ecstatic setting. The dictionary of knowledge and the title of the second poem bode well for the onset of Descartes's career as a philosopher. Unlike the joyful omens in Descartes's dream, Wordsworth's deluge and the half-mad Arab emerge from images of nightmare. Wordsworth takes the two books from Descartes's dream, dichotomizes them into science and poetry, and reinforces the difference between the symbolic dream images, not found in Descartes, of the stone and shell.[7]

As the Arab rides before the impending deluge, he engages in a semi-Quixotic quest to rescue the stone and shell—which he describes to the dreamer as geometry and poetry. The shift from reporting this quest as the dream of a friend (1805) to narrating it in the poet's own person (1850) recalls the alteration of the Dionysiac episode on human sacrifice from the third person in *Salisbury Plain* to the first person reverie in *The Prelude*. The changes indicate a desire, in later life, to resist displacement. The dreams become a more direct index of the poet's own psyche. J. Hillis Miller distinguishes the Arab dream from an actual dream insofar as "Wordsworth himself did not dream it, and it is not so much a real dream as the deliberate invention of a dream sequence." Yet even though Wordsworth borrowed the dream, it works much better as a window into this own allegory of creative consciousness than as the reported dream of a friend. Miller concedes as much when he writes that a full

6. Jane Worthington Smyser, "Wordsworth's Dream of Poetry and Science: *The Prelude, V,*" *PMLA* 71 (1956) 271.
7. Michael Ragussis, *The Subterfuge of Art: Language and the Romantic Tradition* (Baltimore and London: Johns Hopkins, 1978) 19, 23, traces the stone and shell back to Ovid's *Metamorphoses,* where the sea god Triton blows upon a conch shell to halt the rising waters of the deep. Pyrrha and Deucalion are thus left alive on Mt. Parnassus; their pebbles, thrown behind them, spring to human life. This myth thus anticipates the renewal of nature and imagination beyond Wordsworth's nightmare.

interpretation of the Arab dream "would in fact involve an analysis of all Wordsworth's writings."[8] This kind of reticulation in the unconscious discourse of Wordsworth's poems, emerging from the associated parts of *The Prelude,* itself implies a self-analysis.

This change in the dreamer's identity—unlike Wordsworth's many revisions toward orthodoxy—intensifies the poem's psychological ties with the poet's autobiography. Because Wordsworth's dream derives from an actual dream by Descartes that dovetails smoothly with the poet's vocational anxieties about the endangered fruits of imagination, it acquires the allegorical force of an authorial dream.[9] Timothy Bahti, however, downplaying the dream component, interprets the Arab dream as more like a literary text than a dream: "The dream of the Arab, then, is not a dream 'like any other dream,' but is rather at once *sui generis,* 'like' imaginative experience, and related to the discovery and reading of 'texts'—and is itself a text, a 'found text' (found in Baillet, related by a 'studious friend') and a text found—by the reader of *The Prelude* (5.71–140)."[10] A dream by Wordsworth himself might have involved more personal repression and been less subject to the laws of grammar and waking expression. But constructed from another's actual dream, the Arab dream is nearer to an authentic dream than one fashioned out of airy nothing. Bahti's recognition of the unique quality of this dream sets the stage for his own rhetorical reading, yet it also captures the burden of the reader's task. No literary dream, tailored to fit the contexts of fiction, will ever exactly correspond to the live act of dreaming. Wordsworth's nightmare of the Arab, however, meets all of the requirements necessary for a psychoanalytic reading of the text as an authorial dream.

By virtue of recounting his own reverie in the Cave of Montesinos,

8. J. Hillis Miller, "The Stone and the Shell: The Problem of Poetic Form in Wordsworth's Dream of the Arab," *Mouvements Premiers* (Paris: Librairie Jose Corti, 1972) 138, 125.

9. Kenneth Johnston, *Wordsworth and 'The Recluse'* 140, observing that Descartes's original dream was vocational, writes of its appropriation by Wordsworth that "the dream is preeminently a *vocation,* a story about the proper choice of one's life's work."

10. Timothy Bahti, "Figures of Interpretation, The Interpretation of Figures: A Reading of Wordsworth's 'Dream of the Arab,'" *Studies in Romanticism* 18 (1979) 609. Jane Worthington Smyser, "Wordsworth's Dream of Poetry and Science," 270–72, traces this dream to Adrien Baillet, *Vie de Descartes,* 1691. She doubts that Wordsworth had read Baillet himself and favors Michel Beaupuy over Coleridge as the most likely source for Wordsworth's knowledge of Descartes's dream (272).

Don Quixote becomes an author. The *creation* of fiction, and not the fiction itself, is the focus of Cervantes's representation of Don Quixote's dream.[11] Harry Sieber's observation about Don Quixote applies equally well to the 1850 Wordsworth, to the latter-day dreamer of the Arab and the deluge: what is vital about the Cave of Montesinos episode "is merely its existence in the novel where it is presented as a *unique* product of Don Quijote's consciousness."[12] The product comes from the hero's own experience in the cave, where he dreams (or hallucinates, or invents) a vision based on the old Carolingian chivalric ballads. The vision is the residue of his daytime reading of chivalric romance: he enters the cave as a hero bent upon disenchanting Durandarte, Belerma, Montesinos, and Dulcinea. In his role as heroic dreamer entering the fictional world of his own obsessive reading, Don Quixote, under the auspices of his own desire, projects himself as the liberator come to free a cluster of grotesque and superannuated literary figures from the enchantment of Merlin.

No one else can verify this dream, which comes from Don Quixote's own interior world. The narrator, Cide Hamete Benengeli, with his rigid historian's standards of truth or falsehood, doubts the reliability of the whole episode and exonerates himself of any responsibility for the dream. He even credits a rumor about Don Quixote's supposed deathbed retraction of the Cave of Montesinos dream. In a handwritten marginal note, the exasperated Arab narrator finally assigns the work of deciphering to the reader: "Tú, letor, pues eres prudente, juzga lo que te pareciere, que yo no debo ni puedo más [You, prudent reader, must judge for yourself, for I should not, nor cannot, do more]" (2.24).

The poet of *The Prelude*—by adding his own dream interpretation to that of an Arab who, unlike Cide Hamete, does not refuse interpretation—distances himself from his Cervantine model. Wordsworth takes on writerly authority for the Arab dream, a nightmare through which the poet's unconscious discloses itself. His very anxiety about the vul-

11. See John G. Weiger, *In the Margins of Cervantes* (Hanover and London: Published for the University of Vermont by University Press of New England, 1988) 145. Weiger points out that "To depict a dreamer . . . is to depict an authorial figure" (139).
12. Harry Sieber, "Literary Time in the 'Cueva de Montesinos,'" *Modern Language Notes* 86 (1971) 269, n.6.

nerability of books generates the apocalyptic deluge. A kind of self-conscious narrativity haunts the inner landscape of *The Prelude,* where Wordsworth embodies his own emergent poetics of subjectivity.

Dream Interpretation: In and Out of Dreams

In Wordsworth, the Arab is a dream interpreter within his own nightmare. In "the language of the dream," he metaphorizes the stone as 'Euclid's Elements,' and the shell as poetry, as "something of more worth." This shell, "so beautiful in shape, / In colour so resplendent," yields to his ear "a prophetic blast of harmony." Its message, in "an unknown tongue," is a paradox because Wordsworth nonetheless understands its alien language. In contrast to such "beauty" and "harmony," the prophecy of the shell is apocalyptic:

> An Ode, in passion uttered, which foretold
> Destruction to the children of the earth
> By deluge, now at hand. No sooner ceased
> The song, than the Arab with calm look declared
> That all would come to pass of which the voice
> Had given forewarning, and that he himself
> Was going then to bury those two books:
> The one that held acquaintance with the stars,
> And wedded soul to soul in purest bond
> Of reason, undisturbed by space or time;
> The other that was a god, yea many gods,
> Had voices more than all the winds, with power
> To exhilarate the spirit, and to soothe,
> Through every clime, the heart of humankind.
> (*The Prelude* [1850] 5.96–109)

Although the apocalyptic ode foretells "destruction to the children of the earth," the Arab interpreter insists that the generic role of poetry is to uplift and console. The prophetic ode, however, as part of an oneiric dream, predicts the deluge that threatens to engulf dreamer, interpreter, and books. In this deluge that endangers civilization, contraries of ruin and solace emerge, illuminating geometry with its timeless witness to reason, and invigorating poetry within the bad augury of mutual doom.[13]

Thus far we have considered the internalized interpretation of dream images by the Arab himself. But in his ongoing narrative after he awakes, Wordsworth also interprets his dream: the mad quest to save the stone and shell is one that he could share. If he should encounter an event such as the deluge, he might "share / That maniac's fond anxiety, and go / Upon like errand" (*The Prelude* [1850] 5.159–61). Wordsworth's implied reading of the text of his dream includes himself as one of the Arab's doubles. On the distinction between Wordsworth's waking and sleeping relation to his Arab dream, Geoffrey Hartman writes:

> The dream of Book V is, in fact, the closest Wordsworth comes, before this climax, to understanding directly the autonomy of imagination, though his insight is still restricted by the existential and narrative mode of a dream-vision. The dangers of confrontation and engulfment occur only in the "sacred" space of the dream: the poet himself stands firmly in nature and narrative. The special character of any dream not an hallucination is that it is separated from life by a *cordon sanitaire* of the dreamer's consciousness.[14]

Within the action of his dream, Wordsworth both is and is not the Arab; but in his waking state, protected from an actual deluge by his distance from the delusion of his dream, he can both share and judge the "maniac's" quest. For Hartman, this barrier between dream and waking life protects the poet from fully confronting the apocalyptic imagination that is actually beyond nature.

I am less concerned with this insight into the poet's precarious relation to imagination, however, than with the passage's implications for an interpretation by dream contraries. Wordsworth's unconscious investment in his dream figure of the Arab—who rejects the poet-dreamer's attempt to join the doomed quest to save the stone and shell—becomes conscious only in his *a posteriori* waking readiness to share the Arab's futile

13. See Theresa M. Kelley, "Spirit and Geometric Form: The Stone and Shell in Wordsworth's Arab Dream," *Studies in English Literature* 22 (1982) 563–82, for a reconciliation of science and poetry for Wordsworth in the category of enduring knowledge. Kelley also places the stone as geometry in Wordsworth's contemporary scientific thought.
14. Hartman, *Wordsworth's Poetry* 227.

venture. The nightmare threat of deluge and its contrary resurgent imagination, initiated through his role as waking interpreter, allows Wordsworth to have his book and eat it too. As a poet, he faces the conditions of deluge—the revolutionary bloodbath and its tidal ruin.[15] Yet, as we have often seen with the uncanny, Wordsworth can emerge from the shards of ruin to pursue his story, the poet energized by threats of destruction to pluck the fruits of his vocation.

The language of the dream leads to the breaking down of the binaries, madness and reason. Cervantes anticipates this breakdown of opposites, for instance, in Don Quixote's favorite phrase "la razón de la sinrazón" (the reason of unreason). Although Miller maintains that a "binary opposition is as important a structural principle of this text as is the movement of displacement," he does not connect Wordsworth's binaries with Freudian dream contraries. Some examples of these binary opposites are stone/shell, shell/book, desert/sea, and science/poetry. Miller captures the generative function of their opposition: "Poetry is a transformation of the kind of reason which produces geometry. Passion, the generator of poetry, is, says Wordsworth, 'highest reason in a soul sublime.'"[16]

This fusion of passion and reason, akin to Wordsworth's merger of madness and reason, corresponds to Freud's discussion of binaries in dreams. The dream language of contraries, analogous to the principle of wish fulfillment in dreaming, also occurs in myths. In discussing the Moerae (the three fates), Freud describes how the wishful side of the mythic mind acts to replace the disturbing role of the third fate:

> Man, as we know, makes use of his imaginative activity in order to satisfy the wishes that reality does not satisfy. So his imagination rebelled against the recognition of the truth embodied in the myth of the Moerae, and constructed instead the myth derived from it, in which the Goddess of Death was replaced by the Goddess of Love

---

15. See Paulson, *Representations of Revolution* 254, "The natural disaster was introduced in the opening lines and much labored over in the various drafts. Wordsworth's effort to describe his response to this 'deluge,' and the effect it has on his writing, is the center of Book (5). 'Deluge' was, of course, one of the stereotyped images applied to the French Revolution."

16. J. Hillis Miller, "The Stone and the Shell" 140.

and by what was equivalent to her in human shape. The third of the sisters was no longer Death; she was the fairest, best, most desirable and most loveable of women (*SE* 12:299).

Thus the wishful alternative, the goddess of love, emerges from her opposite, death, and their primeval doubling. For Wordsworth, by an analogous process, the nightmare of deluge gives way to the waking world in which the shell's voice of "harmony" prevails. The result is a new covenant between imagination and the cyclical renewal of nature. This nightmare encounter with destruction by water yields to a process described by William Empson as "the Orpheus idea," an idea, found in the *Hymn to David* and *The Ancient Mariner,* that "man gains the strength to control" nature by delighting in its most terrible manifestations.[17] This pattern, now familiar as the trajectory of the sublime, reveals the trauma of self-analysis.

Freudian Dream Contraries

Even before Wordsworth introduces his nightmare of the Arab in *The Prelude* (5), his prologue to the dream suggests that nature would renew itself even after total destruction of the world by earthquake or fire:

> Should the whole frame of earth by inward throes
> Be wrenched, or fire come down from far to scorch
> Her pleasant habitations, and dry up
> Old Ocean, in his bed left singed and bare,
> Yet would the living Presence still subsist
> Victorious, and composure would ensue,
> And kindlings like the morning—presage sure
> Of day returning and of life revived.[18]

This apocalyptic image of Earth's ruin includes the irrepressible life force reborn out of the ashes of its devastation. This play of opposites between scorching and rekindling in the preamble to Book 5 anticipates the Arab

17. William Empson, *Some Versions of Pastoral* (Norfolk: New Directions, 1935) 120–21.
18. *The Prelude* (1850) 155, lines 30–37. The 1850 version will be used for Book 5 because the shift to Wordsworth himself as dreamer, away from the friend who tells the dream to him in 1805, enhances the unconscious dimension of Wordsworth's mind.

dream and its interpretation. Contraries of this kind mark one of the lynchpins of Freudian dream analysis:

> Ideas which are contraries are by preference expressed in dreams by one and the same element. "No" seems not to exist so far as dreams are concerned. Opposition between two thoughts, the relation of *reversal,* may be represented in dreams in a most remarkable way. It may be represented by some *other* piece of the dream-content being turned into its opposite—as it were by an afterthought. We shall hear presently of a further method of expressing contradiction. The sensation of *inhibition of movement* which is so common in dreams also serves to express a contradiction between two impulses, a *conflict of will.* (SE 5:661)

Freud believes so strongly in the principle of contradiction in dream life that, for him, "the alternative *'either-or'* is never expressed in dreams, both of the alternatives being inserted in the text of the dream as though they were equally valid." Because these opposites exist in dreams without canceling each other out, he insists "that an 'either-or' used in *recording* a dream is to be translated by 'and'" (SE 5:661). The ordinary logic of negation, according to Freud, simply does not operate in dreams and the unconscious.

Binaries, already present in *Don Quixote,* appear in different form in Wordsworth's dream: for the poet, these binaries blend into each other precisely in the way accounted for by Freudian dream theory. In Wordsworth's Arab dream, his doublings break down through an authorial merger: Wordsworth, along with Don Quixote, blends with, but does not fully become, the "maniac" Arab on his doomed quest. This principle of opposition is already present in the subtext of Wordsworth's Arab dream, *Don Quixote,* where the Arab, Cide Hamete Benengeli, an unreliable historian, is often at odds with both Cervantes and Don Quixote. At the end of the novel, however, even Cide Hamete affirms his oneness with Don Quixote. Where Wordsworth psychically identifies with his own dream figures, however, Cervantes remains distant, concealing himself behind the screen of his multiple narrators.

Apart from dreams, myths for Freud can also transform love and death into their opposites. His "Theme of the Three Caskets," traces a version of mythic doubling in *King Lear.* When Lear carries his dead daughter, Cordelia, on stage at the end of the play, he is also carrying the mythic figure, death: "She is the Death-goddess who, like the Valkyrie in German mythology, carries away the dead hero from the battlefield." The myth, in its ancient wisdom, "bids the old man renounce love, choose death and make friends with the necessity of dying" (SE 12:301). Even if one objects that tragic reinforcement, not renunciation of love, is the real point of King Lear's closure, the fusion of love and death in this reading by Freud renders his primary argument all the more forceful. Freud's example illustrates the mythic fusion of opposites that, by analogy, generates wishful contraries in dream work.

These contraries also exist in Wordsworth's Arab dream: the shell's oxymoronic "prophetic blast of harmony" contrasts with its destructive forecast to humankind. The deluge about to destroy the civilization of books opposes the endurance of imagination when freed from the shackles of false education. The madness of the Arab/Quixote figure coalesces with reason as the poet/narrator identifies with the insane rider on the dromedary. Like Wordsworth, Cide Hamete Benengeli, who manifests such distance and skepticism toward Don Quixote's exploits, fuses into his protagonist.[19] As Cide Hamete elects to retire his quill upon "a brass wire," he invokes it in an apostrophe, "O my pen, whether of skilful make or clumsy cut I know not; here shalt thou remain long ages, unless presumptuous or malignant historians take thee down to profane thee." His personified pen—warning anyone who might presume to write again with the same "péñola"—conflates Don Quixote and his Arab narrator: "For me alone was Don Quixote born, and I for him; it was his to act, mine to write; we two together make but one, notwithstanding and in spite of that pretended Tordesillesque writer who has ventured or would venture with his great, coarse, ill-trimmed ostrich quill to write the achievements of my valiant knight" (2.74).[20] In spite of that "Tordesillesque" writer (referring to Avellaneda, creator of an apocryphal version of Don Quixote), Cide Hamete finally merges with Don Quixote, at the point of his death: "We two together make but one." For Wordsworth, as for Cervantes, two figures all but become one:

19. Dudley, "Cervantes and Wordsworth" 1102, points out the merging of Cide Hamete and Don Quixote.
20. Miguel de Cervantes, Don Quixote: The Ormsby Translation, Revised Backgrounds and Sources Criticism, eds. Joseph R. Jones and Kenneth Douglas (New York and London: W. W. Norton, 1981) 829–30.

the Arab "to my fancy, had become the knight / Whose tale Cervantes tells; yet not the knight, / But was an Arab of the desert too; / Of these was neither, and was both at once" (*The Prelude* 5.122–25).[21] In the language of the dream, as Freud instructs us, opposites exist side by side, one becoming the other; yet even as extremes meet, differences prevail in the paradoxical twilight of nightmare.

In Book 5, the opposition between the destructive deluge of the dream and the enduring power of poetry operates between the world of nightmare and the waking world. The latter is dominated by the true and false education of imagination. That Wordsworth is using his Arab dream to orchestrate his vocation as poet through contraries emerges at the end of Book 5. By avoiding the confines of modern education that would drive him like a stray sheep into "the pinfold of his own conceit," the young child, left alone among the beautiful and terrible mountains, finds a congenial soil for poetry. The "great Nature," both human and natural, that appears in works of "mighty Poets" takes root more readily in imaginations cultivated in such settings as the Cumberland fells. This education bears fruit in language:

> Visionary power
> Attends the motions of the viewless winds,
> Embodied in the mystery of words:
> There, darkness makes abode, and all the host
> Of shadowing things work endless changes there,
> As in a mansion like their proper home.
> Even forms and substances are circumfused
> By that transparent veil with light divine,
> And, through the turnings intricate of verse,
> Present themselves as objects recognized,
> In flashes, and with glory not their own.
> (*The Prelude* [1850] 5.595–605)

Imagination, for Wordsworth, normally turns outward to the external world, but it now emerges from words on the pages of books, the

---

21. Bahti, "Figures of Interpretation," 620–21. The "both/neither" structure of the dream is the episode's central rhetorical figure: "The figure—fictional and rhetorical—at the moment of its reading both is and is not what it is; insofar as it is both, it also can *be* neither. An either/or *and* both/and structure is actually both/neither, which is itself only another version of *the structure of the rhetorical figure as neither/nor*."

endangered species on the flooded desert of nightmare. Words have their visionary powers, but they also lurk in darkness on shadowy ground (an underground like the shell). The urge to transcend is balanced against an openness to unconscious depth. Just as the nightmare unleashes the surreal and the daemonic, imagination in language is attuned to the visionary noises of the "viewless" winds and to the subliminal shadows of the unconscious.

Daydreaming and Narrative Desire

Although the nightmare need not follow the paradigm of the daydream, Freud's "Creative Writers and Day-dreaming" offers further insight into Wordsworth's contraries of desire. "When scientific work had succeeded in elucidating this factor of *dream-distortion*," Freud writes, "it was no longer difficult to recognize that night-dreams are wish-fulfillments in just the same way as day-dreams—the phantasies which we all know so well." In the analogy between daydreaming and popular novels and romances, Freud finds a device to speculate upon creative writers who shape their actions through their own fantasies. What Freud avers of the novel pertains, as we have seen in earlier chapters, to Wordsworth's ventriloquism in his narrative poems and to his ambivalent relationship to his Arab protagonist: "The psychological novel in general no doubt owes its special nature to the inclination of the modern writer to split up his ego, by self-observation, into many part-egos, and, in consequence, to personify the conflicting currents of his own mental life in several heroes" (*SE* 9:149–50).

That Freud limits himself to minor writers and that he reductively limits these novelists to a conscious process of ego projection into their characters makes this formulation less convincing than Nietzsche's "theogony of creative consciousness" (to borrow a phrase from Tilottama Rajan). Nietzsche's coalescing of the representative "I" of the poet—by means of the dream aspect of Apollo, in a subconscious identification with his or her characters—makes the same point on a deeper level. Yet Freud tentatively speculates that the link between creativity and daydreaming holds, for writers, the secret of making their own personal fantasy representative. A psychoanalytic approach corroborates the insights on creativity articulated by both Nietzsche and Freud. Peter Brooks remarks that psychoanalytic perspectives in literary study must ultimately derive from our conviction that the materials on which psychoanalysts and literary critics exercise their powers of analysis are in some basic sense the same: that the structure of literature *is* in some sense the structure of mind—not a specific mind, but what the translators of the *Standard Edition* call "the mental apparatus," which is more accurately the dynamic organization of the psyche, a process of structuration.[22]

The texts of literature, then, offer patterns for interpretation akin to the dynamics of psychoanalytic tellings. Although the daydream occurs without the distortion, condensation, and displacement of a normal dream, for Freud it functions by the same mechanism of wish fulfillment that occurs in real dreams.

According to Didier Anzieu, the difference between dreams and daydreams is a function of primary and secondary censorship: "The action of the first censorship produces dreams, whereas the action of the second censorship alone produces a waking phantasy." The first censorship occurs between "the unconscious and the preconscious," causing the distortion, displacement, and condensation of latent thoughts that are "represented by mental images associated or not, as the case may be, with word-representations." If the same latent thoughts come up against secondary censorship, "they are not distorted but clearly enunciated in consciousness." In secondary censorship, therefore, the analyst takes literally what the patient says about an "anxiety or symptom."[23] Both the sleeping and the waking dream illustrate a psychic structuring that divulges unconscious processes in literary texts.

If, for Freud, personal fantasies are either repulsive or unlikely to attract the interest of others, how could poets such as Wordsworth succeed in transforming their own wishes into the desires of readers? How does the creative writer cross "the barriers that rise between each single ego and the others"? Freud discovers the secret of attracting a public audience from a private wish:

> The writer softens the character of his egoistic day-dreams by altering and disguising it, and he bribes us by the purely formal—that is,

---

22. Peter Brooks, "The Idea of a Psychoanalytic Criticism," *Critical Inquiry* 13 (1987): 336–37.
23. Didier Anzieu, *Freud's Self-Analysis* 573–74.

aesthetic—yield of pleasure which he offers us in the presentation of his phantasies. We give the name of an *incentive bonus,* or a *fore-pleasure,* to a yield of pleasure such as this, which is offered to us so as to make possible the release of still greater pleasure arising from deeper psychical sources. In my opinion, all the aesthetic pleasure which a creative writer affords us has the character of a fore-pleasure of this kind, and our actual enjoyment of an imaginative work proceeds from a liberation of tensions in our minds. (*SE* 9:153)

By choosing popular novelists and romancers and by referring to the bribery and seduction of literature, Freud implies a secondary place for imaginative fiction in relation to the reality principle. But he also hints at validating the daydream as a model for poetics. By delighting us with wish-fulfilling plots, these writers put us in a position to "enjoy our own daydreams without self-reproach or shame" (*SE* 9:153). The impulse, which underlies Wordsworth's placing a high premium on fairy tales in childhood education, extends to our releasing mental tensions by making another's wish our power.[24] This Freudian model of desire, by its erotics of "fore-pleasure," seduces us into a world of play that engages us, like Coleridge's willing suspension of disbelief on the level of dreams, at a depth beyond our conscious awareness.

Wordsworth's Arab dream is a nightmare, rather than a daydream, yet its mechanism may, by the law of paradox, spring from a primal wish. By making himself the dreamer, and hence the author of this nightmare, Wordsworth is torn between the fleeing Arab's rejection of his desire to share the quest and the oncoming flood. When he sees "a bed of glittering light" on the desert sands, the Arab, dread clouding his face, identifies it as

> "the waters of the deep
> Gathering upon us"; quickening then the pace
> Of the unwieldy creature he bestrode,
> He left me: I called after him aloud;

24. Joel Morkam, "Structure and Meaning in *The Prelude,* Book V," *PMLA* 87 (1972) 251, usefully defines the historical context of education in Wordsworth's time. Morkam cites Kant as deploring fairy tales: "'children have an extremely powerful imagination, which has no need of being further stretched and strained by fairy-tales. It has much more need of being governed and brought under the rules. . . .'" He also objected to children reading romances, "'for they only caused children to fall into reveries and become empty-minded.'"

He heeded not; but, with his twofold charge
Still in his grasp, before me, full in view,
Went hurrying o'er the illimitable waste,
With the fleet waters of a drowning world
In chase of him; whereat I waked in terror,
And saw the sea before me, and the book,
In which I had been reading, at my side.

(*The Prelude* [1850] 5.129–140)

The "glittering light" of the rising deep blends gently into the day's residue, the sea on whose shore the dreamer had been reading *Don Quixote*. Like the "surpassing brightness" of the shell that nonetheless foretells the death of humanity, the light upon the waters contradicts the underlying flood.[25] The Arab dream repeats the pattern we have seen in chapter 4: as in his dreams of being singled out for execution in France, the uncanny here appears in nightmare, this time to threaten his life with death by water. In the spots of time, Wordsworth encountered the deaths of a hanged man and of his father; now his own life is at risk in the general deluge. In the larger context of Book 5, the Boy of Winander and the Drowned Man echo the pattern of the Arab dream. In each episode, death appears like the ghastly body of the drowned schoolmaster from Esthwaite Lake.[26] The "glittering" tide in the Arab dream, by a fusion of contraries, generates its opposite—a birth of poetry from the deluge. Although each incident moves toward consolation, as the apocalypse of Book 5 moves toward rebirth, it is the recurrent encounter with the uncanny that unbinds the death-marked imagination.

These encounters with death, like a leitmotif in music, connect with

---

25. J. Hillis Miller, "The Stone and the Shell" 142–43, notices the antithetical brightness on the waters, and the birth of language in the sounds of sea and wind: "The sound the dreamer hears in the shell is both 'a loud prophetic blast,' like a single note from a trumpet, and at the same time it is 'articulate sounds,' a 'harmony,' a voice which speaks 'in an unknown tongue' the dreamer can nevertheless 'understand' (*Prelude*, V, 93–95), as the inscriptions apparently written by God on nature are in no human tongue and yet may be deciphered."

26. Manning, "Reading Wordsworth's Revisions: Othello and the Drowned Man," 106, shows how tragic allusions to *Othello* in the following episodes have been gradually suppressed to mitigate the violence of the following episodes: "The sequence from the simile in Book IV (247–64) through the Moment of Dedication and the Discharged Soldier (361–504) to the dream of the Arab Knight/Don Quixote and the Deluge (V.49–139) places the power of story against impending death."

the nightmare of the deluge in Wordsworth's Arab dream. Mark Edmundson applies Freudian melancholia to Emerson in a way that I would extend to Wordsworthian self-analysis in *The Prelude*: "Now, having read 'Mourning and Melancholia' in conjunction with Emerson, one can perhaps be more precise—although no less speculative—about the nature of the grief that for Freud, for Emerson, and, if one may include a fictional character, for Hamlet, contributes to Romantic creation."[27] In differentiating between mourning and melancholia, Freud writes about the death of a loved object: "It is a matter of general observation that people never willingly abandon a libidinal position, not even, indeed, when a substitute is already beckoning to them." In the normal grieving process "respect for reality gains the day": after working through the pain, "the ego becomes free and uninhibited again." But for the melancholic a turning away from reality occurs, which takes the form of "a clinging to the object through the medium of a hallucinatory wishful psychosis." The greater the love for the dead person, the more intense is the process of working through the grief: the attempts to withdraw the emotional energy from our lost love is "carried out bit by bit, at great expense of time and cathected energy, and in the meantime the existence of the lost object is brought up and hypercathected, and detachment of the libido is accomplished in respect of it" (*SE* 17:244–45).

Wordsworth's grief for his lost parents obeys the reality principle and leads to mourning rather than melancholia. His later encounters with death, the losses of his brother and children, repeat and revive the earlier pattern of grieving. But working through grieving involves the sublimation of psychic energy to the making of poetry. The very force of his need for consolation in the Boy of Winander, the Drowned Man, and the deluge episode bears witness to a haunting mortality at his creative center. The episode of the Drowned Man illustrates Wordsworth's deep need to control the fact of death:

> The succeeding day—
> Those unclaimed garments telling a plain tale—
> Went there a company, and in their boat
> Sounded with grappling-irons and long poles:

27. Mark Edmundson, *Toward Reading Freud* 152.

> At length, the dead man 'mid that beauteous scene
> Of trees and hills and water, bolt upright
> Rose with his ghastly face, a spectre shape—
> Of terror even.

The fact of death obtrudes from the following use of fairy tales to inure the young poet against the "ghastly face" of the Drowned Man:

> And yet no vulgar fear,
> Young as I was, a child not nine years old,
> Possessed me, for my inner eye had seen
> Such sights before among the shining streams
> Of fairyland, the forests of romance—
> Thence came a spirit hallowing what I saw
> With decoration and ideal grace,
> A dignity, a smoothness, like the works
> Of Grecian art and purest poesy.
>
> (*The Prelude* 5.465–81)[28]

Without detracting from the bold spirit of contradiction in Wordsworth's assertion of the power of romance, one might say that the very act of distancing himself from the fact of death betrays repression. The need for solace to inure the poet to his boyhood trauma emerges from this idyllic reading in fairyland. If the deluge as revolutionary bloodbath infuses Wordsworth's nightmare of the Arab, history emerges again as it did in the episode of human sacrifice on Sarum Plain. The poet's self-analysis subtends the Arab dream as it typifies the creative incentive he earns from confronting death and the potential ruin of literary and mathematical civilization.

Freud's model of daydreaming as a mode of desire, written in a language reminiscent of Wordsworth on poetic composition, involves three levels of time:

> Mental work is linked to some current impression, some provoking occasion in the present which has been able to arouse one of the

---

28. Thanks go to Peter J. Manning for calling my attention to the reading of the final word in line 480 as "works," instead of the Norton *The Prelude*'s reading of "words," originally discovered by Duncan Wu from a fresh reading of the manuscript. The 1850 *Prelude* also reads "works."

subject's major wishes. From there it harks back to the memory of an earlier experience (usually an infantile one) in which this wish was fulfilled; and it now creates a situation relating to the future which represents a fulfillment of the wish. What it thus creates is a day-dream or phantasy, which carries about it traces of its origin from the occasion which provoked it and from the memory. Thus past, present and future are strung together, as it were, on the thread of the wish that runs through them (*SE* 9:147–48).

This model of wish fulfillment is in some ways too simple to account for Wordsworth's "emotion recollected in tranquillity," yet the poet's strategy of memory overlaps with Freud's structure of creative desire. For Wordsworth, however, *passion* rather than *wish* strikes the keynote for desire: "Poetry is the spontaneous overflow of powerful feelings; it takes its origin from emotion recollected in tranquillity: the emotion is contemplated till by a species of reaction the tranquillity gradually disappears, and an emotion, similar to that which was before the subject of contemplation, is gradually produced, and does actually exist in the mind" (*LC* 339). Both Wordsworth and Freud employ memory and desire; both create a dialectic between present and past; both aim to articulate the workings of creativity. For Freud, the wish feeds upon a discrepancy in reality that invites the projection of a fantasy world. Wordsworth, on the other hand, often brings together emotions that are antithetical in dialectic: a present absence provokes a visionary past and generates in turn a disquieting future. If we qualify Freud's dream wish fulfillment as a creative model and incorporate it into his own thinking by contraries, then his paradigm of desire overlaps more precisely with Wordsworth's. Both poet and analyst knit past, present, and future upon the thread of desire: both yield insight into what Brooks calls "the interplay of *form* and *desire*"; both increase our understanding of "how fantasy provides a dynamic model of intratextual temporal relations and of their organization according to the plot of wish, or desire."[29]

Wordsworth understands the ambivalence of fantasy—its potential either for creativity or errancy—especially for imagination's play in politics, poetry, or dreaming. In "The Antithetical Meaning of Primal Words," Freud epitomizes the tendency of dreams to represent any element by its opposite, "so that there is no way of deciding at a first

29. Peter Brooks, "The Idea of a Psychoanalytic Literary Criticism" 339.

glance whether any element that admits of a contrary is present in the dream-thoughts as a positive or as a negative" (*SE* 11:155). We have seen how the apocalyptic deluge in Wordsworth's dream of the Arab leads to the emergence of poetry, in the harmony and destructive prophecy of the shell, from the waters of the deep. In all languages, especially ancient ones, words that contain opposites in a single meaning later branch into new words to express what had been differences of degree in the primal concept. In words such as *light* and *dark,* Freud affirms that we can only define the one by comparison with its opposite: humanity 'only learnt by degrees to separate the two sides of an anti-thesis and think of one without conscious comparison with the other' (*SE* 11:158). We explored in chapter 1 the tendency for *Heimliche* and *Unheimliche* to fuse into each other, for the uncanny to lodge in the commonplace as its proper home.

Freud is quoting above from the philologist, Karl Abel, on the antithetical senses of primal words. His reading of Abel's pamphlet first suggested to Freud the use of the absence of negation in dreams, wherein opposites are sometimes displaced into their contraries. Abel's findings confirmed Freud's belief in "the regressive, archaic character of the expression of thoughts in dreams." If analysts "knew more about the development of language," he affirms that they could become better translators of "the language of dreams" (*SE* 11:161). This antithetical sense of primal words is closely akin to patterns of comparison thinking that occur in other literary forms and stem from the attraction of opposites. The similes in *The Iliad* often juxtapose, in the midst of battle, the opposing realm of rural harmony. The principle of pastoral, as William Empson has pointed out, operates on the same principle of opposites.[30] In "Lycidas," Milton's shepherd poets at the University of Cambridge (students preparing for holy orders) beget their opposites in a corrupt clergy, "the grim wolf with privy paw" stealing into the fold. In *As You Like It,* the Forest of Arden generates a dialectic with a corrupt court, and the ideal retreat to the green world implies a complex reality that is measured by its opposite. The nightmare of the Arab in *The Prelude* involves a cluster of such antithetical terms. In "Lycidas" and *As You Like It,* these opposites remain separate in antagonism; in *The Prelude* (5), contraries fuse into each other and offer clues for interpretation.

By rescuing endangered books from extinction by flood, *The Prelude*

---

30. Empson, *Some Versions of Pastoral* 3–23.

(5) anticipates the renewal of imagination impaired by seduction to political power. The deluges by water and blood blend as symbols and, as a second nature, function in the language of books. Such language is enhanced by would-be poets whose education properly draws its nourishment from external nature.[31] Writers such as Chaucer, Shakespeare, Cervantes, and Milton derive their power from language embodied in books: "Visionary power / Attends the motions of the viewless winds, / Embodied in the mystery of words" (*The Prelude* 5.595–97). Cervantes chose to efface himself behind a proliferation of narrators, who lose authority and control as they become characters in the action and give way to multiple perspectives. Wordsworth, in keeping with the introspection of Romantic poetics, filters his Arab dream through a discourse of desire. By testing his imagination in a trial by water, he releases unconscious fears about the fragility of literature. But Wordsworth also entrusts imagination to the irrational jarring of mighty opposites. Where Cervantes discloses inner energies in an objective narrative frame, Wordsworth uses the dream to reveal the psychic origins of poetic desire.

In thus tracing the language of power to its frail vehicle in books, Wordsworth finds in nightmare what he found in reverie on Sarum Plain—that power, both barbaric and creative, lodges with uncanny force in words. Alan Richardson sees in Wordsworth's early loss of his mother a tendency to cathect libido on to nature and, hence, to overinvest imaginative power in natural objects. Yet I have shown that Wordsworth himself was aware of this penchant to overindulge the imagination. For Cervantes, this overindulgence in fictional desire induced a seriocomic madness that increasingly revealed the lunacy of Don Quixote's surrounding world—a world we recognize today—as more sinister than deluded. Although Richardson's insights regarding Wordsworth's ambivalence toward power are often incisive, he is wrong to call the poet's problems with power mere "indulgence"[32]: they are insepar-

31. W. G. Stobie, "A Reading of *The Prelude*, Book V," *Modern Language Quarterly* 24 (1963): 373, finds, contrary to R. D. Havens, *The Mind of a Poet* (Baltimore: Johns Hopkins, 1941) 375–76, that Wordsworth's phrase, "that great Nature that exists in works / Of mighty poets," here comes from books, not the external world: "Wordsworth means that great poets create in their work another world (see XIII, 367–78), in which we can live in imagination and which has the *power* of forming our minds when we do so, constituting an influence second only to external—'living' (*Prelude* 5.588) nature" [my italics].

32. Alan Richardson, "Wordsworth at the Crossroads: 'Spots of Time' in the 'Two-Part Prelude,'" *Wordsworth Circle* 19 (1988): 18, writes, "a reading of the 'Two-Part Prelude'

able from Wordsworth's creative matrices, and their energy in the Arab nightmare remains a vital preamble to the poet's own critique of impaired imagination, as well as to its renewal.

In Wordsworth's dream, Don Quixote's demented quest is fused to the Arab's, yielding the paradox that this madness contains a core of reason. In the quest for his semi-Quixote, Wordsworth discovers that "in the blind and awful lair / Of such a madness, reason did lie couched" (*The Prelude* [1850] 5.151–52). In this act of troping reason as a savage beast of prey, Wordsworth reveals a Dionysiac depth in keeping with the sublimity of his dream. Both Cervantes's Don Quixote and Wordsworth's Arab engage in a doomed cause on behalf of books, but where Don Quixote finds a sterner reality in his dream than in the waking mania of romantic love, Wordsworth finds reason in madness. Alan Richardson criticizes Wordsworth, as did Hazlitt before him, for problems arising from "indulgence in the will to power" and for a comfortable retreat to a "dependency sublime." Although as a young poet Wordsworth relishes any chance to wrestle with power, his encounters with sublimity are anything but comfortable.[33] As he grows older, this aggressive desire subsides. But in his Arab dream, in his reverie on Sarum Plain, and in his spots of time—all intense bouts of self-analysis—Wordsworth has not yet ceded his sublime vitality to a new stoical control. Imagination requires a descent into the "awful lair" of madness to become fully itself.

---

situated in object-relations theory emphasizes above all the problems that arise from the poet-protagonist's indulgence of the will to power." In the second spot of time, if the child feels partly responsible for his father's death and is "corrected" for excessive desires by "a divine Father," this guilt "makes the turn from a poetics of power to a poetics of submission seem all but inevitable; chastened and subdued, the poet moves even farther from the hiding places of his power" (19).

33. Richardson, "Wordsworth at the Crossroads," 18–19. Much of my argument supports Richardson's position on excess of imagination, yet when he aligns passages from Books 8 and 11 of *The Prelude* to corroborate Wordsworth's comfortable retreat to a "dependency sublime" (8.640) "lying beyond the reach of human will or power" (11.98), this conflation gives me pause.

Index

McConnell, Frank D., 20 n.32
McGann, Jerome J., xii, xiii, 57–58, 82, 112, 127, 135
Meisenhelder, Susan E., 77 n.23, 131 n.30
Mellor, Anne K., 72 n.16, 96 n.26
Memory: and alienation, 59–60, 62, 69, 111, 150; prophetic nature of, 139; and psychoanalytic narration, 19, 25, 33, 38–42, 43; and the uncanny, 30–38; Wordsworthian strategy of, xiv, 54, 56–57, 99, 146, 168, 188
Miller, Alice, 50–51
Miller, J. Hillis, 25 n.4, 172–73, 177, 185 n.25
Milton: influence on Wordsworth, 11, 66, 85, 96, 111, 117, 137–39, 160–61, 163, 167. *Works*: "L'Allegro," 63; *Comus*, 73; "Lycidas," 189; "Methought I saw my late espousèd saint," 30; *Paradise Lost*, xvi, 61–62, 70, 121 n.16, 137–43, 156–58, 166; Adam's dream in *Paradise Lost*, 70–72, 140; Eve's dream in *Paradise Lost*, 139, 140, 143; "Il Penseroso," xii, 63; *Samson Agonistes*, 138; Sonnet 23, 87–88 n.9
Mitchell, W. J. T., 41 n.29
Montale, Eugenio, 158
Moorman, Mary, 50 n.42, 53 n.48, 97 n.27, 123 n.19
Morkam, Joel, 184 n.24
Mudge, Bradford K., 87 n.8
Murillo, Luis Andrés, 170 n.5

Napoleon Bonaparte, 113–15, 119, 154, 165
Narcissism, 6, 64–65
New historicism, xiii–xiv, 57–58, 112
Newton, Sir Isaac, 145 n.8
Nidditch, Peter H., 15 n.24
Nietzsche, Friedrich: concept of dream surface, 80, 118; 36–37; on the "dream scene," 37; and dream theory, 16–17, 21–23; and the Dionysiac, 21, 25, 37, 72–73, 100–102, 109, 117–18, 124, 150, 167, 191; and poetic projection, 40, 84, 98, 135, 182
Nightmare, xi, 18, 19; as characteristic mode of Romantic dream, 71, 74; and

the French Revolution, xvi, 124–26; Wordsworth's exploration of, xiii, xvii, 77, 79, 135, 138–39, 169–91
Novalis (Friedrich von Hardenberg), 1

O'Brien, Conor Cruise, 92 n.17
Object-relations theory, 191 n.32
Onorato, Richard J., 47, 48, 90
Ovid: *Heroides*, 86–87; *Metamorphoses*, 172 n.7
Owen, W. J. B., 61–62 n.6

Paine, Thomas, 104, 163
Parker, Reeve, 84 n.2
Parrish, Stephen Maxfield, 83 n.1, 121 n.17
Patterson, Charles, Jr., 19 n.30
Paulson, Ronald, 111, 137–38, 163, 177 n.15
Perkins, David D., 17, 72 n.16, 147
Perosa, Sergio, 56 n.2
Plato, 19, 31–33, 143; and myth of preexistence, 31–33, 34 n.20
Plutarch, 18 n.28
Pope, Alexander, 92
Postmodern criticism, xv, xviii, 158–60, 162
Projection, 8, 21, 81; as fantasy, 75, 182, 188; into the female, 98, 101, 110, 163–64
Psychoanalysis, in Romantic poetry, xv, 43–44, 168–91
Psychoanalytic criticism, xiii–xiv, 47–48, 95 n.22, 102–3, 104 n.37; 116, 156 n.24, 159–60; competing models of, 5–10, 92–93; and narrative, 38–42; uses of, xvii, 35–36, 98–99

Ragussis, Michael, 172 n.7
Rajan, Tilottama, 23, 182
Rank, Otto, 29
Raysor, T. M., 18 n.28
Reader-response theory, xvii, 16–17, 18 n.28, 19, 45, 78, 82; applied to Romantic poetry, 44–45, 57, 60, 77 n.23, 81–82, 99–100, 106, 109, 128, 132, 134, 173–74, 183–84; and the dream of the book, 169–71

Wordsworth, William (*cont.*)
xv, 42, 49, 60, 65; erotic relationship to
nature, 64; and the feminine, 16, 28, 42–
43, 85–110, 161–63, 166; influence of
Coleridge on, 142; masculinity imputed
to, xv, 43, 85–89, 103, 108–9; and myth
of psychic fall, xv, 31–35, 69, 121 n.16; and
phenomenology, 147, 151; poetic response to death, xvii, 26–30, 37, 45, 47,
50–54, 64, 67–68, 89–90, 150–51, 165,
185–87, 191 n.32; and "sensual tyranny,"
xvi, 47 n.38, 49, 130, 137, 142, 143–52; and
"spots of time," xii, xiv, 19–20, 26, 42–
54, 55, 118, 128, 147–67, 185, 190–91; and
"visionary dreariness," xii, xiv, 26, 46,
48, 50, 52 n.46, 77 n.23, 107 n.41, 117, 128–
35, 148–53. Works: *An Evening Walk*,
107 n.41; *Descriptive Sketches*, 2, 107 n.41;
Essays on Epitaphs, 68; *Excursion* (1814),
119, 145, n.8, 157; (Book 1), 22, 83–84 n.1,
146, tale of Margaret, xv, 84, 90 n.13, 91,
92 n.17, 95 n.22, 98–110, 132–33, 135, 164,
166; (Book 9), 104; *Excursion* (1850),
147 n.11; "The Female Vagrant," 91–94,
96, 101, 108; Five-Book *Prelude*, 117,
121 n.16, 154, 163–65; *Home at Grasmere*,
96, 97 n.26, 138; "Immortality Ode," xv,
19, 31–38, 53, 55–58, 63, 65, 69–70, 75–77,
107, 109, 112 n.2, 125 n.21, 127, 147–48;
"Laodamia," 2, 72, 85–89, 92, 94, 96, 105,
106; "The Leech Gatherer," 75; *Lyrical
Ballads*, 30, 70, 78, 91–97, 119, 127; *Michael*, 127, 132 n.31; "My Heart Leaps
Up," 31; "The Mad Mother," 91, 94, 96,
101, 108; political sonnets of, 96, 97 n.26;
"The Power of Sound," 145; *The Prelude*
(1805), (Book 1), 44, 148; (Book 2), 45,
56, 89, 90, 95 n.22, 144, 145; (Book 3),
166; (Book 4), 39, 121 n.16, dedication to
poetry, 128, 134, 169, reverie on Dis-

charged Soldier, xv, 2, 16, 107–8, 111,
128–35, 169, 185 n.26; (Book 5) xi, xvii,
169, 189, 190; 140, 154–55, 159, 168, 177,
178, 181, 184 n.24, 190; Boy of Winander,
xvii, 185–86, Drowned Man episode,
xvii, 185–87; (Book 9), 119, Vaudracour
and Julia episode, 96, 162–63; (Book 10),
120, 121; (Book 11), xv, 42, 46–50, 53, 151,
157, 165; Girl with Pitcher, 45–47, 150–51;
(Book 12), 4, 111, 116; Sarum Plain reverie, xv, 4, 15, 16, 20, 111–19, 124–27, 132,
134–35, 150, 153, 170, 172, 187, 190–91;
(Book 13), 149, 155, 156, 161–62, 164–66,
190 n.31; Mount Snowdon episode, 163–
65; *The Prelude* (1850), (Book 2), 119;
(Book 4), 128–29, 131–32; (Book 5), 95,
175–91, Arab Dream, xi, xvi–xvii, 4, 7,
17, 140, 167, 168–91; (Book 8), 120;
(Book 10), 122–25; (Book 11), 119; (Book
12) 144, 149; (Book 14), 156; "Prospectus
to *The Recluse*," 139; *The Recluse*, 96, 139,
116, 173; "Reply to 'Mathetes,'" 146, 153,
166; "Resolution and Independence,"
xv, 19, 22, 55, 56, 74, 75, 76–82, 107, 132–
35; *The Ruined Cottage*, 90 n.15, 98, 99,
103–5, 107; *Salisbury Plain*, 125–26, 172;
"A Slumber Did My Spirit Seal," 130;
The Story of Margaret, 98; "Strange Fits
of Passion," 26; "Surprised by Joy," 30;
The Tale of a Woman, 98; "Thanksgiving
Ode," 114–15, 133; "The Thorn," 83, n.1,
121 n.17; "Tintern Abbey," 46, 48, 49, 55,
58–64, 69–70, 90, 98; "To the Cuckoo,"
41; "Two April Mornings," 29; Two-
Part *Prelude*, 190–91 n.32; *The Vale of Esthwaite*, 53, 126; "The Wanderer," 105
Wu, Duncan, 187 n.28

Zall, Paul M., 26 n.5